AN INTRODUCTION TO THE LEGAL SYSTEM OF THE UNITED STATES

FOURTH EDITION

AN INTRODUCTION to the Legal System of the United States

FOURTH EDITION

E. Allan Farnsworth

Edited by

Steve Sheppard

Originally Published for the
Parker School of Foreign and Comparative Law
Columbia University in the City of New York

OXFORD
UNIVERSITY PRESS

2010

OXFORD
UNIVERSITY PRESS

Oxford University Press, Inc., publishes works that further Oxford University's objective of excellence in research, scholarship, and education.

Oxford   New York
Auckland   Cape Town   Dar es Salaam   Hong Kong   Karachi   Kuala Lumpur   Madrid   Melbourne
Mexico City   Nairobi   New Delhi   Shanghai   Taipei   Toronto

With offices in
Argentina   Austria   Brazil   Chile   Czech Republic   France   Greece   Guatemala   Hungary   Italy
Japan   Poland   Portugal   Singapore   South Korea   Switzerland   Thailand   Turkey   Ukraine
Vietnam

Copyright © 2010 by Oxford University Press, Inc.

Published by Oxford University Press, Inc.
198 Madison Avenue, New York, New York 10016

Oxford is a registered trademark of Oxford University Press
Oxford University Press is a registered trademark of Oxford University Press, Inc.

Library of Congress Cataloging-in-Publication Data

Farnsworth, E. Allan (Edward Allan), 1928–
   An introduction to the legal system of the United States / E. Allan Farnsworth;
edited by Steve Sheppard. — 4th ed.
      p. cm.
   Includes bibliographical references and index.
   ISBN 978-0-19-973310-1 ((pbk.) : alk. paper)
1. Law—United States. I. Sheppard, Steve, 1963– II. Title.
   KF387.F3 2010
   349.73—dc22   2009053017

10

Printed in Canada

Note to Readers
This publication is designed to provide accurate and authoritative information in regard to the subject matter covered. It is based upon sources believed to be accurate and reliable and is intended to be current as of the time it was written. It is sold with the understanding that the publisher is not engaged in rendering legal, accounting, or other professional services. If legal advice or other expert assistance is required, the services of a competent professional person should be sought. Also, to confirm that the information has not been affected or changed by recent developments, traditional legal research techniques should be used, including checking primary sources where appropriate.

(Based on the Declaration of Principles jointly adopted by a Committee of the American Bar Association and a Committee of Publishers and Associations.)

You may order this or any other Oxford University Press publication by
visiting the Oxford University Press website at www.oup.com

To Patricia

CONTENTS

Appendices

EDITOR'S INTRODUCTION

The Study of the Law of the United States

Welcome to the study of American law. For nearly half a century, *An Introduction to the Legal System of the United States* has been a leading basic text on American law, read both by students in the United States and by students and lawyers around the world. Earlier editions of this book have been translated into twenty languages, and it has been studied in hundreds of universities, colleges, and schools in every corner of the globe.

This book is popular because it is clear in describing the law, and it makes sense to a person who has not studied law before. Its simplicity is not simpleminded, however, and American law is presented rich with history and in its many categories, with an eye to explain its differences from the other legal systems of the world, as well as to make it sensible when either history or good sense is its origin. Another reason for its popularity, however, is the unusual grace and influence of its author, the great contracts lawyer and theorist, Allan Farnsworth.

Allan Farnsworth, the Law, and This Book

Edward Allan Farnsworth was born in Providence, Rhode Island, in 1928, where his father, Harrison Farnsworth, was on the physics faculty of Brown University. Harrison became especially well known for the study of atomic surfaces, a tradition that Allan initially followed, taking his bachelor's degree in applied mathematics from Michigan in 1948 and a master's in physics from Yale in 1949. He had planned to take a doctorate in physics but changed to law, later saying he changed his course of study at his father's suggestion because the younger Farnsworth wanted "to do something which had a human element in it as opposed to an inanimate object."

.Farnsworth attended Columbia Law School in New York, which he chose over Harvard and Yale because its midterm grades would allow him to see if he could succeed in legal study. He did succeed, earning the unusually high grades required to be named a Kent Scholar (including perhaps the only A++ in the school's history) and winning the school's John Ordonaux Prize, given to one graduating law student for outstanding general proficiency in legal study. He graduated in 1952, entering the U.S. Air Force, becoming a captain in the JAG Corps, posted as a judge advocate to Mitchell Field on Long Island. Aside from his Air Force duty, he also spent six months working full time for the Central Intelligence Agency, where he appears to have made many interesting friends. He got a taste of private practice in a San Francisco law firm before joining the Columbia law faculty in 1954. He was twenty-six years old, the youngest teacher in the school, a bit of a tenuous position, but he would stay through a highly celebrated career, becoming the Alfred McCormack Professor of Law in 1970.

Working alongside his mentor, the contracts maven Edwin Patterson, Farnsworth taught Commercial Transactions, Admiralty, Legal Aspects in Foreign Trade, and Contracts and began to produce not only extraordinary scholarship but also very attractive teaching materials, including his casebooks, which are still in print in subsequent editions: *Negotiable Instruments* (1959), *Contracts* (1965), and *Commercial Law* (1965).

A brilliant, funny, and passionate teacher, Farnsworth was revered by Columbia students as much for his engagement with them as for the unrelenting brilliance of the class, though this could be daunting. On the first day of the course, every student found the teacher had committed to memory the student's name and home town; was able to address each student by name on sight; and throughout the year, would call on any student to discuss a case that had a mention of the student's home city. Farnsworth's slide shows, culture, and seemingly inexhaustible energy were evident both in class and out, and his mentoring of student research, engagement in student life, and squash game were the stuff of law-school legend.

While a student, Allan had met a young biology student named Patricia, whom he pursued through his tennis game and with whom he started a family. A marriage of equals, Patricia completed a doctorate in physiology. She taught at Barnard, Harvard, the University of Medicine and Dentistry of New Jersey, and elsewhere, including creating a marine biology study center in St. Croix for Fairleigh Dickinson University. Allan was deeply engaged in the lives of their children, who were bright and athletic—basketball player Gigi; tennis pro Pam; son Teddy, the tennis ace and a Navy pilot (who died tragically in 1993); and daughter Karen, the only lawyer among them, whom Allan followed in a boat during long-distance swims around the island of Manhattan (she swam the English Channel in 1987).

In 1960, Farnsworth gave the first of many lectures abroad, giving the courses at the University of Istanbul that would become the basis for this book, which was first published in 1963 under the auspices of the Parker School of Foreign and Comparative Law. Over the next four decades, he traveled widely, lecturing sometimes in English and sometimes in his fluent French, as a visiting professor and lecturer in Argentina, Austria, Australia, Belgium, Brazil, Canada, China, England, France, Germany, Hungary, Italy, Japan, the Netherlands, Poland, Romania, Russia (when it was still the USSR), Rwanda, Senegal, Singapore, Switzerland, and Turkey.

This work was complemented by his efforts as the U.S. representative to the UN Commission on International Trade Law, with which he worked from 1970, and as a member of the governing council of the International Institute for the Unification of Private Law. He had great influence in these roles, particularly as a member of the working group on UNIDROIT Principles of International Commercial Contracts.

Despite the significance of his international work, Farnsworth's most famous work remains his efforts in American contract law. His treatise is the standard text in the field. His labors for a decade as a reporter for the American Law Institute's *Restatement (Second) of Contracts* helped establish its principles as the dominant source of contract law in the United States. His lectures throughout the United States and his many articles brought clarity and a much larger degree of uniformity to the commercial law of the fifty states.

After an illness through which he continued to teach, he died of cancer in January 2005. He is buried at Arlington National Cemetery, not very far from his son Teddy. His influence continues unabated. As of 2008, his works on contracts had been cited in over two thousand published judicial opinions and over twenty-five hundred U.S. scholarly articles, still averaging a hundred cites per year in each.

A Note on How to Use This Book

An Introduction to the Legal System of the United States is intended to give the reader a very basic understanding of the elements of American law and its legal system, with a particular eye to the historical context necessary to understand it. In his teaching, Professor Farnsworth stressed the knowledge of facts, and this book is a wealth of facts; yet he also valued carrying forward this knowledge to acquire more knowledge from it and to develop the skills needed to use facts effectively with the law. The selected readings at the end of each section were important to him, and with each edition of this book, he carefully updated the selections, removing some and adding others, in the obvious hope they would aid the reader with new tools to understand each of the many topics he explored. The appendix was updated from the first edition to the second, in an effort to place before the reader cases that would be relevant to learning the nature of case reading in the United States with opinions relevant to the law one might encounter. (The first edition reprinted *Greenberg v. Lorenz*, 9 N.Y.2d 195 (1961).)

Study and practice are essential to develop the basic information provided in this book. The topic and purpose of this *Introduction* being what they are, the book is not only a primer but also an invitation to further work, to further understanding, and to further interest in American law.

Toward that end, one of Professor Farnsworth's colleagues, George P. Fletcher, and I wrote a book of cases on American law from a comparative viewpoint, which we deliberately modeled in certain ways on this *Introduction*. We selected cases of particular importance in the study of the fields highlighted here, often reprinting with context, questions, and analysis of the cases talked about by Professor Farnsworth. I have therefore noted the particular links between these books in some chapters below. Whether a reader of one book uses the other as a reference is unimportant; what matters is to understand that the initial taste of the law here is an invitation to the feast of the law to be found in the cases and statutes. That is where you will understand the strengths—and the weaknesses—of American law. It is a banquet not to be missed.

A Note of Thanks

The assistance of Patricia Farnsworth and of Karen Farnsworth Einsidler were invaluable in preparing this edition. I am deeply grateful for their kindness in finding materials and in sharing their own stories. I am also grateful to Kent McKeever of the Diamond Law Library of Columbia Law School, to the anonymous public information officer of the Central Intelligence Agency, and to Mr. Nathan Berry for their assistance in pursuing other information and sources that improved this edition.

Suggested Readings

On the life and achievements of Professor Farnsworth, see: Jennifer Bayot, *Obituary: Allan Farnsworth, Law Professor, Dies at 76,* New York Times, Feb. 6, 2005, *at* http://query.nytimes.com/gst/fullpage.html?res=9D01EEDF1E3BF935A3 5751C0A9639C8B63. Michael Joachim Bonell, *Remembering Allan Farnsworth on the International Scene,* 105 Colum. L. Rev. 1417 (2005). Jean Braucher, *E. Allan Farnsworth and the Restatement (Second) of Contracts,* 105 Colum. L. Rev. 1417 (2005). Rayner M. Hamilton, *Memorial for Professor E. Allan Farnsworth,* 105 Colum. L. Rev. 1427 (2005). Lance Liebman, *Allan Farnsworth, ALI Reporter,* 105 Colum. L. Rev. 1429 (2005). Carol Sanger, *Remarks for Allan Farnsworth Memorial,* 105 Colum. L. Rev. 1432 (2005). Megan Manni, *The Ace: Remembering the Englewood Resident and Columbia Professor of Law* (201) Magazine 95 (2005). Perhaps the best among his celebrations is Karen Einsidler, *Gedenkschrift in Honor of E. Allan Farnsworth (1928–2005),* 19 Pace Int'l L. Rev. 1 (2007).

Steve Sheppard
Fayetteville, Arkansas
2010

PREFACE TO THE THIRD EDITION

This book had its genesis when I delivered a series of lectures on American law in a class in comparative law at the University of Istanbul, and it occurred to me that there was a need for a brief introductory text on the legal system of the United States. This thought has been confirmed by the appearance of the first two editions in a dozen languages. This third edition is intended to serve the same purpose as the first two, for both American and foreign readers.

This book does not pretend to explain the political or economic system within which our law has developed, nor does it purport to compare our law with that of any other country. Its object is to set forth those fundamentals of our legal system that are most important as background in the event of further inquiry and most likely to be novel or troublesome to one not trained in it.

In order to present this complex subject in small compass, I have taken liberties that would not be fitting in a more detailed exposition. It is only fair to warn the reader of the obvious fact that what follows is general rather than specific and illustrative rather than exhaustive. Prevailing or conventional views on controversial points may be presented without notation of conflicting or dissenting opinion, and significant matters may be omitted entirely. The reader who would be on firmer ground may find guidance in the list of readings suggested in each chapter.

I owe more than the usual author's debt of gratitude to the colleagues who have read the manuscript and given criticism, suggestion, and encouragement and to the librarians who have patiently responded to many requests. Thanks go to Foundation Press for permission to adapt some material in Chapter 1 from N. Dowling & G. Gunther, *Cases on Constitutional Law* 21–31 (7th ed. 1965). Responsibility for remaining vices rests upon my own shoulders.

E. Allan Farnsworth
New York
May 1996

A NOTE ON TERMINOLOGY

It will be helpful, at the outset, to clear up the considerable ambiguity that surrounds the terms "law" and "common law." The word "law" in the English language is used to refer to both the sum of all legal rules (*ius, droit, diritto, derecho, Recht*) and the express rule laid down by legislative authority (*lex, loi, legge, ley, Gesetz*). Originally the term "common law" described that part of the law of England which was understood mainly through cases decided by judges and which was common to the whole land rather than local to one place or another. It may still be used in much the same sense, as in the phrase "at common law," to refer to the law, usually of England, during the early part of its development and before widespread legislation. The American lawyer may use it in at least three other senses.

The first use is to refer to the law that is laid down by the courts rather than by the legislatures. In this book, the term "case law" is used for this purpose; "decisional law" is used to include the law as laid down by other tribunals, such as administrative tribunals, in addition to courts. "Statute law" is used to refer to the enactments of legislatures; "legislation" is used in its broadest sense to include such similar forms of law as constitutions, treaties, administrative regulations, and the like, as well as statute law.

The second use of the term "common law" is to refer to the body of rules applied by the common-law courts as distinguished from the special courts of equity or of admiralty. The term is not used in this sense in this book.

The third use is to refer to this country as a "common-law" country, whose law is based on English law, as opposed to a "civil-law" country, whose law is derived from the Roman law tradition. This is the sense in which these terms are used in this book.

The term "civil" is also sometimes used in the United States in opposition to "criminal." It is used in this book in this sense only in such terms as "civil case" and "civil procedure." The term "civil law" is not ordinarily used in the United States to refer to the subject matter of a civil code, in opposition, for example, to "commercial law."

Suggested Readings

See Fletcher & Sheppard, *American Law in a Global Context,* Chapter 3. For more discussion of the relationship of the civil law and the common law in the context of other legal systems, see H. Glenn, *Legal Traditions of the World: Sustainable Diversity in Law* (3d ed. 2007).

I

Sources and Techniques

ONE

Historical Background

American law has two distinctive ingredients: a singular variety of federalism and a common law tradition. How did federalism take shape during the establishment of the union? How did the common law win acceptance during the formative era?[1]

Establishment of the Union

Rapid change has been the rule rather than the exception during the course of American history. Less than four centuries have passed since the start of the colonial period, which is commonly dated from the first English settlement at Jamestown, Virginia in 1607. In the roughly 240 years since they declared their independence in 1776, the thirteen colonies of under three million inhabitants clustered near the Atlantic Seaboard have become

---

[1] A fuller development of this chapter, written later by Professor Farnsworth, is in *The Evolution of the Common Law in the United States of America, in Evolution des systemes juridiques, bijuridisme et commerce international / The Evolution of Legal System: Bijuralism and International Trade* 81–93 (L. Perret, A.F. Bisson & N. Mariani eds., Montreal 2002).

50 states of over three hundred million inhabitants, spreading from ocean to ocean and beyond.

Along with change there has, from the outset, been diversity—of religions, of nationalities, and of economic groups. To the colonies came Anglicans, Baptists, Huguenots, Jews, Presbyterians, Puritans, Quakers, and Roman Catholics, as well as the native Indians with their own religion. Among the English majorities of settlers were pockets of Africans, Dutch, French, Germans, Irish, Scots, Spanish, Swedes, and Swiss. They lived as merchants, artisans, plantation owners and workers, small farmers, and pioneers. But most important, there was diversity in the political organization of the colonies, which were entirely separate units under the English crown. Some were royal provinces ruled directly by a royal governor appointed by the king. Others were proprietary provinces with political control vested by royal grant in a proprietor or group of proprietors. Still others were corporate colonies under royal charters that generally gave them more freedom from crown control than either of the other forms. Each of the colonies had its own independent evolution and its own largely separate existence until the events that led up to the Revolution put an end to their self-sufficiency. No adequate comprehension of the American legal system is possible without an understanding of the way in which these individual colonies were welded together into a single nation under a Constitution which has, with relatively little amendment, withstood the stress of diversity and the strain of change from 1789 until today.

The events that provoked the American Revolution arose in large part out of the measures taken by Britain to solve three of that country's major problems of the mid-eighteenth century: first, the need for additional revenue for the British treasury, some of which, it was thought, the colonists should contribute; second, the demand by British merchants for enforcement of commercial regulations to preserve colonial markets and sources of supply; and third, the difficulty of control of new territories, involving administration, land organization, and protection against Indians. In reaction to these measures, which the colonists found oppressive of their liberties, the First Continental Congress met in Philadelphia in 1774. Composed of some 55 delegates from almost all the colonies, it was a harbinger of union among the colonies and of war with England. The colonists were anxious to assure their enjoyment of rights that they felt they had been deprived though they believed they were assured them from English case law, the English Bill of Rights of 1689, and other great enactments reaching back to the Magna Carta in 1215. This 1774 assembly, unauthorized by the Crown, represented a great advance toward united colonial action. From this moment forward, there was always in being a public body devoted to the common cause of the colonies. The forceful Declaration and Resolves issued by this First Congress set out the arguments of the colonists and demanded that Parliament cease its interference in matters of taxation and internal polity. But the Congress rejected a proposed plan of colonial union.

By 1775, when the Second Continental Congress convened, fighting between the colonists and the British had already begun. Despite its dubious status, this body assumed authority over the colonies as a whole and instigated preparations for war. In spite of the hostilities, there was reluctance to break with England, and only after long delay were all of the colonies brought into line and independence declared in July 1776. The Declaration of Independence detailed the colonists' grievances and epitomized much of the revolutionary theory. The Declaration, at least in its preamble, calls attention both to the "station to which the Laws of Nature and of Nature's God entitle" the colonists and to the "unalienable rights" with which "all men . . . are endowed by their Creator" and reflects the influence of theories of natural law under which the Revolution was justified. The language is, however, not that of union but only that of "free and independent states." It did not unite the colonies among themselves but only severed their ties with England.

By 1777, a committee of the Second Continental Congress, at work on the problem of colonial union, had drafted Articles of Confederation, but these were not finally ratified until 1781. This was the first serious attempt at a federal union. However, each state was jealous of its newly asserted sovereignty, conscious of its own special interests, and hopeful of its own distinctive kind of reform. The Continental Congress created under the Articles resembled an association of diplomatic representatives of the various states in which each one had an equal vote. There was no provision for a separate national executive or judiciary. The most conspicuous reason for the ultimate failure of the Confederation was the lack of powers granted to Congress. It had no authority to levy taxes, to regulate interstate or foreign commerce, or to ensure state compliance with treaties. It was against this background that many of the best minds in America came to the Constitutional Convention in Philadelphia in May of 1787, to try to preserve the union.

They approached their task equipped not only with the governmental theories of their day but also with an impressive degree of realism. Beginning in 1776, state constitutions had been adopted, occasionally amid bitter political rivalries. A number of the delegates had participated in the drafting of these documents and had been members of the Continental Congress. It was, in large measure, experience on which they relied—experience under colonial rule, under state constitutions, and under the Articles of Confederation. The chief problem before them was to form a strong union without obliterating the states as constituents—in some respects, autonomous parts of the system; it was through the states that experience gained in the colonial period was to be preserved. Widely differing points of view were ably represented among the delegates, and the result was inevitably a compromise. As the Convention progressed, the movement away from a loose league of sovereign states, as the Confederation had been, grew more pronounced. Instead of adding coercive and other powers to patch up the old league, the delegates ultimately arrived at the crucial decision of the Convention: to have a central government with widened powers designed to operate on individuals rather than states.

In September 1787, the Constitution was signed and submitted to Congress, to become effective upon its acceptance by two-thirds of the states. This occurred in July of 1788, and the first president of the United States, George Washington, was inaugurated the following April. The final text of the Constitution shows the influence of principles developed in the course of history. The notions that the people are sovereign and that their government is based on a social compact may be found in the preamble, in the provisions for state conventions to ratify the completed Constitution, and in the idea that powers are "granted" to the central government. The theory that the federal government is one of limited powers is evidenced by their enumeration, including the power to tax, to wage war, to regulate interstate and foreign commerce, and to make treaties; as to the residue of powers, each of the states has the capacity to make law. The concept of the separation of the federal legislative, executive, and judicial powers is implied by the form of the Constitution with three separate major articles, each of which delineates one of these three major, and presumably distinct, powers. And the belief that constitutional rights should be embodied in a written instrument is evident from the document itself. The Constitution as ratified contained no guarantees of basic human rights. But in 1789, the first Congress promptly proposed the first ten amendments to the Constitution, which are popularly known as the Bill of Rights because many of them are concerned with the rights of the individual against the federal government. Their ratification was completed in 1791.[2]

One of the tenets of the framers of the Constitution was that the interpretation of constitutional rights should be entrusted to specialists. The judiciary article provides for an independent judicial power operating, like the legislative and executive, upon both states and individuals and vests this power in a Supreme Court and in such inferior courts as Congress "may from time to time ordain and establish." Their jurisdiction expressly includes cases arising under the Constitution. Coupled with this is the Supremacy Clause, a statement that the "Constitution, and the Laws of the United States which shall be made in Pursuance thereof, and all Treaties made, or which shall be made, under the Authority of the United States, shall be the supreme Law of the Land." But there is no specific provision giving the federal courts the power of judicial review[3] over either federal or state legislation, though many of the delegates must have assumed it would have that power.

In 1789, Congress passed the First Judiciary Act which, on its face, contemplated federal judicial review of state court decisions in certain cases. The Act implemented the judiciary article of the Constitution by creating lower federal courts and by defining their jurisdiction along with that of the Supreme Court. The state courts had already exercised judicial review over state legislation under state constitutions and continued to do so, and the newly created lower federal courts began to strike down state legislation as contrary to the federal Constitution itself. Judicial review was natural because of colonial experience with review of legislation and because federal and state constitutions had come to embody notions of limitations on government. Since the federal government was a government of limited powers only—those granted to it by the Constitution—it could be inferred

---

2 The Bill of Rights initially had twelve amendments of which ten were ratified by the states by 1791. An additional amendment proposed in the same bill, limiting pay raises for members of Congress to benefit only those who serve after the subsequent election, was ratified as the Twenty-Seventh Amendment in 1992.

3 Judicial review, as that term is used in American constitutional law, refers to the power of a court to pass upon the constitutionality of legislation and to refuse to give effect to legislation that it decides is invalid on constitutional grounds.

that the federal judiciary was also to determine whether Congress had exceeded these powers.

This inference was borne out by the opinion of Chief Justice John Marshall[4] in the landmark case of *Marbury v. Madison*,[5] decided in 1803. In that case, the Supreme Court refused to give effect to a section of a federal statute, on the ground that Congress in enacting it had exceeded the powers granted it by the Constitution. The Court thereby firmly established that federal legislation was subject to judicial review in the federal courts.[6] A few years later, it affirmed its authority under the federal Constitution to pass upon the validity of state statutes,[7] an authority which has been one of the great unifying forces in the United States. Justice Oliver Wendell Holmes, Jr.,[8] of the Supreme Court of the United States observed, "I do not think the United States would come to an end if we lost our power to declare an Act of Congress void. I do think the Union would be imperiled if we could not make that declaration as to the laws of the several states."[9] A state court, too, may refuse to enforce a state or federal statute on

---

[4] John Marshall (1755–1835) was the fourth Chief Justice of the United States, from 1801 until 1835. He had previously served in a number of public offices, including that of Secretary of State. His only formal education consisted of two months of law lectures at The College of William & Mary. He was the author of many of the most significant opinions of the Court during this crucial period and is generally regarded as its greatest Chief Justice.

[5] 5 U.S. (1 Cranch) 137 (1803).

[6] The Court's first declaration of the unconstitutionality of an executive act was Little v. Barreme, 6 U.S. (2 Cranch) 170 (1804), also called the *Flying Fish* case.

[7] Fletcher v. Peck, 10 U.S. (6 Cranch) 87 (1810). This power was elaborated in Martin v. Hunter's Lessee, 14 U.S. (Wheat.) 304 (1816).

[8] Oliver Wendell Holmes, Jr. (1841–1935), a graduate of Harvard College and the Harvard Law School, practiced law in Boston, served briefly as professor of law at Harvard, and then for twenty years as justice and later chief justice of the Supreme Judicial Court of Massachusetts. In 1902, he was appointed an associate justice of the United States Supreme Court, where the quality of his dissenting opinions won him the title of the "Great Dissenter." He resigned because of ill health in 1932. His most famous book is *The Common Law* (1881), based on a series of lectures.

[9] OLIVER WENDELL HOLMES, COLLECTED LEGAL PAPERS 295–96 (1920). According to The Constitution of the United States of America: Analysis and Interpretation (Senate Doc. 99-16 1987), the Supreme Court from its inception through 1986 had held unconstitutional in whole or in part only 124 acts of Congress as opposed to roughly a thousand state acts.

the ground that it violates the federal Constitution, but this determination is subject to review by the Supreme Court of the United States.[10]

The subject of judicial review is discussed in more detail in later chapters, as is the hierarchy of such authorities as constitutions, treaties, statutes, regulations, and judicial decisions, among the various sources of law in the newly formed union. For present purposes, it is sufficient to note that in spite of the surrender by the states of some of their sovereignty when they joined the union, each state was left to work out its own law as best it might, subject only to the restraints imposed under the Constitution.

Origins of American Law

Just as there was no uniform evolution of political organization in the colonies, there was no uniform growth of colonial law. The same diversity as to the extent of crown control, date of settlement, and conditions of development resulted in 13 separate legal systems, each with its distinct historical background. Furthermore, as the boundaries of the United States were extended, large areas were added which had been subject to Spanish, Mexican, French, or Russian sovereignty for substantial periods of time. Many states, most notably Louisiana, still show the imprint of such origins, and the civil law institution of community property can be found in eight states today and in their influence on the family law of rest of the nation. Nevertheless, the similarities among state law far outweigh the differences, and there is on the whole an unmistakable family resemblance to the law of England. That the influence should have been English is hardly surprising in view of the language and nationality of most of the colonists; that this influence should have met with the resistance that it did calls for some explanation.

There were at least three impediments to the immediate acceptance of English law in the earliest colonial period. The first was the dissatisfaction with some aspects of English justice on the part of many of the colonists, who had migrated to the New World in order to escape from what they regarded as intolerable conditions in the mother country. This was particularly true for those who had come in search of religious, political,

---

[10]   *See* Chapter 4, *infra*.

or economic freedom. A second and more significant impediment was the lack of trained lawyers, which continued to retard the development of American law throughout the seventeenth century. The rigorous life in the colonies had little attraction for English lawyers, and few among the earliest settlers had received any legal training. The third impediment was the disparity of the conditions in the two lands. Particularly in the beginning, life was more primitive in the colonies, and familiar English institutions that were copied often produced rough copies at best. The early settlers did not carry English law in its entirety with them when they came, and the process by which it was absorbed in the face of these impediments was not a simple one.

During these early years, the extent to which English case law, as distinguished from statute law, was in effect, either in theory or in practice, during the early history of the colonies is not free from dispute. The legislative power that the British Parliament had over the colonies had not been fully exercised. Although acts passed prior to the initial settlement of a colony, if adapted to the circumstances, were generally regarded as being in force in that colony as well as in England, acts passed after initial settlement did not extend to the colonies unless expressly provided. Power to legislate had been conferred upon the colonies themselves, and each had its own legislature with at least one elective branch and with considerable control over internal affairs. Codification was common in the early stages of some of the colonies, partly because of the scarcity of English law books and the lack of a trained bar and partly because of colonial notions of law reform. Colonial legislation was reviewed by administrative authorities in the mother country and might be set aside if it was "contrary" or "repugnant" to the laws or commercial policy of England. Colonial legislation was also subject to judicial review and might be held to be void when appeals from judgments of colonial courts were taken to England. But no systematic control was exercised until the end of the seventeenth century.

During the 1600s, colonial justice often lacked English legal technicality and was sometimes based on a general sense of Right as derived from the Bible and the law of nature. Court procedure, at least outside of the superior courts, was tailored to suit American needs and was marked by an informality of proceedings, a simplicity of pleading, and judges untutored in the law. The model may have been the local courts in England, which would have been familiar to many of the colonists. Substantive law, as well as procedure, began to respond to colonial needs. In England, the feudal policy in favor of keeping estates in land intact had resulted in the rule of primogeniture, the exclusive right of the eldest son to inherit the land of the father.[11] In America, however, this rule was rejected in favor of equal distribution among all of a father's children, subject to varying rights of a surviving spouse. This practice began in the northern colonies, was confirmed there by statute, and had spread southward by legislation to all of the states by the end of the eighteenth century.

The beginning of the eighteenth century saw considerable refinement of colonial law and a concurrent increase in the influence of English case law. Review of colonial legislation had become more thorough. With the growth of trade and the increase in population—to some three hundred thousand in 1700—the ranks of trained lawyers swelled, and the courts of review began to be manned by professionals. Some were English lawyers who had immigrated, while others were native lawyers who had studied in London or as apprentices in law offices in the colonies. English law books, especially those of Sir Edward Coke,[12] had become increasingly available. It has been said that, by the time of the Revolution, William Blackstone's[13] widely read *Commentaries on the Laws of England*, which first appeared between 1765 and 1769, had sold nearly as many copies in America as in England. Interest in English law was stimulated by the necessity of dealing in commercial matters with English merchants trained in its ways and by the desirability of reliance upon its principles to support the colonists' grievances against the Crown. By the time of the Revolution, English law had come to be generally well regarded and each colony had a bar of trained, able, and respected professionals, capable of working with a refined and technical system. The colonial legal profession, especially in the cities, had achieved both social standing and economic success. It was also

---

[11] The rule of primogeniture was not changed in England until the Administration of Estates Act in 1926.

[12] Sir Edward Coke (1552–1634), an English lawyer and judge, was personally involved in the establishment of some of the English colonies in America. His opinions and law books, especially his *Reports* and *Institutes* were the core of most colonial law libraries and remained influential long after independence.

[13] William Blackstone (1723–1780), an English barrister, began the first university lectures on the common law in England at Oxford in 1753. In 1758, he was appointed to the first professorship of English law at that university. He is remembered chiefly for his *Commentaries*, which went through eight editions in his lifetime.

politically active: 25 of the 56 signers of the Declaration of Independence were lawyers.

It is therefore not surprising that most of the 13 original states formally "received"—that is, adopted, by constitution, judicial order, or statute—some part of the law of England along with their own colonial enactments. The formulas varied, but a typical reception provision might include that part of English law that "together did form the law of said colony" prior to such a specific date as 1607 or 1776. As additional states were carved out of the Western territories, similar procedures were followed with regard to reception. While the details of the reception of English law differ considerably from state to state, it is clear that the changes and developments in English law after the date of reception for a particular state have no binding force at all in that state.

The Revolution resulted in a setback to the influence of English law in some of the new states because of political antipathy. In a few, anti-British sentiment was implemented by statutes prohibiting the citation of English decisions handed down after independence.[14] At the same time, the quality of the practicing bar as a whole declined. Some lawyers, who had been loyalists, had left the country before the end of the war; others, seizing the opportunity for leadership, accepted political or judicial posts under the new government. The standards and repute of the remainder deteriorated in many communities. The era of the lay judge was not entirely over, and during the early nineteenth century, the state of Rhode Island had a farmer as chief justice and a blacksmith as a member of its highest court. There was not even an adequate body of American case law that could be used by those judges who had the ability and inclination to do so. Although reports of cases began to be published at the end of the eighteenth century, they were few in number. The opportunity for broadening the base of American law was considerable. There was some inclination to look to French and Roman law, and European writers were cited, particularly in the fields of commercial law and conflict of laws where English treatises

---

14 New Jersey and Kentucky enacted statutes forbidding the citation of common-law authorities, and a common toast of the time is said to have been, "The Common Law of England: may wholesome statutes soon root out this engine of oppression from America." E. HAYNES, THE SELECTION AND TENURE OF JUDGES 96 (1944). *See also* Stein, *The Attraction of the Civil Law in Post-Revolutionary America,* 52 VA. L. REV. 403 (1966).

were inadequate. But few judges were versed in modern foreign languages and, while English treatises and reports were available, the Code Napoleon did not appear until after the beginning of the nineteenth century. Blackstone's *Commentaries*, which were available in numerous American editions throughout the nineteenth century, became particularly influential, not only to present the English law as received but also to describe local extensions and departures from it by American authors, courts, and legislatures.

During the first part of the nineteenth century, agriculture and trade dominated the economy as energies went into the Westward Expansion and the production of staples for European markets. Judges labored to shape English legal materials to fit the conditions of their particular jurisdictions. They examined the pre-Revolutionary English law to determine its applicability to American conditions and laid the foundations of such fields as contracts, torts, sale of goods, real property, and conflict of laws. There was constant legislative intervention in such areas as procedure, criminal law, marriage and divorce, descent and distribution, wills, and administration of estates. Sometimes the law grew out of local usages or needs. The customs of western farmers and gold miners formed the basis for water and mining law in some of the western states. Some of the prairie states in which raising cattle was the means of livelihood and wood for fences was scarce, changed the English rule that the owner of cattle is liable without fault for damage that they may cause to a neighboring crop owner. But it was also an era of great "national" treatises such as James Kent's[15] *Commentaries on American Law*, published from 1826 to 1830, and nine works by Joseph Story[16] published from 1832 to 1845. These treatises, which went through many revisions, played an important role in promoting uniformity by helping to counter the forces which contributed to diversity.

---

[15] James Kent (1763–1847) became the first professor of law at Columbia College in 1793. He resigned in 1798 for the New York Supreme Court and was appointed chancellor of the state in 1814. Upon his retirement in 1823, he returned to Columbia and published his *Commentaries on American Law*, from his lectures dealing with nearly all phases of contemporary law, including one of the first American studies of international law.

[16] Joseph Story (1779–1845) was appointed to the United States Supreme Court in 1811 at the age of 32. In 1829, while retaining his seat on the Court, he became the first Dane professor of law at the Harvard Law School, where he reorganized the curriculum and revitalized the school. His nine commentaries developed from his lectures on subjects ranging from the Constitution to conflict of laws. For more on Justice Story, *see* Chapter 2, *infra*.

Out of the first half of the nineteenth century came institutions and procedures that still survive. But the functions they now perform and the issues they now deal with often differ from those of this earlier, formative period. The years of the Civil War, 1861 to 1865, mark a rough but convenient division between this period and the later development of American law. The years after the war saw a rapid increase in population and its concentration in the cities. They witnessed the growth of large-scale industry, transportation, and communication, with attendant complexities in the corporate form of organization. For example, from 1850 to 1860, the population of the state of Minnesota increased from 6000 to 172,000. In 1790, only about 3 percent of the people in the United States lived in the six cities that had 8000 or more inhabitants; by 1890, about one out of three Americans lived in a city of 4000 or more. From 1869 to 1900, railway mileage grew from 30,000 to 166,000 miles, running from the Atlantic to the Pacific Oceans. In 1876, the first telephone message was sent; and in 1882, Edison's electric power plant began operation in New York City.

In this rapidly expanding industrial society, the creation of a stable system of law took on increased importance. Development continued in such fields as corporations, public service companies, railroads, and insurance. But during the final quarter of the century, much of the law of the formative era began to crystallize, and the role of the judge became one more of systematizing rather than of creating. As the volume of case law increased, the uncertainty that had been inevitable in earlier years became unpopular, and efforts turned toward a search for predictability. The principal achievements of the courts were the ordering of the system and the logical development of details. It is significant that the legal treatises of this period were more specialized than those of the first half of the century. Some creative activity was to be found in the legislatures, which had been more active in reform than the judiciary until the Civil War, but popular esteem for the courts was at its height, and aggressive judges asserted their judicial authority in holding legislation to constitutional standards.

By the turn of the century, however, the methodical accretion of rules, case by case, had begun to lose some of its popular appeal. The watchword of the courts was still stability, but the courts had failed to keep pace with the demands of the rapidly changing political and economic order. The shape of things to come might have been foretold from the organization in 1886 of the American Federation of Labor, the first of the great national labor unions; from the creation in 1887 of the Interstate Commerce Commission, the first of the great national regulatory agencies; and from the enactment in 1890 of the Sherman Act, the first of the great federal antitrust statutes. And so the twentieth century ushered in a new era of change and creativity in law, marked by an increased pace of legislation, particularly legislation over social relationships, and by greater reliance upon administrative agencies instead of courts. During the second decade of the 1900s, most of the state workers' compensation laws were enacted. At about the same time, modern administrative power began to take its present shape, both in the nation and in the states. Some of these more recent developments will be dealt with later.

The direct influence of contemporary English law in America, which was fading by the time of the Civil War, is negligible today. Only infrequently are the more recent English cases cited in contemporary American judicial opinions, and even more rarely will a question arise that turns on the reception of English law. Yet the fundamental approach, much of the vocabulary, and many of the principles and concepts of the common law are as familiar in the United States as in England. English cases, though in relatively small numbers, are still part of the "taught tradition" in American law schools. And while American lawyers and judges may commonly ignore English authorities, they are nevertheless conditioned by English ideas that were imported into American law two centuries ago. Foremost among these are first, the concept of supremacy of law, as exemplified in this country by the distinctive principle that even the state is subject to judicial review under constitutional standards; second, the tradition of precedent, according to which later decisions are based on earlier cases; and third, the notion of a trial as a contentious proceeding, a contest, often before a jury, in which the adversary parties take the initiative and in which the role of the judge is that of umpire rather than of inquisitor. These will be explored in later chapters.

Suggested Readings

L. Friedman, *A History of American Law* (3d ed. 2005) and K. Hall & P. Karsten, *The Magic Mirror: Law in American History* (2d ed. 2008) are comprehensive treatments that begin with colonial times. More controversial works are M. Horwitz,

The *Transformation of American Law, 1780–1860* (1977) and M. Horwitz, *The Transformation of American Law, 1870–1960: The Crisis of Legal Orthodoxy* (1992). For three lively lectures, see G. Gilmore, *The Ages of American Law* (1977).

For the influence of British immigration on the colonies, see D. Fisher, *Albion's Seed: Four British Folkways in America* (1989). The colonial legal experience is now undergoing a renewed study, with a new and greater breadth of context and archival reach. See W. Nelson, *The Common Law of Colonial America* (2008); M. Bilder, The *Transatlantic Constitution: Colonial Legal Culture and the Empire* (2008); D. Hulsebosch, *Constituting Empire: New York and the Transformation of Constitutionalism in the Atlantic World, 1664–1830* (2005). For a newly classic reinterpretation of a telling moment of unprofessional colonial law, see M. Norton, *In the Devil's Snare: The Salem Witchcraft Crisis of 1692* (2003). For the period of the transitions following independence, generally, see G. Wood, *Empire of Liberty: A History of the Early Republic* (2009).

On William Blackstone, see W. Prest, *William Blackstone: Law and Letters in the Eighteenth Century* (2008). On Edward Coke, see *The Selected Writings of Sir Edward Coke* (S. Sheppard ed., 2005). On John Marshall, see R. Newmyer, *John Marshall and the Heroic Age of the Supreme Court* (2007). On Oliver Wendell Holmes, Jr., see G. White, *Oliver Wendell Holmes, Jr.* (2006).

For cases and notes on these topics see G. Fletcher & S. Sheppard, *American Law in a Global Context: The Basics*, Chapters 5 through 8 and 15.

TWO

Legal Education

In spite of their diversity, American law schools have as common character-istics their graduate level and professional objective and their use of the case method of instruction. Why did legal education take this form, and what is the role of the case method?

Diversity

The development of the American legal system has been influenced by the kind of education that lawyers have received, and legal education, in turn, reflects the diversity of that legal system. The study of law for more than one hundred and fifty thousand law students today means study in one of over two hundred law schools that have been approved by the American Bar Association.[1] Nearly all lawyers currently admitted to practice in the United States hold degrees from these schools. But because the number of

---

[1] The great majority of these schools have also met the somewhat stricter standards for membership in the Association of American Law Schools. The list of ABA law schools is available online *at* http://www.abanet.org/legaled/.

institutions is large and because there is no federal control of education, the diversity among these institutions is much greater than in countries where the number of law faculties is smaller or where there is some regulation by the national government. Most law schools are part of a university. The university may be private, with no state connection, as are Chicago, Columbia, Harvard, Stanford, and Yale; or it may be supported by one of the fifty states, as are California, Michigan, and Virginia. The school may be regarded as a "state" law school in the sense that its students come from and intend to practice in the state where it is located, and its curriculum emphasizes the law of that state, or it may be one of the "national" law schools which, like the ones just named, attempts to prepare its graduates more generally for practice in any state. It may have only a full-time program of study lasting for three years, or it may also have a part-time program, usually of evening study, requiring a longer time to complete the standard course.[2] It may be one of the few law schools with more than fifteen hundred students, or one of the handful with less than four hundred.[3] Yet in spite of the great variety in American law schools, there are several characteristics that they have in common, which distinguished them from their sister institutions in most of the rest of the world. The most striking of these are their graduate level and professional objective and the case method of instruction, each of which had its origin in the development of legal education during the nineteenth century.

Graduate Level and Professional Objective

It may seem surprising that legal education should be thought of as being on the university graduate level in a country where an established tradition of university education for the practice of law is only a century old.

---

[2] Less than a fifth of all law students study part time.

[3] Even among the schools named above, the enrollments of J.D. candidates vary. In 2010, they ranged from close to 2,000 for Harvard and between 1,200 and 1,500 for Columbia, Michigan, and Virginia to about 1,000 for California (Berkeley) and about 600 for Chicago, Stanford, and Yale. Tuition and fees range from about $10,000 a year (for state residents at some state schools) to more than $40,000 a year but may in case of need be more than offset by scholarship or loan aid. Most U.S. law students borrow the money to pay for tuition, books, and expenses.

After the Revolution, legal education deteriorated along with the bar.[4] Until well past the middle of the nineteenth century, it was principally in the hands of the practitioners, as at the Inns of Court in England and the accepted way of preparing for the bar was by "reading law." This usually meant a more or less casual apprenticeship, consisting largely of the performance of routine tasks in the office of a practicing lawyer, together with the reading of cases and statutes, as well as with whatever law books were in the office, initially Coke's *Institutes*, then likely an American edition of Blackstone's *Commentaries* and later, Kent's *Commentaries* or Story's *Treatises*, and by the end of the century, some of the more specialized treatises in narrower areas of practice.[5]

There were some exceptions. In 1753 at Oxford University, William Blackstone had begun the first university lectures on the common law in England and before the turn of the century, a small number of American universities had followed this example. A chair of law was established at the College of William & Mary in 1779; James Kent became professor of law at Columbia College in 1793; and there were a few others. In addition, independent schools of law, in which a lawyer undertook to instruct more students than could be accommodated in an office, grew up outside the universities as offshoots of the apprenticeship system. The most notable of these was the Litchfield Law School, which lasted from 1784 to 1833.

However the present-day American law school did not begin to take shape until Justice Joseph Story reorganized the Harvard Law School in 1829, twelve years after its establishment. Story helped to set the dominantly professional orientation of the American law school. The occupants of the early university chairs of law had, like Blackstone, regarded law as a part of liberal education. But under Story, legal and liberal education were divorced, and Law was taught on the assumption that the student had acquired a sufficient background in the liberal arts before commencing legal study. The idea took hold, and the number of such university law schools with one- or two-year courses had increased to thirty-one by 1870. However, these schools had no academic admissions requirements and few graduation requirements, and no attempt was made to ensure that the

---

[4] *See* Chapter 1, *supra*.
[5] Many lawyers, including President Abraham Lincoln, prepared for the bar largely by self-directed reading of such works, as well as preparing later lawyers by the same means.

students had the background of liberal education that Story had assumed. Most schools had faculties of from one to three professors. The first half of the century had been a period of rampant Jacksonian democracy,[6] marked by the exaltation of the common man and carrying with it the implication that one had an almost inherent right to practice law.[7] The legal profession in the United States has never been the province of a select elite, and egalitarian feeling ran especially high at this time. Even the general requirements of preparatory study or apprenticeship for admission to the bar that had existed in the early 1800s had been abandoned. The new law schools, in spite of their university connections, were vocational and lacking in distinction.

Beginning in about 1870, the expansion and industrialization that followed the Civil War gave new vitality to the training of the lawyers who were to practice the more complex law of this era. The American Bar Association was formed in 1878, and its section on legal education evidenced the interest of the organized bar in this field. From this group, the Association of American Law Schools was organized in 1900 for the improvement of legal education. By 1905, the association was able to require of its members the present minimum of three years of law study. By 1952, it had established three years of college education as a prerequisite for admission to law school, and most students today have completed the four years necessary for the college bachelor's degree.[8]

So it is that an American law student usually does not enter law school until the age of twenty-one or older, usually after at least four years of college. Many schools have several times as many applications as they have

---

6 "Jacksonian democracy" took its name from Andrew Jackson, who was president from 1828 to 1836 and had as a premise that the popular mandate is the basis of all governmental activity.

7 From 1851 to 1933, the Constitution of the State of Indiana provided that "Every person of good moral character, being a voter, shall be entitled to admission to practice law in all courts of justice."

8 The American student usually graduates from high school, the end of the tuition-free public school system, at the age of seventeen or eighteen. The student may then seek admission to a state or private college or university for a general college education, leading to a bachelor's degree at the end of four years, by the age of twenty-one or –two. An institution that includes several faculties, *e.g.*, an undergraduate faculty, graduate faculty, and professional schools, is usually called a "university"; while one with only an undergraduate faculty is ordinarily called a "college." A bachelor's degree is also commonly required for the study of medicine, which is itself a four-year course.

vacancies, and places are filled on the basis of the applicant's college record and a nationwide day-long examination used to test aptitude for law study. Where selection in law school admission is careful, fewer than one in a hundred will be lost because of academic failure; where it is not, the rate of failure will be higher. Although the typical law student was once a white male, recent decades have seen a dramatic increase in both women and students of many racial backgrounds in law schools. Women now account for nearly half of all law students, and students from the six groups defined by race or nationality studied by the ABA account for roughly one out of four law students.

The American law student is usually interested in some form of public or private law practice.[9] The three years at law school are devoted to such technical subjects as contracts, torts, real and personal property, trusts, evidence, procedure, criminal law, commercial law, corporation law, taxation, trade regulation, constitutional law, administrative law, labor law, family law, and conflicts of laws,[10] together with a few broader offerings such as jurisprudence, comparative law, law and economics, and legal history. It is assumed that the student has been exposed to such subjects as history, literature, art and music, economics, sociology, political science, and government before entering law school. The curriculum for the first year of law school is entirely or largely prescribed but in later years is mostly elective. The requirement of a college education as a prerequisite to the study of law, coupled with the disappearance of any requirement of an office apprenticeship, has increased the professional emphasis of law training in most law schools. During this three-year period of intensive professional training, the student is subjected to that peculiarly American method of instruction known as the case method.

Case Method

The introduction of the case method on a large scale in American law schools came with the appointment in 1870 of Professor Christopher

---

9 Some law students pursue joint degree programs combining law with such fields as business administration or public administration. These programs generally require an additional year.

10 These fields are described in Part Two, *infra*.

Columbus Langdell[11] as Dane Professor and then dean of the Harvard Law School. He taught his class on contracts not from a treatise but from a casebook, an ordered collection of cases—appellate court opinions—he arranged and published for the use of his students. He had concluded that the shortest and best way of mastering the few basic principles on which he thought the law to be based was by studying the opinions in which they were embodied. He also believed that the instruction should be of such a character that the pupils "might at least derive a greater advantage from attending it than from devoting the time to private study." Once law professors began to put collections of cases in the hands of their students, the next step was to abandon the traditional lecture method and to pose questions and discuss with the students the cases which they were to have read before class—the so-called Socratic method. Because the cases came from many jurisdictions, they were not always consistent, and the method took on a comparative aspect in which the student was required to evaluate conflicting rules in the context of an actual situation. By the end of the first decade of this century, these techniques had been generally accepted in law schools throughout the country.

But if Langdell thought that all of the law could be learned from cases, he was badly mistaken. Much of American law is found elsewhere than in cases, and the role of legislation, regulation, and academic commentary in the curriculum is increasing. Furthermore, the case method is inordinately time consuming if the objective is to learn all or even a substantial part of the law. In recent times, the case method has been justified on the ground that by requiring the student to state, analyze, evaluate, and compare concrete fact situations, to use sources as they are used by lawyers and judges, and then to formulate basic propositions, the method serves to develop the skills and techniques of the profession and to strengthen powers of analysis, reason, and expression. These goals are valued more highly than encyclopedic knowledge of legal rules.[12] Although the case method is suited to the

---

[11] Christopher Columbus Langdell (1826–1896) was a New York lawyer who became professor of law at Harvard Law School in 1870. His principal achievement as professor and later dean was the introduction of the case method of instruction.

[12] The case method is reflected in the typical law school examination question, which poses a hypothetical fact situation unfamiliar to the student, often based on a borderline case in which the law is not clearly settled. The question may ask the student to decide the case and present supporting reasons or perhaps to argue the case for one side or to advise a client in

peculiarly professional character of legal education in the United States, it has helped to isolate law from other branches of learning. An increasing awareness of this difficulty, of the limitations of appellate court opinions, and of a slackening of student interest, has lead to some diminution in the stress on cases, and the pure case method is now rare in classes after the first year of law school. The casebooks that once contained only cases now contain text, statutes, legal forms, and writings from other disciplines such as economics, philosophy, sociology, and history. Cases are often supplemented by problems that may call for counseling or drafting or that challenge the student to apply professional and personal ethics. Many courses seek to develop the abilities to analyze and to resolve questions of policy, as well as to impart the traditional skills of the lawyer. But the emphasis is still on development of the student's critical faculties by requiring preparation in advance of class and the exercise of independent judgment, as well as on the student's ability to engage publicly in the independent exercise of those faculties through a dialogue with the professor in the classroom.

So it is that the American law student still finds the case method the basic pattern in most large classes, especially in the first year. Because the class may number over a hundred students,[13] the student called on to speak at any given time joins in a dialogue with the professor, and the other students learn by both listening and imagining their own answers to the professor's questions. The student is expected to spend two hours reading casebooks and treatises or other readings in preparation for each hour of class, and there are usually twelve to fifteen hours of class per week. There is, to be sure, a wide variety of teaching styles in law schools today, especially in small classes and classes in the upper years, although the case method remains a hallmark of U.S. legal education.

A number of other activities are available to enrich this educational experience. In a small course or seminar, discussion is more collaborative and informal. In courses that emphasize legal practice, the student may get practice in research and writing[14] and perhaps also in advocacy, counseling,

---

the situation of one of the hypothetical characters. Emphasis is on analysis and reasoning rather than on a "correct" conclusion. Law school examinations are written.

[13] In many schools, classes are often taught in sections so as not to exceed one hundred students.

[14] Law students are required to make extensive use of the library for research, although great libraries support scholarship and archives for advanced consultation. Harvard holds more

negotiation, or drafting. In a clinical program, the participants may receive practical experience by doing supervised work on actual cases, often in cooperation with an organization that furnishes legal services to those in need.[15] In moot court, students participate as counsel, usually on appeal, in simulated cases that the students argue before judges who are drawn from the faculty, the bar, the judiciary, and the student body. And those students who are fortunate enough to succeed in a competition, usually based at least in part on first-year grades, are invited to help to write and edit the many law reviews published by nearly two hundred law schools. These periodicals include America's most distinguished legal journals and are traditionally run by students.[16] After three years of this kind of training,[17] the law student is awarded the degree of *juris doctor* (J.D.) and becomes a candidate for admission to the bar.[18]

Suggested Readings

The classic lecture on the modern law school is K. Llewellyn, *The Bramble Bush: The Classic Lectures on the Law and Law School* (S. Sheppard ed., 2008). For a comprehensive history of U.S. law schools, see S. Sheppard, *The History of Legal*

---

than two million volumes (including microfilm) in its law library. Columbia and Yale have over one million each, and the libraries of other law schools are usually of well over one hundred thousand volumes.

[15] Virtually all law schools offer some form of clinical legal education, often involving actual problems but sometimes, as in the case of instruction in trial practice, involving simulated problems. In addition to practical work of this kind, most law students are exposed to some aspect of law practice through summer or part-time employment.

[16] Law reviews are discussed in Chapter 8, *infra*.

[17] Periodic reexaminations of the curriculum are common in American law schools. The landmark study conducted by the Columbia Law School in the 1920s under the influence of the "legal realists" is described in Currie, *The Materials of Law Study* (pt. 2). 8 J. Legal Educ. 1 (1955).

[18] In spite of the graduate character of legal study, most law schools awarding the degree of juris doctor (J.D.) once awarded a bachelor's degree in law (LL.B.), which is still awarded by some schools for three years of graduate study. While some institutions offer additional work leading to the degree of master of laws (LL.M.) and doctor of the science of law (J.S.D. or S.J.D), these degrees are rarely taken as preparation for the practice of law. Candidates for the degree of doctor of the science of law usually intend to teach law. (The degree should not be confused with that of doctor of laws (LLD.), which is an honorary rather than an earned degree.)

Education in the United States: Commentaries and Primary Sources (2007). For a summary of the development of the case method, see W. LaPiana, *Logic and Experience: The Origin of Modern American Legal Education* (1994). Current thinking in the field can be found in the Journal of Legal Education, the quarterly periodical of the Association of American Law Schools.

Some idea of nontraditional offerings in American law schools can be gotten from A. Polinsky, *An Introduction to Law and Economics* (4th ed. 2003); L. Freidman, S. MacAulay & J. Stookey, *The Law and Society Reader* (1995), and the schools of contemporary criticism of law and legal education derived from the critical movements of the 1970s and 1980s. Two books of readings on the feminist movement in legal thought are N. Levit, R. Verchik & M. Minow, *Feminist Legal Theory: A Primer* (2006). Critical Race Theory is described in K. Crenshaw, *Critical Race Theory: The Key Writings that Formed the Movement* (1996). On the critical legal studies movement generally, which stresses the internal contradictions in traditional legal thought, see M. Kelman, *A Guide to Critical Legal Studies* (1987), and D. Kennedy, *Legal Education and the Reproduction of Hierarchy: A Polemic Against the System* (2007).

See G. Fletcher & S. Sheppard, *American Law in a Global Context: The Basics*, Introduction, and Chapters 1 through 4.

THREE

Legal Profession

The American lawyer is fortunate in the wide range of activities in which he or she may engage and in the ease with which he or she may move from one branch of the profession to another. Who are American lawyers, what functions do they perform, how are they organized, and what have been their contributions to the profession?

The Bar

The regulation of the legal profession is primarily the concern of the states, each of which has its own requirements for admission to practice law. Most require three years of college and a law degree. Each state administers its own written examination to applicants for its bar and makes its own inquiry into the applicant's character. Almost all states, however, make use of the multistate bar examinations; multiple choice and essay tests, to which the state adds its own essay examination; and other examinations emphasizing its own law. The test in some states requires three days. A substantial fraction of all applicants succeed on the first try, and many of those who fail pass on a later attempt.[1] In all, over fifty thousand applicants are admitted to the bar each year[2] in their respective states. No apprenticeship is required either before or after admission. The rules for admission to practice before the federal courts vary with the court, but generally those entitled to practice before the highest court of a state may be admitted before the federal courts upon compliance with minor formalities.

A lawyer's practice is usually confined to a single community for, although a lawyer may travel to represent clients, one is only permitted to practice in a state where one has been admitted.[3] It is customary to retain local counsel for matters in other jurisdictions. However, one who moves to another state can usually appear in a single matter by the grant of a motion before the court to be admitted *pro hoc vice*, or one be admitted to practice routinely without examination if one has practiced in a state where admitted for some time, often five years.

A lawyer may not only practice law but is permitted to engage in any activity that is open to other citizens. It is not uncommon for the practicing lawyer to serve on boards of directors of corporate clients, to engage in business, and to participate actively in public affairs. A lawyer remains a member of the bar even after becoming a judge, the employee of a government or of a private business concern, or being appointed a law teacher. Lawyers often return to private practice from these other activities. A relatively small number of lawyers give up practice for responsible executive positions in commerce and industry. The mobility as well as the sense of public responsibility in the profession is evidenced by the career of Harlan Fiske Stone[4] who was, at various times, a successful New York lawyer,

---

[1] Roughly three-fourths of applicants pass the exam in their state, with pass rates varying widely from jurisdiction to jurisdiction. In 2008, 91 percent of takers passed the Montana bar exam, but only 54 percent passed in California. The National Conference of Bar Examiners maintains such statistics. *See* http://www.ncbex.org.

[2] Originally the "bar" was a partition in the courtroom separating the general public from the judges, lawyers, and others involved in the proceeding. It is now used to refer generally to the legal profession.

[3] A lawyer may, however, be admitted in more than one state and one may by special permission be permitted to appear before a court in a state where one is not admitted. A law firm may have offices in more than one state.

[4] Harlan Fiske Stone (1872–1946) combined teaching and the practice of law for a time after his graduation from Amherst College and the Columbia School of Law. He served as dean of the law school at Columbia from 1910 to 1923. In 1924, he was appointed attorney general.

a professor and Dean of the Columbia School of Law, Attorney General of the United States, and Chief Justice of the United States.

There is no formal division among lawyers according to function.[5] The distinction between barristers and solicitors found in England did not take root in the United States, and there is no branch of the profession that has a special or exclusive right to appear in court, nor is there a branch that specializes in the preparation of legal instruments.[6] The American lawyer's domain includes not only advocacy but also counseling and drafting. Furthermore, within the sphere broadly defined as the "practice of law," the domain is exclusive and is not open to others. In the field of advocacy, the rules are fairly clear: any individual may represent himself or herself in court but, with the exception of a few inferior courts, only a lawyer may represent another in court. Nonlawyers are, however, authorized to represent others in formal proceedings of a judicial nature before some administrative agencies. The lines of demarcation are less clear in the areas of counseling and drafting of legal instruments; for example, it is sometimes hard to find the line between the practice of law and the practice of accounting in the field of federal income taxation. However, the strict approach of most American courts is indicated by a decision of New York's highest court[7] that a lawyer admitted to practice in a foreign country but not in New York is prohibited from giving legal advice to clients in New York, even though the advice is limited to the law of the foreign country. A foreign lawyer may, however, be admitted to the bar of one

---

In 1925, he was appointed to the Supreme Court, and in 1941, he succeeded Charles Evans Hughes as chief justice.

[5] Where the terms "lawyer," "attorney," "attorney-at-law," "counselor," and "counselor-at-law" are used, it is generally for their elegance rather than for any difference in meaning. In those states with an equitable bench separate from their law courts, though, "counselor in equity" refers only to the lawyers licensed to practice equity. *See* Chapter 9, *infra*.

[6] In the United States, the office of notary or notary public is a minor office in each state, with the power to perform such routine functions as the attestation of writings and the administration of oaths. It requires no legal training, its function is often assigned to a clerk or secretary, and it cannot be compared with professions bearing similar names in other legal systems.

[7] Matter of New York County Lawyers Association (Roel), 144 N.E.2d 24 (N.Y. 1957), *appeal dismissed*, 355 U.S. 604 (1958) (advice on Mexican divorce law).

of the states[8] and may, even without being admitted, advise an American lawyer as a consultant on foreign law.

Because of the wide range of activities open to lawyers in the United States, the number of persons admitted to practice is large, now over a million, or one lawyer for every three hundred persons. Their income is good, though they are seldom rich, and the average lawyer earns considerably less than the average medical doctor. Nevertheless, the young law graduate who enters the employ of a law firm or a corporation can usually earn enough immediately to support a family. Lawyers are concentrated in metropolitan areas, with nearly a quarter of the total in California and New York. Roughly three-quarters of all lawyers are in private practice. Most of the rest are employed by private business concerns or are in government service, with smaller numbers in the judiciary or the teaching profession.

Lawyers in Private Practice

Among lawyers in private practice, just about half are solo practitioners. Most lawyers in private practice are in law firms, which range in size from two partners in a single office to many hundreds of lawyers in offices across the globe, many of them practicing in specialized groups, each of which focuses on a given field. About a third of lawyers in firms are in firms of one hundred or more. Firms are generally organized as partnerships of lawyers, the lawyers with an ownership interest are partners, and the other lawyers are associates, who are paid a salary by the firm.[9] This trend toward group practice is of relatively recent origin. Throughout most of the nineteenth century, law practice was general rather than specialized, its chief ingredient was advocacy rather than counseling and drafting, and the prototype of the American lawyer was the single practitioner. Marked specialization began in the latter part of that century in the large cities near the financial centers. With the growth of big business, big government, and big labor, the

---

[8] In the case of In re Griffiths, 413 U.S. 717 (1973), the Supreme Court of the United States held unconstitutional a state requirement that a person be a citizen of the United States in order to be admitted to the bar. However, in most states a nonresident lawyer, even if admitted, may not practice without maintaining an office there.

[9] In recent decades, lawyers have increasingly organized themselves into a new form of organization known as the professional service corporation.

work of the lawyer accommodated itself to the needs of clients for expert counseling and drafting to prevent as well as to settle disputes. Able lawyers were attracted to this work, and leadership of the bar gravitated to persons who rarely, if ever, appeared in court and who were sought after as advisors, planners, and negotiators. Today, the lawyer regards it as sound practice to be continuously familiar with clients' business problems and to participate at all steps in the shaping of their policies. Major business transactions are rarely undertaken without the advice of counsel.

The breadth of vision required of the today's attorney has been suggested by one American judge: "The modern lawyer almost invariably advises his client upon not only what is permissible but also what is desirable . . . His duty to society as well as to his client involves many relevant social, economic, political, and philosophical considerations."[10] Often the challenge cannot be met by one person alone. The complexity of American law and the flexible and malleable character of American business organizations make increasingly necessary a specialized knowledge of many fields as well as a substantial library.

In response to this need, the large law firm has developed. Although generally each client looks to one particular partner, there are partners specializing in such fields as taxation, commercial transactions, corporation law, antitrust law, bankruptcy law, real estate transactions, wills and estates, and litigation.[11] Large law firms claim a goodly share of the business of the giants of industry and commerce, whose problems seem to call for the cooperation of specialists, and each year they hire many of the top graduates of the leading law schools. These young men and women do much of the painstaking legal research,[12] and while they hope for partnership, they know that, in any case, after five or six years of experience as an associate in such a firm, other attractive opportunities will be open to them. Even outside of the relatively small number of such large firms, specialization is becoming more common, with lawyers whose practice consists largely or exclusively, for example, of personal injury cases, criminal cases, tax matters,

---

[10] Judge Wyzanski in United States v. United States Shoe Machinery Corp., 89 F. Supp. 357, 359 (D Mass. 1950).

[11] There is no regulation of practice in specialties as such, though a few states have taken steps to regulate a lawyer's description as a "specialist" in certain fields.

[12] Routine work is sometimes done by persons called "paralegals" who have not had the legal training that a lawyer has and who are not admitted to the bar.

or labor cases. The same need has brought about an increase in the number of lawyers engaged as house or corporate counsel.

House Counsel

Of the lawyers who are not in private practice, many are employed by private business concerns, such as industrial corporations, insurance companies, and banks, usually as house counsel in the concern's legal department.[13] The growth of corporations, the complexity of business, and the multitude of problems posed by government regulation make it desirable for such firms to have in their employ persons with legal training who, at the same time, are intimately familiar with the particular problems and conditions of the firm. In large corporations, the legal department may number one hundred or more. The general counsel, who heads the office, is usually an officer of the company and may serve on important policy-making committees and perhaps on the board of directors. House counsel remain members of the bar and are entitled to appear in court, though an outside lawyer is often retained for litigation. However, it is the house counsel's skill as advisor rather than as advocate that is a valued asset. Constantly in touch with the employer's problems, house counsel is ideally situated to practice preventive law and may also be called upon to advise the company on its broader obligation to the public and the nation.

Lawyers in Government

A parallel development has taken place in government, and many of the lawyers who are not in private practice are employees of the federal, state, county, and municipal governments, exclusive of the judiciary. Those entering public service are often recent law graduates who find government salaries sufficiently attractive at this stage of their careers and seek the training that such service may offer as a prelude to private practice.

---

[13]   There is no significant difference among the terms "house counsel," "in-house counsel," "corporate counsel," "general counsel," or "vice president for legal affairs" when applied to an officer or employee of a corporation who is an attorney.

Limitations on top salaries, however, discourage some from continuing with government employment, though others enter public service toward the end of a lucrative career. Most government lawyers serve by appointment in the legal departments of a variety of federal and state agencies and local entities. The United States Department of Justice alone employs over ten thousand lawyers,[14] and the Law Department of the City of New York about six hundred. Others are engaged as public prosecutors. Federal prosecutors, the United States attorneys, and their assistants, are appointed by the president and are subordinate to the Attorney General of the United States. State prosecutors, sometimes known as district attorneys, are commonly elected by each county and, together with their assistants, are not under the control of the state attorney general. As a rule, lawyers in government are directly engaged in legal work, since law training is infrequently sought as preparation for general government service. However, a small but important minority that constitutes an exception to this rule consists of those who have been appointed to high executive positions and those who have been elected to political office. Though the participation of lawyers in government has declined somewhat, for two centuries, lawyers made up roughly half of the Congress of the United States and of the state governors.[15] These figures bear out the comment of Chief Justice Harlan Stone that "No tradition of our profession is more cherished by lawyers than that of its leadership in public affairs."

Judges

A small number of those admitted to practice law serve as federal, state, county, or municipal court judges. Except for some inferior state courts, judges are generally required to be admitted to practice but do not practice while on the bench. There is so little uniformity that it is difficult to generalize further than to point out three salient characteristics that relate to the ranks from which judges are drawn, to the method of their selection, and to their tenure.

---

[14] More than half of these are employed in the offices of the United States attorneys, who serve in the federal districts under the Department of Justice.

[15] Somewhat less than half of the members of Congress now have law degrees.

Judges are drawn from the practicing bar and, less frequently, from government service or the teaching profession. There is in the United States no career judiciary like that found in many other countries, and there is no prescribed route for the young law graduate who aspires to be a judge—no apprenticeship that must be served, no service that must be entered. The outstanding young law graduates who act for a year or two as law clerks to the judges of the federal and state courts have only the reward of the experience to take with them into practice and not the promise of a judicial career. While it is not uncommon for a vacancy on a higher court to be filled by a judge from a lower court, even this cannot be said to be the rule. The legal profession is not entirely unaware of the advantages of a career judiciary, but it is generally thought that they are outweighed by the experience and independence which American lawyers bring to the bench. Many of the outstanding judges of the country's highest courts have had no prior judicial experience. Criticism has centered instead on the method of selection of judges.

State court judges are usually elected, commonly by popular vote, but occasionally by the legislature.[16] Popular election has been the subject of much disapproval, including that of the American Bar Association, on the ground that the public lacks interest in and information about candidates for judicial office and that therefore the outcome is too often controlled by leaders of political parties or by interested litigants who fund judicial election campaigns.

In a majority of states, judges of the highest court are now appointed by the governor. In most of these states, the judge then periodically stands unopposed for reelection by popular vote on the basis of his or her record.[17] In many states, however, judges of the highest court are elected, though in most of these states the election is nonpartisan.

---

[16] It has not always been so. The first state constitutions generally provided for selection of judges either by the legislature or by the governor, or both, and for life tenure. This system was swept away during the wave of Jacksonian democracy in the middle of the nineteenth century when, to limit the power of judges and the power of elected officials generally, there was a shift to popular vote and short judicial terms.

[17] Such a system is sometimes called "the Missouri Plan," after the first state to adopt one.

Federal judges are appointed by the President of the United States, subject to confirmation by the Senate.[18] Even under the appointive system, the selection of judges is not immune from political influence and appointees are usually of the president's or governor's own party. But names of candidates for the federal judiciary are submitted to a committee of the American Bar Association, and appointment is usually made only after the committee has found that the candidate is qualified. The office of chief judge or chief justice is usually filled in the same manner as other judicial offices, although in some states, it is filled from among the members of the court by rotation, by seniority of service, or by vote of the judges. The Chief Justice of the United States is appointed by the president, subject to Senate confirmation.

The third characteristic is that state judges commonly serve for a term of years rather than for life. For courts of general jurisdiction, it is typically four, six, or eight years, and for appellate courts, six, eight, or ten years. Happily, even where selection is by popular election, it is customary to return to office sitting judges whose service has been satisfactory. In a few state courts and in the federal courts, the judges (except for magistrate judges) sit for life. Whether on the bench for a term of years or for life, a judge may be removed from office only for gross misconduct and only by formal proceedings. Instances of removal have been rare indeed, and only a handful of federal judges have been removed by formal proceedings.[19] The independence of the judiciary is also encouraged by the rule that a judge incurs no civil liability for judicial acts, even if guilty of fraud and corruption. The American Bar Association's *Code of Judicial Conduct* has been widely adopted as a standard to which judges are expected to adhere. Salaries for the higher judicial offices are usually good although much less than the income of a successful private practitioner; the prestige of these offices is high, and the bench has been able to attract many of the country's ablest legal minds. The great names in American law are in large part the names of its great judges.

---

[18] Appointments of federal judges below the Supreme Court are subject to a rule of "senatorial courtesy" under which a senator from the president's own party approves appointments within the senator's state. Refusal to confirm is rare, although recent arguments between the political parties in the Senate have altered and slowed this process.

[19] Federal judges can be removed by impeachment proceedings in the Senate. Judges have, on occasion, resigned rather than face impeachment.

Law Teachers

American law teachers, like American judges, serve no formal apprenticeship before their appointment and, like judges, they are often drawn from the practicing bar. Their most common titles are assistant professor, associate professor, and professor. Although many successful candidates for teaching positions have engaged in the graduate law study toward a master of laws or a doctoral degree in law or another field, or in a period as a teaching fellow, neither is essential.[20] In spite of the practical background of many law teachers, the leading law schools, with few exceptions, demand that the members of their faculties devote their full time to teaching and research and give up the regular practice of law. American law teachers seem to be given to introspection, and the attention which they pay to the educational process itself is probably unsurpassed in any other country. A striking characteristic of the American law faculty is the independence accorded to even its youngest members. One teaches one's own courses and prepares and grades one's own examinations. Although a faculty committee or a faculty mentor may be appointed to guide junior professors, no faculty member is under the direction of another,[21] and the academic freedom of each is jealously guarded.

Professional Organizations

Bar associations existed in colonial times and through the first few decades of the nineteenth century, but they fell into disuse long before the middle of that century. The history of the revival of lawyer's professional organizations in the United States therefore can be dated from 1870. In that year, the Association of the Bar of the City of New York was organized for the immediate purpose of fighting corruption in local government. It set the pattern for such organizations for the next fifty years: it was unofficial, voluntary, selective in its membership, and included only a small fraction of

---

[20] It must be remembered, however, that the degree of juris doctor usually evidences seven years of university education.

[21] The "chairs" that are occupied by distinguished professors at many American law schools may carry honor and stipend, but they give no supervisory responsibility over other faculty members or scholars.

the members of the profession in New York City. It remains today one of the most influential and active.

By 1923, every state and territory had a bar organization; and by 1930, city and county groups were said to number over one thousand. Their purposes include reforming and unifying the law, improving the administration of justice, advancing legal education, upholding the standards of the profession, providing continuing legal education for their members, increasing the availability of legal services, and furnishing library facilities. In 1878, the first and most important of the nationwide associations, the American Bar Association, was formed on the pattern of the Association of the Bar of the City of New York. Although one of its objectives was to coordinate and correlate the activities of the entire organized bar, it is a separate entity rather than a true federation of state or local organizations. Its membership was at first highly selective, but it has made efforts to broaden its base and now includes somewhat under half of those admitted to the practice of law in this country.

It was not until 1921 that the first state enacted legislation, which was patterned after a model act recommended by the American Bar Association and the American Judicature Society, to require that every lawyer practicing in the state be a dues-paying member of the state bar association. Such a mandatory bar is said to be "integrated." Well over half of the states now have integrated bars, which give the profession a way to express its opinions as a body. One purpose of integration is to improve the discipline of lawyers in relations with their clients, a matter that traditionally has been handled by the high court of the state. Disciplinary measures may include fines and imprisonment for contempt of court, censure, suspension, and disbarment. Only a few thousand public disciplinary orders are issued annually among the one million members of the bar. In almost all of the integrated states, the bar has investigatory function in disciplinary proceedings, and in many it has a trial function as well, leaving the courts with only a power of review. In non-integrated states, voluntary bar associations have rarely been given functions in disciplinary matters. All states require attorneys to subscribe to an oath to serve their office in good faith and to comply with rules governing professional conduct patterned after those promulgated by the American Bar Association.[22]

---

[22] In 1969, the American Bar Association adopted a Model Code of Professional Responsibility, on which rules in all states came to be based. In 1983, the Association adopted the

Aside from the general professional organizations, a number of groups seek to serve special needs. The most notable of these is the American Law Institute, which was organized in 1923 to overcome the uncertainty and complexity of American law. It is a select group of fewer than three thousand elected lawyers, judges, and law teachers, whose projects have included the Restatements of the Law, uniform and model laws, and the educational programs mentioned below.

Availability of Legal Services

One of the objects of many bar associations is to increase the availability of legal services, particularly to segments of society that have difficulty in affording such services. Legal assistance to those who can afford to pay may be handled through lawyer referral services, by which one may be referred to a lawyer who is available for consultation for a fee.[23] A lawyer's fee is a matter to be arranged between lawyer and client. Contingent fees[24] are generally permitted if they are not excessive, and they often help claimants to obtain counsel in personal injury cases. Some persons, notably members of labor unions, participate in group legal service arrangements in which they make periodic payments that entitle them to legal services that may be needed in the future. And in many cities, there are small claims courts with jurisdiction in most civil matters of perhaps $5,000 and an informal procedure in which costs are minimal, and a lawyer is not needed.

The middle of the twentieth century saw major developments in the availability of legal services to the poor in both criminal and civil cases. Traditionally, heavy reliance has been placed on private voluntary efforts.

Model Rules of Professional Conduct, intended to replace those rules. Many states have now adopted the Model Rules, but many others have retained the Model Code.

[23] In recent decades, lawyers have begun to advertise their services. Although many lawyers still do not advertise, traditional prohibitions of advertising have been relaxed since the Supreme Court of the United States held that some advertising by lawyers is constitutionally protected commercial speech. *See* Bates v. State Bar of Arizona, 433 U.S. 350 (1977), together with its progeny.

[24] A contingent fee is fixed as a percentage of the client's recovery in a dispute against another party. In the event that there is no recovery, no fee is due to the lawyer, though the client is still liable for expenses.

Some of these are by individual lawyers, who do work *pro bono publico* (for the public good) in their spare time by, for example, serving without compensation as counsel assigned by the court in criminal cases or participating in the preparation of briefs in civil rights cases. Many law firms encourage such work, and some have programs to promote it. Legal assistance to the needy in civil cases is furnished by legal aid societies, which have traditionally relied largely on private contributions to support this work. And privately supported organizations such as the American Civil Liberties Union and the Legal Defense and Education Fund provide representation in cases in which public issues are involved.[25] This has now been supplemented by the involvement of government in furnishing legal services to the needy.

Beginning with a landmark case in 1963,[26] the Supreme Court of the United States has held not only that indigent defendants who are accused of all but minor criminal offenses have a constitutional right to counsel in both state and federal courts but also that the government is obliged to provide such assistance. In most instances, especially in large urban areas, this is done by a public defender system in which lawyers serve on a regular basis, either by a contractual arrangement or as public employees. Sometimes, however, it is still done in the traditional manner, by a system of counsel assigned on a case-by-case basis, using local lawyers approved by the court who serve with or without compensation.

There is no constitutional requirement that counsel be furnished in civil cases. In 1965, however, the federal Office of Economic Opportunity began a legal services program for the poor, recognizing that the traditional private efforts could not meet the full range of their legal needs. In 1974, Congress replaced this program by establishing an independent but federally funded Legal Services Corporation to provide legal aid to the poor. Through its support of state and local legal service organizations, the corporation helped the needy with such everyday matters as consumer complaints, divorces, and evictions. It also helped them, sometimes through class actions, to assert their rights against government agencies and private interests. At the height of its activities, it distributed money to several hundred legal service organizations with more than a thousand offices, where

---

[25]   A few firms have now been formed for the practice of "public interest law."
[26]   Gideon v. Wainwright, 372 U.S. 335 (1963).

more than six thousand lawyers handled over a million and a half cases a year. However, this aspect of the corporation's activities became politically controversial and led to restrictions on the corporation's activities.

Continuing Legal Education

Another relatively recent phenomenon has been the growth in continuing legal education of the profession. A pioneer in this field has been the Practising Law Institute, a nonprofit educational corporation.[27] Since 1947, the American Law Institute and the American Bar Association have collaborated through a joint committee which supervises postadmission legal education programs throughout the nation.[28] These institutions offer lecture programs and publish materials in a wide variety of fields. Law schools also sponsor lectures and institutes on professional topics, and most state bars have continuing legal education programs. Many large law firms offer free programs as a means of recruiting and ingratiating themselves to clients. Most states now require that a lawyer periodically attend a specified number of hours of continuing legal education in order to remain qualified to practice. The expansion of continuing legal education is likely to continue in coming years, with a growing use of Internet distribution of such courses.

Suggested Readings

R. Abel, *American Lawyers* (1991) is slightly dated but remains one of the most useful studies of the practicing bar in America, and the same materials are considered in a comparative light in *Lawyers in Society: An Overview* (R. Abel & P. Lewis, eds., 1996). The law firm is chronicled and analyzed in M. Galanter & T. Palay, *Tournament of Lawyers: The Transformation of the Big Law Firm* (1994), while on the other side of the spectrum, public interest lawyers are described in *Cause Lawyers and Social*

---

[27]   See *Continuing Legal Education, Treatises, Books and Webcasts for Lawyers and Legal Professionals—Practising Law Institute,* http://www.pli.edu/.

[28]   See *ALI–ABA for CLE—Continuing Leadership in Professional Education,* http://www.ali-aba.org/.

Movements (A. Sarat & S. Scheingold eds., 2006). A magisterial review, appreciation, and criticism of the profession is presented in D. Rhode, *In the Interests of Justice: Reforming the Legal Profession* (2000). On the legal aspects of law practice, see *Restatement (Third) of the Law Governing Lawyers* (1988–) and G. Hazard, *The Law of Lawyering* (2001).

FOUR

The Judicial System

A salient characteristic of the American judicial establishment is its cleavage into parallel systems of state and federal courts. How are these systems organized and what are the limits of their jurisdiction?

A Dual System of Courts

For the most part, law in the United States can be conveniently classified, according to its sources, as decisional law or as legislation.[1] The judicial system is the best starting point for an inquiry into the sources of law for, though decisional law stands below legislation in the hierarchy of authorities, and case law is subject to change by statute, the judiciary has been the traditional fountainhead of law in America as in other common-law countries.

---

[1] Custom, a third possibility, is usually thought to be relatively insignificant as a source of law in the United States. It may be used, for example, in interpreting a contract or in determining whether a prescribed standard of conduct has been met, but rarely has it given rise to a new legal rule. *But see* Chapter 1, *supra*, for an example of the use of custom as a source of water and mining law.

One of the results of the particular form of federalism that has grown up in the United States is a judicial structure in which a nationwide system of federal courts functions alongside the state courts.

State Courts

The great bulk of all litigation comes before the state courts. Each state by constitution and statute has established its own system, and the lack of uniformity from state to state makes it impossible to give a detailed description to fit all states. Too often, the state courts bear the stamp of conditions and concepts belonging to the time of their origins, which are now changed or outmoded. In the late eighteenth century, when the first court systems were established, travel was difficult, and communication was slow. The response was to create a number of courts of general jurisdiction to bring justice close to the people, who soon came to regard the state court in their locality as their own particular possession. This policy of multiplication of courts and decentralization of the court system has persisted until modern times. In recent years, however, considerable progress has been made in the simplification of state court systems and in the improvement of judicial administration. This is perhaps best illustrated with the growth of electronic records of the courts, allowing litigants, lawyers, and others to observe the work of the state courts without travelling to each courthouse.

In each state, there are trial courts of general jurisdiction, which are called by such names as the superior courts, circuit courts, or courts of common pleas.[2] A single judge presides, whether there is a jury or not, and is generally competent to hear all cases, civil and criminal, that are not restricted to special courts or divisions. Such special courts or divisions with limited jurisdiction may include criminal courts, domestic relations or family courts, juvenile or children's courts, and probate or surrogates' courts for decedents' estates. In addition, there are courts of inferior jurisdiction that handle petty matters. These were traditionally the justice of the peace courts, which are now often called justice courts, but they have often been

---

[2] Circuit courts are so called because at one time judges traveled about "on circuit" to hold court. In New York, the court of general jurisdiction is known as the Supreme Court, Trial Term.

supplanted by county, municipal, small claims, police, and traffic courts. Neither at the state nor the federal level are there special commercial courts like those in some countries.

At the top of the state judicial system is the highest appellate court of that state. In most states, it is called the supreme court; in some it is known by another name, such as the New York Court of Appeals or the Massachusetts Supreme Judicial Court. The number of judges ranges from five to nine, with seven the most common number, including a chief justice and associate justices. In most states, there are intermediate appellate courts, usually called courts of appeal or appellate courts,[3] which are between the courts of general jurisdiction and the highest court and which are sometimes divided into specialized courts, such as a court specially tasked to hear criminal appeals.

Federal Courts

The decision of the framers of the Constitution to leave to Congress the power to create the lower federal courts, if it chooses to do so, has given flexibility and the opportunity for experiment within the federal judicial system. This system has three principal levels: the district courts, the courts of appeals, and the Supreme Court. There are also such special courts of limited jurisdiction as the U.S. Court of Federal Claims, the U.S. Court of International Trade, and the U.S. Tax Court.[4] Although there is no special system of administrative courts, there are many federal administrative tribunals that have adjudicatory functions within the various departments and agencies but that are not properly courts.[5]

The United States District Courts are the federal trial courts of general jurisdiction for both civil and criminal matters, including admiralty (or maritime) cases. They also review the decisions of some federal administrative agencies. There are some ninety-four district courts located throughout

---

[3] In New York, where the Court of Appeals is the highest court, the intermediate appellate court is called the Appellate Division of the Supreme Court.

[4] The Court of Federal Claims hears certain claims against the United States. Appeals from the Court of Federal Claims and from the Court of International Trade go to a special court of appeals, the Court of Appeals for the Federal Circuit.

[5] On judicial control of administrative actions, see Chapter 12, infra.

the fifty states, the District of Columbia, and some territories. Some states contain only one judicial district, while other states are divided into as many as four. Although a judicial district may have a number of judges, depending on the volume of cases, a single judge generally presides over any given case, whether it is heard with a jury or not. The work of the district court judges is eased by magistrate judges and bankruptcy judges.

Appeals from a district court are generally heard in the United States Court of Appeals for the circuit in which the district is located.[6] In very rare instances, an appeal may be from a district court directly to the Supreme Court. There are thirteen such circuits, eleven comprising geographical divisions of the states and including a number of districts, a twelfth for the District of Columbia, and a thirteenth that reviews cases from specialized federal courts. These are the intermediary appellate courts in the federal system, but because of the limitations on review by the Supreme Court, they are, in practical matter, the courts of last resort for most federal cases. In addition to hearing appeals from the district courts, they also review decisions of certain federal administrative agencies such as the National Labor Relations Board. The number of judges in each circuit varies, but the judges ordinarily hear appeals in panels of three. In a few rare cases, all of the active judges of a court will reconsider a decision reached by a panel, in a proceeding *en banc*.

Appellate review of the decisions of the U.S. courts of appeals is in the hands of the U.S. Supreme Court, which since 1869 has consisted of nine members—one chief justice and eight associate justices—who sit as a body and not in panels. Their number has varied over time and is fixed by Congress.[7] It is the only federal court created by the Constitution; all others are creatures of congressional enactment under a grant of power in the Constitution. As will be explained shortly, it not only holds the highest appellate authority in the federal system but also has a limited power of

---

[6] A map of the districts and of the circuits is available at www.uscourts.gov/images/CircuitMap.pdf.

[7] The most recent attempt to change the number of judges on the Supreme Court came in 1937, when President Franklin Delano Roosevelt proposed what came to be known as his "court-packing" bill, an attempt to increase the size of the Supreme Court in response to Court decisions holding parts of his legislative program unconstitutional. That proposal was abandoned after the Court altered its philosophy regarding his program.

review over the state courts. However, the proportion of cases in which the Supreme Court reviews either federal or state courts is very small.

Federal Jurisdiction

The determination of the jurisdiction of the state and federal courts is a part of the more general problem of the distribution of state and federal power. Under the Constitution, the federal government has only those powers that are granted to it, and the residual powers are left to the states or to the people. Whatever judicial jurisdiction has not been given exclusively to the federal courts remains in the state courts, and so by determining what jurisdiction is given exclusively to the federal courts, what jurisdiction is given nonexclusively to the federal courts (which is concurrent jurisdiction), or that has not been given to the federal courts, the jurisdiction of both systems may be understood. It is therefore customary to discuss the division of judicial power in terms of federal, rather than state, jurisdiction.

Because the federal district courts were created by congressional enactment, their jurisdiction is defined not only by the constitutional grant of federal judicial power but also by the implementation of that power by federal legislation that began with the First Judiciary Act of 1789. Congress need not grant, and indeed has not granted, jurisdiction to the district courts to the full extent of the power given it by the Constitution.

The criminal jurisdiction of the district courts, which accounts for a substantial minority of all cases, includes all offenses against federal law. This includes federally recognized offenses against international law and state law.

Most of the civil business of these courts is of three kinds: first, cases in which the United States is a party; second, cases between private parties involving federal laws, under the so-called "federal question" jurisdiction; and third, cases between citizens of different states, under the so-called "diversity" jurisdiction.

The first category embraces not only criminal actions but also other actions brought "by the United States, or by an agency or officer thereof expressly authorized to sue by Act of Congress," as well as certain actions against the United States in which Congress has conferred jurisdiction upon the district courts. Its reason is evident: actions in which the

United States is a party, whether as plaintiff or defendant, are heard not in state courts but federal courts.

The second category, cases under federal question jurisdiction, consists of controversies arising under the Constitution, laws, or treaties of the United States. The reasons for this category are also apparent. The federal courts are thus charged with the vindication of federally created rights and the settlement of federally recognized causes of action.

The third category, diversity jurisdiction, includes cases in which the dispute is between citizens of different states including foreign states and the amount in controversy exceeds \$75,000.[8] The reason for this category of jurisdiction is not entirely clear, but the conventional explanation is that the framers of the Constitution sought to avoid the partiality that might result if, for example, a New York creditor were obliged to try a claim against a Massachusetts debtor before a Massachusetts state court. In any event, some litigants prefer to be in federal courts today less from a fear of prejudice than from a belief that the court, the procedure, or the court calendar is more favorable to their interests. Diversity jurisdiction has been criticized from time to time and remains the most controversial ground of federal judicial power.

In some cases, Congress has made the jurisdiction of the federal courts exclusive. Thus, in cases under the federal criminal laws, in some admiralty (maritime) cases, in bankruptcy proceedings, and in cases under most patent doctrines and copyright laws, the matter cannot be brought before a state court. In most matters, Congress has not given the subject matter exclusively to the federal courts, and the jurisdiction of federal and state courts in these matters is concurrent, which means that the plaintiff can bring the action in either court. Cases of diversity jurisdiction and many cases of federal question jurisdiction are instances of concurrent jurisdiction. Thus, state-created rights may be enforced in the federal courts, and federally created rights may be enforced in the state courts. Where jurisdiction is concurrent and suit has been brought in the state court, however,

---

[8] This amount, which is a realistic assessment of the potential damages that might be paid to the plaintiff, is set by Congress and varies from time to time. *See* 28 U.S.C. § 1332 (2009). For the purpose of determining whether there is diversity, a corporation is regarded as a citizen not only of the state where it has been incorporated but also of the state where it has its principal place of business. Resident aliens are considered citizens of the state in which they are domiciled.

the defendant usually has the right to have the case removed to the federal district court. In these cases of concurrent jurisdiction, either party may select the federal courts, the plaintiff by the original choice of forum and the defendant by removal.[9]

Under the Constitution, the Supreme Court itself has original (or trial) jurisdiction over a few categories of cases, the most usual being disputes between states or between a state and the federal government. The trial is conducted by an officer of the court known as a special master, who is appointed for that case and who reports findings on the evidence to the Court for review and adjudication of the law. However, such cases are not common. The Court's jurisdiction is in the main appellate and is assigned, within constitutional limits, by Congress. The mechanism of review is designed to limit those cases that are to be decided on the merits with full consideration to a relatively small and manageable number, which are usually of some concern to the public at large as well as to the litigants.

One of the most important limitations on the work of the Supreme Court, as well as the lower federal courts, is that its jurisdiction extends only to "cases and controversies." It will decide lawsuits only between adversary litigants who have real interests at stake in a ripened controversy. Unlike some state courts, the U.S. Supreme Court will not give advisory opinions, even on constitutional questions, and even at the request of the president or Congress.[10] Another restriction is that federal questions must be "substantial" in order to confer jurisdiction on the Supreme Court. And in no event will the Court review decisions of the state courts on questions of state law that do not affect a federal law or constitutional interest. The state courts are themselves the final arbiters of state law, and their decisions are conclusive on such matters.

The principal method of review by the Supreme Court that has been provided by Congress is by writ of certiorari, a command issued from

---

[9] There are some exceptions. A resident defendant who is sued in a state court by a nonresident plaintiff cannot remove on the ground of diversity.

[10] However, the Declaratory Judgment Act authorizes federal courts, in certain circumstances including the existence of an "actual controversy," to render a judgment declaring the rights of the parties in advance of any claim for damages or other relief. The highest courts of several of the states are empowered to give advisory opinions to the state legislature or the governor.

the Supreme Court to the lower federal court or to the state court of last resort,[11] requiring it to certify and return the record of the proceedings in the case.[12] Even in a proper case, the issuance of such a writ is within the discretion of the Court.[13] It may be granted upon the petition of a party to any case before a federal court of appeals. It may also be granted to review a judgment of a state court of last resort where, for example, a state statute has been held to be invalid under the Constitution or other federal law. But certiorari will only be granted for "special and important reasons," and the fact that the decision below is erroneous is not such a reason. Circumstances that may influence the Court to grant certiorari include the existence of a conflict either between decisions among federal courts of appeals for different circuits or between a decision by a state court on a federal question and the decisions of the Supreme Court itself. While the bulk of the cases disposed of annually by the Court consists of requests for certiorari, it grants less than five percent of these and rejects the remainder as unsuitable for review. Thus, while the Court may dispose of nearly seven thousand cases a year, it decides very few on the merits and writes full opinions in only about one hundred.[14]

Law Applied in the Federal Courts

Because the federal government has only such powers as are conferred upon it by the Constitution, federal law is supreme only in limited areas. Litigation in American courts often involves complex problems of accommodation of state and federal law. In either a state or federal court, an action based on a right derived from state law may be met by a defense based on federal law, or conversely, one based on federal law may be met by a defense

---

[11] The state court of last resort is the highest state court to which a particular case could be taken on appeal. It is usually, although not always, the highest court of the state.

[12] Appeal is another method of review, but it is of limited significance in U.S. Supreme Court practice.

[13] It is the practice to grant certiorari only on the concurrence of at least four justices.

[14] The calendar of cases pending before the court and the opinions of the Court that have recently been announced are both available at http://www.supremecourtus.gov/. A survey of the work of the Court during the preceding year appears annually in the *Harvard Law Review*.

based on state law. The federal courts are thus frequently called upon to apply state law, and while the problem of giving effect in one jurisdiction to the laws of another is not peculiar to American federalism, the role of state law in the federal courts has had a unique history.

In 1842, in the landmark case of *Swift v. Tyson*,[15] the Supreme Court recognized the duty of the federal courts to give effect, on questions within the law-making competence of the states, to state law that was distinctively "local" in character, meaning in most instances that state statutes would be applied, because statutes were presumed more to regulate local matters. But if the subject matter of the case was considered to be "general law" (*i.e.*, the general provisions of the common law), the federal courts were under a duty both to ascertain the relevant legal principles independently and to apply these principles regardless of what the courts of the particular state would have done. Thus, there grew up a "federal common law," binding upon the federal courts but not upon the state courts, and the outcome of litigation might depend upon which court, state or federal, heard the case. Critics deplored the resulting "forum shopping" and the frustration of state policies. Defenders of the decision maintained that it contributed toward a needed national uniformity in the law.

In 1938, when the doctrine of *Swift v. Tyson* had been in force for almost a century, it was overruled by the U.S. Supreme Court in *Erie Railroad Co. v. Tompkins*.[16] The opinion of the Court in this historic case, by Justice Brandeis,[17] rested finally upon the constitutional ground that, in the absence of applicable federal legislation, the federal courts were bound to apply state case law no less than state statutory law. This decision has in turn given rise to a host of new problems.

The Supreme Court has interpreted the principle of the *Erie* case as requiring, in cases of diversity jurisdiction, that a federal court adjudicating

---

[15] 41 U.S. (16 Pet.) (1842).

[16] 304 U.S. 64 (1938).

[17] Louis Dembitz Brandeis (1858–1941) practiced in Boston, Massachusetts, for about forty years after graduation from Harvard Law School, during which he argued many major cases and became famous for his long written arguments, or briefs, citing social science in support of his legal claims. He was appointed an Associate Justice of the Supreme Court of the United States in 1916, although he had previously held no judicial or other public office. In part, because of his allegedly "radical" position on social and economic issues, his confirmation aroused some of the most substantial opposition to meet any successful appointee to the Court. He served with great distinction until his retirement in 1939.

claims arising under state law arrive at substantially the same statement of the law as would a court of the state in which it sits.[18] The impact of this approach on choice of law is unique. Under this approach, a court hearing a case that might be subject to the substantive laws of a different forum, departs from the general rule that a court applies the choice-of-law rules of its forum to determine what foreign law, if any, it should apply. Instead, the federal forum gives effect to state law, and the federal court must follow the choice-of-law principles of the state in which it sits, in the manner that a state court would apply them.[19] Furthermore, the extent to which federal courts may apply federal rather than state law to matters that have usually been regarded as procedural is not free from doubt.[20] The issues raised by state law in the federal courts are generally complex and still in a state of flux.[21]

Suggested Readings

There is no comprehensive treatise on both federal and state courts, but a nice summary is in D. Meador, *American Courts* (2000). H. Abraham, *The Judicial Process: An Introductory Analysis of the Courts of the United States, England, and France* (7th ed. 1998) is a helpful comparative work. On the federal system, see C. Wright & M. Kane, *Handbook of the Law of Federal Courts* (6th ed. 2002). A biennial tabulation of information on state courts is contained in Council of State Governments, *The Book of the States*, Chapter 4, State Judicial Branch. For an introductory analysis of the role of the state and federal judiciary in government, see A. Tarr, *Judicial Process & Policymaking* (2009). Although very much a study of the U.S. Supreme Court, many of the insights also apply to state courts high courts in T. Van Geel, *Understanding Supreme Court Opinions* (5th ed. 2006).

---

[18] Guaranty Trust Co. v. York, 326 U S. 99 (1945).
[19] Klaxon v. Stentor Electric Manufacturing Co., Inc., 313 U.S. 487 (1941).
[20] *Compare* Hanna v. Plumer, 380 U.S. 460 (1965), *with* Ragan v. Merchants Transfer & Warehouse Co., 337 U.S. 530 (1949), discussed in C. WRIGHT & M. KANE, HANDBOOK OF THE LAW OF FEDERAL COURTS, section 59 (6th ed. 2002).
[21] The extent to which the federal courts are bound by decisions of inferior state courts is discussed in *id*.

FIVE

Case Law

Case law has special significance in the United States because of the common law tradition. What is its form, where can it be found, and what authority does it have?

Form of Reported Cases

Because of the modern doctrine of precedent in the United States, some knowledge of the form of reported cases is particularly important to an understanding of American law. Case law is found primarily in the decisions of appellate courts. Except for the federal trial courts—and those of a few states—trial court opinions are not published.[1] The typical case is entitled by the names of the parties who oppose one another, which are

---

[1] Publication was once an important requirement for an opinion to be considered as precedent, but whether an opinion is published or not has grown less important in recent years. An unpublished opinion may not be cited as authority in every court, although it now may be in federal courts. With the growth of the publication of opinions by the courts on authorized Web sites, this distinction will grow even less significant.

separated by "v." for "versus," for example, as in *Jones v. Smith*. Usually the name that appears first is the name of the original plaintiff in the trial court, but in some jurisdictions, it is the name of the party taking the appeal. A criminal case may appear as *State v. White* or *California v. Brown* or *Green v. United States*. Occasionally only one name appears, as, for example, *In re Brown* in a bankruptcy proceeding, which means "in the matter of Brown." In published versions of opinions, after the title will come a headnote or syllabus summarizing the opinion, occasionally a digest of the arguments of counsel, and then, perhaps, a statement of the facts by the reporter of the case. After the name of the judge or justice writing the opinion is printed follows the portion of the report that carries authority—the opinion of the court, which usually concludes in its decision disposing of the case.

An opinion may vary in length from less than one to more than twenty pages, but five pages in the official reports is typical. Although a decision is announced in the "opinion of the court," this opinion is commonly written on behalf of the court by a single judge, whose name precedes the opinion. The judge will usually summarize the facts and the procedural history of the case, state the issues before the court, and give a full and careful statement of the reasons for the decision, citing statutes, cases, and other authorities.[2] Judges are expected to have the time to do this. In a year, a member of the Supreme Court of the United States may write fewer than three dozen opinions, including concurrences and dissents. A judge on the highest court in some states may write only somewhat more, although the courts in other states have grappled with increasingly growing dockets. In preparing opinions, judges are assisted by law clerks, often high-ranking recent law school graduates with writing experience on a law review, who have served as a law clerk to a judge of one of the courts of appeals. The decision of the court itself is by majority vote[3] and is stated at the end of the opinion. It may affirm, reverse, or modify the decision of the court below and may contain directions for further proceedings by the lower court. The members of the court who concur may then be listed. A judge

---

[2] A judge in writing an opinion may well be influenced by experience at the bar, and individual literary styles vary considerably. On the writing of opinions, including dissenting and concurring opinions, *see* R. Leflar, Appellate Judicial Opinions ch. 7 & 8 (1974).

[3] If an even number of judges should sit, perhaps because of the disqualification of one member of the court, and a tie vote results, the decision of the lower court is thereby affirmed.

who agrees with the decision but for reasons different from the opinion's rationale for it may write a separate concurring opinion, stating reasons for the concurrence. However, in contrast to the practice in England and other jurisdictions, concurring opinions are the exception rather than the rule in the United States. A judge who disagrees with the decision may dissent from it, with or without an opinion.[4] Opinions need not be signed, however, and it is not uncommon for a court to write an unsigned and usually shorter opinion *per curiam* (by the court) when, for example, the point in issue is thought to be well settled. In most jurisdictions, a court need not give any reasons for its decision, and many appeals, particularly upon affirmance, are disposed of without opinion by what are known as memorandum decisions.

Finding Case Law

The sheer number of decisions is an obvious obstacle to finding case law, which has customarily been a matter of research in printed books. Reported decisions of the Supreme Court of the United States and of many of the state appellate courts can be found in the official reports of those courts.[5] Those decided from at least 1887 to date can also be found in a system of unofficial reports, the National Reporter System of the West Publishing Company, with over ten thousand volumes, with some volumes of over 1,500 pages.[6]

In the West system, state court decisions are published in seven regional sets of volumes, each covering a geographical area of the country, plus three additional sets devoted solely to decisions of the California, Illinois, and New York courts. Federal decisions are published in five sets, one each

---

[4] The dissent has become peculiarly frequent in the Supreme Court of the United States, where well over half of the decisions have dissents. For an entertaining discussion of the "chores of the dissenter," *see* Guilmet v. Campbell, 188 N.W.2d 601, 610–11 (Mich. 1971) (Black, J., dissenting).

[5] In a substantial and increasing number of states, however, the publication of official reports has been abandoned, and in many states, the official opinions of the courts are released only in an electronic file from the court's Web site.

[6] This estimate of the number of volumes does not include those devoted solely to the California, Illinois, and New York courts.

for the Supreme Court, the courts of appeals, and selected cases from the district courts, along with one for bankruptcy cases and one for decisions involving the federal rules of procedure.[7] Other decisions of the lower federal courts are not published officially.[8] Opinions as reported in the unofficial reports are sometimes preferred by lawyers because they are available sooner through publication in temporary pamphlets known as advance sheets, are coordinated with a system of digests or annotations, and are more compact. A second and highly selective system of unofficial reports—the American Law Reports—publishes only that small fraction of all reported cases that is thought to be of special interest and appends extensive annotations that discuss and cite related cases.

In the past it was usual, when referring to a case, to cite both official and unofficial reports. Thus, a correct citation was *Wangen v. Ford Motor Co.*, 97 Wis. 2d 260, 294 N.W.2d 437, 13 A.L.R. 4th 1 (1980), meaning that the case was decided in 1980, is found at page 260 of volume 97 of the second series of official Wisconsin reports, at page 437 of volume 294 of the second series of the Northwestern set of the National Reporter System, and at page 1 of volume 13 of the fourth series of American Law Reports, where it is followed by annotation.

Today it is common to cite only one official or unofficial report, as required by the style manual of the court or firm in which the writing is to be read. Thus, in most cases, one would cite the case as *Wangen v. Ford Motor Co.*, 294 N.W.2d 437 (Wis. 1980). In this manner are collected well over one hundred thousand reported court decisions that each year add to the existing millions of reports.

This flood of cases is somewhat manageable because of two well-developed systems, one of digests and the other of citators. The American Digest System is coordinated with the National Reporter System and covers the appellate court reports from 1658 to the present. The several points

---

[7] The seven regional sets are now in a second series of numeration and the federal set is in a third series.

[8] Decisions of the Supreme Court of the United States may be found not only in the official United States Reports and now on the Court's Web site, but also in unofficial printed reports, particularly the *Supreme Court Reporter* of the National Reporter System, the *Supreme Court Reports, Lawyers' Edition*, and *U.S. Law Week*, as well as many other online databases, including Westlaw and Findlaw, Loislaw, Jurist, and Lexis. Each system employs the volume and page of the official reports, and all print the docket number as well as the official names of the parties, so location is normally not difficult.

in an opinion are digested in short paragraphs and are then numbered and classified by subject matter according to an elaborate classification scheme. The numbered digest paragraphs are printed as the headnotes to the cases as they are reported in the National Reporter System and are also collected in a series of analytically arranged digest volumes. Subject to the vagaries of the classification system, one trained in the use of these digest notes can, in a relatively short time, collect the reported cases, with a few minor exceptions, decided by the courts upon a particular point. Shepard's Citations, an index of citations, covers the National Reporter System and the official state reports. It indexes decisions which have been cited in later opinions so that in a few minutes, it is possible to compile a list of subsequent opinions in which a particular decision has been mentioned.

Computer technology has now been developed to save time and ensure thoroughness in researching case law. Several computer systems, LEXIS, WESTLAW, LOISLAW, and an increasing array of search engines available on the Web have to a considerable extent replaced the traditional systems based on the printed page. They enable the user to retrieve most published and many unpublished federal and state court opinions. In searching for cases, one may use, for example, the name of the case, the citation of the case, the name of the judge, specific words or phrases contained in the opinion or (in Westlaw) particular digest headings, as well as assess the case (in Lexis) through an automated Shepard's index.

The increasing practice of courts to publish the opinions of the court on a database on the Internet has increased the difficulty of searching through case law without using computers, although more material is available. Many courts, such as the Massachusetts Supreme Judicial Court, now publish a wider array of judicial materials than in the past, and with the aid of a computer provide free access to such materials to anyone who wishes to read them.[9] The federal courts provide a single consolidated service by which to access a range of materials from the trial and appellate courts, including not only opinions but filings. This service is cost-free to access, although a nominal fee is charged for downloading or printing materials.[10]

---

[9] See the official Web site of the office of the Reporter of Decisions of the Massachusetts Supreme Judicial Court and the Appeals Court. Massachusetts Supreme Judicial Court, http://www.massreports.com/welcome.htm.

[10] The PACER Service Center is the federal judiciary's centralized registration, billing, and technical support center for PACER. See PACER Service Center's home page, http://pacer.psc.uscourts.gov/.

Opinions of administrative agencies remain harder to find, although they, too, are increasingly available online. Although Shepard's Citations covers the decisions of some agencies, they are not reported or indexed in the National Reporter System. The most important federal regulatory agencies publish their own sets of reports, and unofficial loose-leaf services, usually in special fields, also contain agency opinions.

The Judicial Function

A judicial decision has two functions in a common-law system. The first, which is not, to be sure, peculiar to the common law, is to define and to dispose of the controversy before the court. Under the doctrine of *res judicata*, the parties may not re-litigate issues (whether in the same forum or another) that have been determined between them by a final and valid judgment. This determination is the responsibility of the court. It cannot abdicate its duty even should the case be a novel one for which there is no controlling authority. An old view was that the court in such a contingency was to discover the law among the principles of the common law, much as a scientist discovers a natural law, and then declare it. Today, it is more usual to admit that the court creates the law somewhat as a legislature creates law but within the narrower bounds set by the facts of the case before it and the analogous legal principles from distantly related doctrines.

Whether the court discovers or creates the law that it applies, its resolution of the controversy has an impact that extends beyond the parties before it. This is because the second function of a judicial decision, and one that is characteristic of the common law, is that it establishes a precedent so that a similar case arising in the future will probably be decided in the same way. This doctrine is often called by its Latin name, *stare decisis*—from *stare decisis et non quieta movere* (to stand by the decisions and not disturb settled points).[11] Reliance on precedent developed early in English law, and the practice was received in the United States as part of the tradition of the common law, though it was much developed in the nineteenth century as a means of restricting the powers of the appellate courts. As a tradition,

---

[11]   The doctrine of *stare decisis* is used here as synonymous with the doctrine of precedent, and the latter term will generally be employed.

the doctrine has not been reduced to a written rule and is not to be found in constitution, statute, or oath of office.[12] The justifications commonly given for the *stare decisis* may be summarized in four words: equality, predictability, economy, and respect. The first argument is that the application of the same rule to successive similar cases results in equality of treatment for all who come before the courts. The second is that consistent following of precedents contributes to predictability in future disputes. The third is that the use of established criteria to settle new cases saves time and energy. The fourth is that adherence to earlier decisions shows due respect for the wisdom and experience of prior generations of judges.

For several reasons, the doctrine of precedent has never enjoyed in the United States the absolute authority that it is said to have attained in England. The great volume of decisions, with conflicting precedents in different jurisdictions, has detracted from the authority of individual decisions. The rapidity of change has often weakened the applicability of precedents to later cases that have arisen after social and economic conditions have altered with the passage of years. Nevertheless, the doctrine of precedent, though less rigidly applied than in England, is still firmly entrenched in the United States.

Techniques in the Use of Precedent

Skill in the use of precedent is more art than science. It is no easier to acquire by reading a discussion of the doctrine than it is to learn to ride a bicycle by studying a textbook on mechanics, and the subject matter is considerably more controversial. It is possible, however, to set down the vocabulary, to make some of the more obvious generalizations, and to raise

---

[12] It is reported that the Supreme Court of the United States, where the doctrine of precedent is not at its strongest, overruled itself only ninety times in nearly a century and a half from 1810 to 1957. Blaustein & Field, *Overruling Opinions in the Supreme Court*, 57 MICH. L. REV. 151 (1958). That the constraint is in the nature of a tradition only is illustrated by the extraordinary example of Judge James E. Robinson, who served as a judge and briefly as chief justice of the Supreme Court of North Dakota and who attained some notoriety for his disapproval of the doctrine of precedent. Toward the end of his tenure, he stated the facts of cases with great brevity and rarely cited authority in his opinions. *See Note*, 33 HARV. L. REV 972 (1920).

a few of the interesting problems. What follows is, of course, a simplified explanation that assumes that each case involves only a single "case in point" as a precedent. More often, there is a line of decisions, or perhaps several divergent lines, and the task of advocate and court includes the synthesis of a number of cases. In this synthesis may be seen both the development and elaboration of a rule and the rule's broadening or narrowing to meet changing conditions and to take account of the great variety of situations that arise. Occasionally, at the other extreme, the problem before the court is a novel one, without precedent, and the court must reason from general principles, from analogy, and from what it conceives to be public interest and community understanding and expectation.[13] In between these two extremes, earlier decisions are considered more or less authoritative according to the degree their facts are similar; a case resulting from very similar facts in the past holds greater authority in a later dispute than does a case with very different facts, which may be "distinguished" on the grounds of the different facts by the later court.

Assuming the facts giving rise to an earlier and a later case are similar, the authority of the earlier case law is frequently divided into two classes: "persuasive" and "binding," a division that depends upon the relationship of the court that authored the opinion and the court in which the opinion would be applied. Persuasive authority includes decisions of courts of other jurisdictions and decisions of coordinate courts of the same jurisdiction, for example, other intermediate appellate courts of the same state or other federal courts of appeals.[14] The persuasiveness of such a decision will depend largely on the similarity of the facts, the force of the reasoning in the opinion, and the apparent soundness of the result. It may also depend on whether the decision has support in other jurisdictions: when there is a conflict among a number of jurisdictions on a given point, it is common to speak of a "majority" and a "minority" rule, and the majority rule may be followed because of its wider acceptance. The persuasiveness of a decision may also depend on the prominence of the court that decided it and of the judge who wrote the opinion: the opinions of such renowned judges as

---

[13]   In such situations, courts have often been receptive to data from the social sciences.

[14]   The authority of state court decisions in the federal courts is discussed in connection with Erie Railroad Co. v. Tompkins, discussed in Chapter 4, *supra*.

Holmes and Cardozo[15] carry more weight than those of lesser minds. And its persuasiveness may depend on the similarity of the law and of circumstances in the two jurisdictions: on a problem of commercial law, the courts of the eastern industrial state of New Jersey may be more influenced by a decision from their neighboring eastern industrial state of New York than by a conflicting one from the midwestern agricultural state of Iowa. But in any event, if it is only persuasive authority, the doctrine of precedent does not apply, and the court is not bound to follow it.

Binding authority, to which the doctrine of precedent does apply, includes decisions of higher courts of the same jurisdiction and decisions of the same court. Since a lower court is not likely to disregard a prior decision of a higher court,[16] which has the power of reversal on appeal,

---

[15] Benjamin Nathan Cardozo (1870–1938) practiced in New York City after graduation from Columbia College and the Columbia School of Law, served as judge and later chief judge on the Court of Appeals of New York, and was appointed an associate justice of the Supreme Court of the United States in 1932 to fill the vacancy left by Holmes. His best-known work is a series of lectures entitled *The Nature of the Judicial Process* (1921).

[16] Very rarely, a lower court will decline to follow a decision of a higher court in anticipation that the higher court will overrule its earlier decision if the case is appealed to it. An example is a New York case involving the question of whether a child can recover for breach of warranty (without any proof of fault) for injuries caused by impure food in an action against the retail seller from whom the child's father had purchased the food. Under decisions of the Court of Appeals of New York, the highest state court, in 1923 and 1927, the child could not recover for breach of warranty because the remedy was contractual in nature and since the father made the purchase, there was no contract of sale between the retailer and the child. In spite of these precedents, the trial court, the City Court of the City of New York, in 1957 allowed the child to recover. Greenberg v. Lorenz, 178 N.Y.S.2d 404 (N.Y. City Ct. 1957). An intermediate appellate court, the Appellate Term of the Supreme Court, affirmed, stating that, "Though it is not within the competence of an intermediate appellate court to disregard controlling precedent, nevertheless when the higher appellate courts— breaking new ground—establish a new trend and render it clear that if the instant question were before them they themselves would overrule earlier pronouncements, it becomes the right, nay the duty, of an intermediate appellate court to take cognizance of it." One of the three judges dissented. Greenberg v. Lorenz, 12 Misc.2d 883, 178 N.Y.S. 2d 407 (1958). A higher intermediate appellate court, the Appellate Division of the Supreme Court, reversed in a short per curiam opinion based on precedent. Two of the five judges dissented. Greenberg v. Lorenz, 7 A.D.2d 968, 183 N.Y.S.2d 46 (1959). But this decision was in turn reversed by the Court of Appeals of New York, which reinstated the trial court's judgment for the child and, as the Appellate Term had predicted, overruled the earlier decisions insofar as they applied to the case. Greenberg v. Lorenz, 9 N.Y.2d 195, 173 N.E.2d 773, 213 N.Y.S.2d 39 (1961). The situation in the federal courts is discussed in Kniffin, *Overruling Supreme Court Precedents: Anticipating Action by United States Courts of Appeals.* 51 FORDHAM L. REV. 53 (1982).

the significant question is the extent to which a court will follow one of its own prior decisions. The question is squarely raised by a single decision, for though the weight of persuasive authority may vary with the number of similar decisions, one of a court's own prior decisions is enough to constitute a precedent.

Fundamental to the answer of when an earlier opinion will bind a later court is the distinction between the "holding"[17] of a case and the "dictum."[18] The distinction stems from the common law's faith in adversary proceedings and the resultant belief that judges have the competence to decide only those matters that are necessary for the decision in the case. As to these matters, which have presumably been thoroughly argued by the parties, judges' decisions are to be treated as precedent and are "binding" authority. But judges, unlike legislators, have no power to lay down rules for cases that are not before them, and what they say on such other matters is not binding. In the words of Chief Justice John Marshall, "It is a maxim, not to be disregarded, that general expressions in every opinion, are to be taken in connection with the case in which those expressions are used. If they go beyond the case, they may be respected, but ought not to control the judgment in a subsequent suit when the very point is presented for decision. The reason of this maxim is obvious. The question actually before the court is investigated with care and considered in its full extent. Other principles which may serve to illustrate it, are considered in their relation to the case decided, but their possible bearing on all other cases is seldom completely investigated."[19] It is characteristic of the common law that a point of law may remain unsettled until some losing party determines to assume the burden of presenting that issue in an adversary proceeding on appeal. The "holding," then, is the rule of law that was necessary for the decision. Whatever else the judges said that was not necessary to their decision is only "dictum."

---

[17] In the United States, the word "holding" is generally used instead of the term *ratio decidendi*, used in England.

[18] Dictum is short for *obiter dictum*, Latin for "things said in passing." The plural is dicta. When the term *obiter dictum* is used to refer to an older judicial statement, the emphasis may suggest that the dictum is not reliable.

[19] Marshall made this statement in avoiding an application of Marbury v. Madison, in which he himself had written the opinion eighteen years earlier. Cohens v. Virginia, 19 U.S. (6 Wheat.) 264, 399 (1821).

Dictum is, nevertheless, authority worthy of respect. It may well be followed by the same court in later cases; it is usually sufficient to persuade a lower court, and it is often regarded by lawyers as a reliable basis for counseling. But, at least in principle, it is only persuasive authority and, unlike the holding, is not binding on any court. "Judges," said Justice Cardozo, "differ greatly in their reverence for the illustrations, and comments and side-remarks of their predecessors, to make no mention of their own."[20]

The holding of a case must be determined from an analysis of the material facts, from the decision, and from the reasoning of the opinion. Even this may be more difficult than it would seem at first. It is often hard to know how far the process of abstraction should be continued, to know how broad a statement of the rule is justified. The formulations of rules of law contained in the opinion cannot always be relied upon as authoritative; the rule that the court actually applied may never have been articulated or may have been stated in several different ways in the course of the opinion. Furthermore, the facts may have been stated so concisely that it is hard to tell what they were, or they may have been set forth in such ample detail that it is difficult to determine which facts the court thought material. Fortunately, no case is decided in isolation, and some of these difficulties may be resolved when the opinion is read against the background of other related decisions and general principles.

The rule that the court intended to lay down in one case may not, however, be the holding in the eyes of a later court. When a court is called upon to apply the doctrine of precedent, it is faced with not one but two concrete fact situations, that of the earlier decision and that of the case then up for decision. With both fact situations in mind, the court derives a rule from the first and decides whether it is applicable to the second, that is, the court determines whether the second case is a "like" case. In many instances, the precedent gives a decently clear and reasonable rule that the court will apply, more often than not with no inquiry into its merits. At other times, a desirable precedent may not seem to cover an appropriate case, or an undesirable precedent may seem to cover an inappropriate case.

At this point, it should be recognized that the doctrine of precedent does not demand unbending adherence to the past but admits of more supple techniques that permit an able court to profit from earlier wisdom

---

[20]   B. Cardozo, The Nature of the Judicial Process 29 (1921).

and experience while rejecting past folly and error. If it seems desirable to the judge in the later case to extend the principle of a prior decision to the present case, the holding of that prior decision may be read more broadly than had been intended by the court that handed it down; differences in the facts of the two cases will be treated by the later court as immaterial; and what might have been considered as dictum upon a narrow reading of the earlier case may be regarded as its holding. If, on the contrary, the later judge deems the rule of the earlier decision to be undesirable in deciding the case at hand, the later court may narrow the holding of that prior case in order to distinguish it from the one before it; differences in the facts of the two cases will be treated by the later court as material; and what might have been considered as holding upon a broad reading of the earlier case will be regarded as dictum—as not "necessary" to the disposition of the dispute then before the court.

Within limits, every decision is subject to such broadening and narrowing. Just where the limits are and just what attitude a given court will take on a given set of facts can be predicted—if at all—only on the basis of experience in working with a tradition that has been handed down through generations of common-law students, common-law lawyers, and common-law judges. As Justice Cardozo put it, "Back of precedents are the basic juridical conceptions which are the postulates of judicial reasoning, and farther back are the habits of life, the institutions of society, in which these conceptions had their origin, and which, by a process of interaction, they have modified in turn. None the less, in a system so highly developed as our own, precedents have so covered the ground that they fix the point of departure from which the labor of the judge begins. Almost invariably, the first step is to examine and compare them. If they are plain and to the point, there may be need of nothing more. Stare decisis is at least the every-day working rule of our law."[21]

But even a decision that is a "binding" authority is not absolutely binding. On rare occasions, a court will be faced with a situation in which it cannot render what it regards as a just decision and still stay within what it sees as the limits imposed by the doctrine of precedent. It may resolve the dilemma by following precedent in spite of the injustice in the particular case on the ground that the policies underlying the doctrine outweigh those

---

[21]   *Id.* at 19–20.

in favor of the opposite decision. Perhaps it will explain that any change is for the legislature and not the court to make. This result might not be surprising in a case involving commercial law or property law, where predictability is particularly important and where remedial legislative action is generally feasible. On the other hand, the court may be unwilling to follow precedent. The decision may have been clearly wrong when rendered, it may be so old that altered conditions have made it inappropriate,[22] or the composition of the court may have changed so that what was formerly the view of a vehement minority is now that of the majority. For any of these reasons, or for others, the court may refuse to follow precedent and may overrule its earlier decision. This result might not be surprising on a constitutional issue where legislation is not an available remedial device,[23] or on a procedural question where retroactive change is not exceptional. Tradition demands that where possible, the doctrine of precedent be honored by careful distinguishing rather than by outright overruling of objectionable decisions. But in point of fact, the decision which has been distinguished and expressly "limited to its particular facts" by a later opinion is often so whittled down as to be virtually overruled.[24]

Two Puzzles in Precedent

Among the puzzling problems that arise out of the doctrine of precedent, two are especially intriguing. The first concerns the weight to be given to a

---

[22] As in the case of wines, some precedents improve with age, while others deteriorate. Certainly the accretion of supporting authorities with the passage of time lends strength; on the other hand, changing circumstances erode it.

[23] "Stare decisis is usually the wise policy, because in most matters it is more important that the applicable rule of law be settled than that it be settled right. . . . This is commonly true even where the error is a matter of serious concern, provided correction can be had by legislation. But in cases involving the federal Constitution, where correction through legislative action is practically impossible, this Court has often overruled its earlier decisions. The Court bows to the lessons of experience and the force of better reasoning, recognizing that the process of trial and error, so fruitful in the physical sciences, is appropriate also in the judicial function." Justice Brandeis dissenting in Burnet v. Coronado Oil & Gas Co., 285 U.S. 393, 406–08 (1932).

[24] Occasionally, a court will simply ignore an embarrassing precedent. This questionable technique leaves the prior decision of doubtful validity in later cases.

multi-legged holding. It should be apparent that, even among the so-called binding precedents, the value of a decision may be lessened by a number of factors. For example, dissenting or concurring opinions, while they may indicate that the particular judges have hotly disputed the point and are not apt to change their views, usually weaken the authority of a decision and make it less likely that it will be followed by a later court of different composition. Similarly, a memorandum decision, which sets forth no reasons, may have effect as precedent if it affirms a decision of a lower court which stated the facts and its reasons in an opinion, but its weight is much lessened by the circumstance that the higher court gave no reasons for its affirmance of the opinion below.[25] What is the weight of a multi-legged holding—a decision that is based upon several grounds rather than a single ground?

Suppose the case of an appeal from the judgment of a trial court in which three distinct errors are cited as reasons for reversal. Clearly, if the appellate court affirms the judgment, it has held that each of the three grounds was insufficient, since rejection of each was necessary for affirmance. But suppose that it reverses, stating that the first and second grounds were sufficient but that the third ground was not. What has the court held? Has it held anything as to the first and second grounds? Since either one without the other would have been sufficient for reversal, it can be argued that neither one was necessary to the decision and that there is therefore no holding, and the entire opinion is dictum. But each of the points was disputed and was argued before the court, and the trial court will be expected to observe both upon any rehearing before it. While neither is the sole ground of the decision, it is usual to treat each as an alternative or multi-legged holding. Yet holdings though they may be, no prudent lawyer can ignore the fact that precedents stand more firmly when they stand on only one leg, and alternate grounds make a holding less reliable. The same words of caution apply with even greater force to the third ground, which was also disputed and was argued before the court and is to be observed by the trial court upon any rehearing, but which was clearly not necessary to the reversal. Whether it be dignified with the name of holding or be classified as dictum, it is obviously an authority of a still lower order than the decision on the first two points.

---

[25] A memorandum decision, however, is valueless as a precedent if the facts of the case cannot be determined.

The second puzzling problem relates to the retroactive effect of a decision that overrules a prior decision. Of course, to the extent that a court in reaching any decision announces a new principle of law and applies it to the case already before it, there is an aspect of retroactivity, but the effect is particularly apparent where an earlier decision has been overruled. Suppose that two similar transactions have been concluded, one between A and B, the other between C and D. In a dispute between A and B, the highest court of the state decides that such transactions are invalid. After this decision, yet a third similar transaction is concluded between E and F. Then in a dispute between C and D, the highest court decides to overrule its earlier decision in the case of *A v. B* and holds that such transactions are valid. Which decision, that in *A v. B* or that in *C v. D*, determines the validity of the transaction between E and F that was concluded in the interval between the two decisions? Is the decision in *C v. D* retroactive in its effect, or does it apply only to transactions entered into after it was handed down? According to the older theory that judges merely discover existing law and then declare it, the decision of the court in *A v. B* was simply an erroneous interpretation of what the law was then and still is, an interpretation that was later corrected in *C v. D*. And since the law was always as stated in *C v. D*, the transaction between E and F was therefore a valid one, even though it took place before the court had discovered its error. According to the newer theory that judges actually create or make law by their decisions, the decision in *A v. B* made law that was good law until it was changed in the decision in *C v. D*. Because the transaction between E and F was concluded after the first decision and before the second, during the time when the decision in *A v. B* was law, the transaction was invalid. Over the years, the conflict between these opposing theories has been reflected in conflicting cases, though other considerations may be more important than either theory. Clearly, for example, the case for retroactivity would be weaker if the decision in *A v. B* had held that the transaction was valid, and the decision in *C v. D* had held that it was invalid. And it would be still weaker if E and F had in fact relied upon the decision in *A v. B* when entering into their transaction.

The problem of the overruled decision, like that of the multi-legged holding, admits of no simple solution.[26] Occasionally a court, in an attempt

---

[26] For more on the overruled decision, Chafee, *Do Judges Make or Discover Law?* 91 PROC. AM. PHILOS. SOC'Y 405 (1947); Lobinger, *Precedent in Past and Present Legal Systems,*

to avoid the unsettling effect of retroactivity, has refused to overrule an earlier decision but has expressed disapproval of the precedent and issued a warning that the old rule will not be followed as to facts arising after the new decision.[27] Occasionally a court has overruled the earlier decision but has indicated that the new rule is not retroactive and will not be followed as to facts arising before the new decision.[28]

Suggested Readings

K. Llewellyn, *The Bramble Bush: The Classic Lectures on the Law and Law School* (Steve Sheppard ed., 2008) is the classic narrative of modern case analysis. A more advanced work by the same author on the process of judicial decision is K. Llewellyn, *The Common Law Tradition: Deciding Appeals* (1960). A nice new synthesis of legal analysis is in F. Schauer, *Thinking Like a Lawyer: A New Introduction to Legal Reasoning* (2009). Though cited above in the notes, the reader should also remember B. Cardozo, *The Nature of the Judicial Process* (1921). Suggested readings on legal research are cited at the end of Chapter 8, *infra*.

See G. Fletcher & S. Sheppard, *American Law in a Global Context: The Basics*, Introduction and Chapters 1 through 4 and the appendices, which discuss the briefing of cases and provide illustrations of briefs compared to case opinions.

44 MICH. L. REV. 955 (1946). A more recent and magisterial consideration is M. GERHARDT, THE POWER OF PRECEDENT (2008).

[27] *E.g.*, Hare v. General Contract Purchase Corp., 249 S.W. 2d 973 (Ark. 1952). It has been held that such decisions by a state court do not violate the guarantee of due process in the federal Constitution. Great Northern Railway v. Sunburst Co., 287 U.S. 358 (1932).

[28] Molitor v. Kaneland Comm. Unit Dist. No. 302, 163 N.E. 2d 89 (Ill. 1959). For discussion of solutions to the problem of retroactivity, *see* James B. Beam Distilling Co. v. Georgia, 501 U.S. 529 (1991).

SIX

The Legislative System

In spite of the emphasis on court decisions in a common law system, legislation is of great and increasing importance in American law. What is the hierarchy of authority among the various legislative materials? How do the United States Congress and the fifty state legislatures function? What other special sources of legislation exist?

Hierarchy of Legislation

Although case law is traditionally the core of a common-law system, legislation has so increased in quantity and importance in the United States during the past century that it is the dominant creative force in many fields. While this is particularly true of federal law,[1] legislation also pours

---

[1] In 1947, Justice Felix Frankfurter of the Supreme Court of the United States said: "Inevitably the work of the Supreme Court reflects the great shift in the center of gravity of law-making. Broadly speaking, the number of cases disposed of by opinions has not changed from term to term. But even as late as 1875 more than 40% of the controversies before the Court were common-law litigation, fifty years later only 5%, while today cases not resting on statutes are reduced almost to zero. It is therefore accurate to say that courts have ceased to be the

ountless lawmaking bodies on the state and local levels. Under
in doctrine of judicial review, the validity of this legislation is
the courts to decide. A court may refuse to apply a legislative
to a case on the ground that the enactment is invalid because it
conflicts with some more authoritative legislative source. For this reason, it
is important to have an understanding of the hierarchy of these sources.[2]

1. **The Constitution of the United States.** The Constitution is, to use
   its own language, the "supreme Law of the Land" to which all other
   legislative sources are subject. The ultimate arbiter of constitutional
   disputes is, of course, the Supreme Court of the United States. Amendments to the Constitution may be proposed by a two-thirds vote of
   both houses of Congress and must be ratified either by the legislatures
   of three-fourths of the states or by conventions in three-fourths of the
   states. Twenty-seven amendments have been ratified, of which thirteen
   have come since 1791.[3]

2. **Treaties**. Treaties made by the United States have equal authority
   with federal statutes and are subject only to the Constitution. Thus,
   in the case of a conflict between a treaty and a federal statute, the
   more recent one controls. A treaty may be entered into by the president with the consent of two-thirds of the senators voting. If it is a
   self-executing treaty, it takes effect immediately on ratification; otherwise it takes effect as a matter of domestic law on implementation
   by a federal statute. The president also has limited powers to make
   executive agreements with foreign nations without the approval of
   Congress. Such agreements have been given the same effect as treaties
   by the courts and have, in fact, been more numerous than treaties.

3. **Federal statutes**. In addition to specifically enumerated legislative
   powers, the Constitution gives Congress the power to "make all Laws
   which shall be necessary and proper for carrying into Execution"

primary makers of law in the sense in which they 'legislated' the common law. It is certainly
true of the Supreme Court that almost every case has a statute at its heart or close to it."
Frankfurter, *Some Reflections on the Reading of Statutes*, 47 COLUM. L. REV. 527 (1947).

[2] The list here is not exhaustive. It omits, for example, interstate compacts.

[3] All but one of the twenty-seven amendments were ratified by state legislatures rather
than by conventions. The Twenty-Seventh Amendment, on congressional pay, was originally
proposed in 1789 but ratified in 1992.

the powers expressly vested in any department of government, and this clause has been broadly construed. The statutes enacted by Congress are, like treaties, subject only to the Constitution, and a statute will be interpreted, if possible, so as to avoid constitutional questions. In the words of Chief Justice Charles Evans Hughes,[4] "We have repeatedly held that as between two possible interpretations of a statute, by one of which it would be unconstitutional and by the other valid, our plain duty is to adopt that which will save the act."[5] The process of enactment will be described presently.

4. **Federal executive orders and administrative rules and regulations.** The president has a limited power to issue executive orders, which usually are legislative in character. Federal administrative bodies may also be empowered to make rules and regulations of a legislative character, which, if validly made pursuant to federal statute, have the force of law and are superior to state law.

5. **State constitutions.** The constitution of a state is subject to valid federal legislation,[6] but is the paramount authority within the state itself. State constitutions are often more detailed than the federal Constitution and require more frequent amendment.

6. **State statutes.** The enactments of state legislatures, while subject to valid federal legislation and to the state constitution, are of the greatest importance in the many fields of law that have been left to the states. Under the Tenth Amendment to the Constitution, "The powers not delegated to the United States by the Constitution, nor

---

[4] Charles Evans Hughes (1862–1948) graduated from college at Brown University and in 1884 received a law degree from Columbia University. After practice in New York City, several years as professor of law at Cornell University, and service as special counsel for a state legislative committee, he was elected governor of New York. In 1910, he was appointed an associate justice of the Supreme Court of the United States. In 1916, he ran for President of the United States and, after a narrow defeat by Woodrow Wilson, returned to practice. He subsequently served as United States Secretary of State and as a member of the Permanent Court of International Justice. He was appointed Chief Justice of the United States in 1930 and served until ill health forced him to resign in 1941.

[5] National Labor Relations Board v. Jones & Laughlin Steel Corp., 301 U.S. 1, 30 (1937).

[6] Of course, a federal statute must have been enacted under a power granted to Congress in order to prevail over a state constitution or statute.

prohibited by it to the States, are reserved to the States respectively, or to the people." Even where Congress has the power to legislate under the Constitution, its power may not be exclusive, and the states may have concurrent power, at least on matters on which federal legislation has not occupied the field. Since federal legislation is chiefly interstitial in nature, it rarely "preempts" state law or occupies a field to the exclusion of state law on that subject.[7] State statutes are, for the average lawyer, the most common form of legislation. State legislative processes will be discussed shortly.

7. **State administrative rules and regulations.** Rules and regulations of state administrative bodies are similar in form and purpose to those of federal agencies. They may concern such matters as the licensing of various activities within the state.

8. **Municipal charters, ordinances, rules, and regulations.** Units of local government are extremely varied and are therefore difficult to describe. They do not have the kind of independent political existence that the states have within the federal scheme. Each state is divided into counties, which may have legislative powers. Within a county, there may be a number of municipalities, which are usually independent of the county in most things. They are most often governed by an elected mayor and a council, under powers conferred by the state in the charter of the municipality.[8] Municipal enactments, commonly called ordinances, are usually of only local interest. In addition, local administrative bodies may promulgate rules and regulations.

This, then, is the hierarchy of legislative sources of the law.[9] The remainder of the discussion will be confined to the principal legislative bodies: Congress and the state legislatures.

---

[7] In recent years, the Court has become quite nuanced on the scope of preemption. *Compare* Wyeth v. Levine, 129 S. Ct. 1887 (2009), *with* Altria Group, Inc. v. Good, 129 S. Ct. 538 (2008) and Riegel v. Medtronic, Inc., 128 S. Ct. 999 (2008).

[8] The delegation to a county or municipality of the power to frame and adopt its own charter for self-government is called "home rule." It may be required by the state constitution or may be a product solely of legislative initiative.

[9] Rules of court, sometimes considered as a variety of legislation, are discussed in Chapter 10, *infra.*

The United States Congress

Federal statutes are enacted by the United States Congress, a bicameral legislature that consists of a lower house, the House of Representatives, and an upper house, the Senate. The former was intended by the authors of the Constitution to give each state a voice in national affairs proportional to its population. It is made up of 435 members, each of whom is elected for a two-year term by the voters of one of the congressional districts into which each state is divided. The number of representatives from each state depends on its population, and districts are generally redrawn by state legislatures every ten years on the basis of the national census so as to be as nearly equal in population as possible. The Senate, by contrast, was intended to preserve the equality of the states. The voters of each state, regardless of population, elect two senators, for a total of one hundred.[10] Senators are elected for six-year terms, which are so staggered that only about one-third of the total number, and at most one senator from any one state, is elected at each biennial election. Each house serves as a check on the other, because legislation requires approval of a majority in both the Senate and the House of Representatives. The life of a Congress is two years, commencing in January of odd-numbered years, and each Congress has two regular annual sessions beginning in January. The president may also call a special session if Congress has adjourned.

Although members of Congress spend most of their time on matters other than the enactment of legislation, it is the legislative process that is of concern here. It is useful to have some knowledge of that process because, as will be explained shortly, the history of a federal statute before its enactment may influence a court in interpreting its language. Most federal legislation takes the form of an Act of Congress, which is introduced in the

---

[10]   The senators from the most populous state, California, represent nearly seventy times as many persons as those from the least populous state, which in 2009 is Wyoming. In the Constitution as written, senators were elected by state legislatures, a method rejected in favor of a direct election in 1917 by ratification of the Seventeenth Amendment.

form of a bill.[11] It may originate with the member of Congress[12] but may come from constituents as individuals or as organized groups or from the executive branch. Each house has an Office of Legislative Counsel to aid in the drafting of proposed legislation. Except for bills to raise revenue, which must originate in the House of Representatives, a bill may be introduced in either house, but only by a member of that house.

With rare exceptions, the bill will then as a matter of course be referred to one of the standing committees of the house where it was introduced. Each of the two major parties assigns members to serve on committees, with the larger number and the chairmanship going to the majority party. In most cases, subcommittees of the standing committees have been created, which report to the parent committees. Since the workload in Congress is too heavy to permit detailed consideration of every proposal by every member, much of the serious work is done in committee, and the committee system is of immense practical significance. Once in committee, the bill may be studied by the experts on its staff, and departments of the executive branch may be requested to submit their views in writing. If the bill is of sufficient importance, there may be public hearings at which interested parties are heard. Finally, the committee members vote to determine the fate of the bill. They either report it favorably with or without amendments or postpone its consideration by tabling it, which normally prevents further action upon the bill. A large percentage of all bills die in committee.

If the bill is reported favorably, it is customary for the committee to submit a report to Congress with its recommendation. The committee report will rehearse the purpose of the bill, the need for legislation, and the legislative history. It will give a section-by-section analysis of the bill; an estimate of its cost to implement; reports and comments from appropriate

---

[11]   On occasion, a joint resolution is used instead of an act, though there is little practical difference between the two. Congressional legislation, in whatever form, can be divided into "public" and "private" enactments. The latter, enacted for the benefit of a particular individual or group, as for example for the relief of one injured by governmental action, are of limited interest. This discussion is restricted to "public" laws, which are of general application.

[12]   It may also result from an investigation by a House or Senate committee. The power of congressional committees to investigate stems from the constitutional grant of "all legislative powers." It is, however, not necessary to the validity of an investigation that legislation actually result.

governmental agencies and departments; and, sometimes, minority views in the committee. A verbatim transcript of the hearings is usually published in advance of the committee report. The bill is then brought to the floor of the house for debate, at which time further amendments may be proposed.[13] If the bill is approved by a majority vote, it then goes to the other house where a similar procedure of referral to committee followed by debate on the floor is observed. Should the versions passed by both houses be identical, it goes directly to the president for signature. If there are minor differences, they may be accepted by vote in the house where the bill originated. But should the differences in the two versions be substantial, they must be adjusted by a conference committee consisting of members of both houses, followed by approval of the compromise by a majority vote of each house. Once the bill is approved in the same form by both houses, it is then sent to the president, who has veto power over federal legislation. The president has ten days to sign it into law. If the president fails to act within this time, the bill becomes law automatically without his signature.[14] If the bill is vetoed, it is returned to the house where it originated, with a veto message stating the president's reasons for doing so. A two-thirds vote of each house is then necessary to override the veto and enact the bill into law.

State Legislatures

In addition to Congress, each of the fifty states has its own legislative body which is usually termed a "Legislature" or a "General Assembly." These bodies are almost universally bicameral, a tradition going back to colonial times; only one state, Nebraska, has changed to a unicameral legislature. The smaller upper house is called the "Senate," and the larger lower house is commonly known as the "House of Representatives." Senates range in size from twenty members for Alaska and twenty-one for Nevada to sixty-one for New York and sixty-seven for Minnesota. Lower houses range in size from forty for

---

[13] The proceedings of Congress are published in full in the Congressional Record, which is available in a searchable format online *at* http://www.gpoaccess.gov/crecord/.

[14] However if Congress has adjourned within the ten days following presentment of the bill, the president's failure to sign is known as a "pocket veto," and the bill does not become law.

Alaska and forty-one for Delaware to two hundred and three for Pennsylvania and four hundred for New Hampshire. Members are elected for terms of either two or four years, the former being more common for the lower houses and the latter more usual for the senates. Although some states hold sessions only biennially, an increasing majority meets annually.

Records of state legislative activity are inadequate compared to congressional records. Hearings and reports of state standing committees are not usually available, nor is any comprehensive record generally kept of statements made during debates on the floor. For this reason, a detailed understanding of the mechanics of the legislative process is of less importance in the interpretation of state than of federal statutes. The process is similar to that in Congress, but the effectiveness of the committee system and the quality of enactments are impaired by the fact that members of state legislatures, unlike members of Congress, usually do not devote full time to their duties. Technical assistance in drafting legislation is available to committees and individual lawmakers through a legislative reference bureau or library, through a bill drafting staff on the congressional model, or through the office of the state attorney general. Efforts are being made to improve these services, and special commissions may be used to prepare legislation in important fields.[15] Generally, the governor—the elected state executive—has veto power over legislation, which can be enacted over a veto only by a two-thirds vote of each house.[16] State legislation, like federal legislation, is subject to judicial review, and a state or federal court may refuse to enforce a state statute on the ground of its validity.

Special Sources of Legislation

The role that legislation should play in the common-law system of the United States, particularly in those fields of private law that are chiefly the concern of the states, has long been a matter of lively concern. A general

---

[15] *See* National Conference of State Legislatures, *About Us: National Conference of State Legislatures*, http://www.ncsl.org/AboutUs/tabid/305/Default.aspx.

[16] In a number of states, a constitutional provision for initiative and referendum allows the people to propose or enact legislation or adopt constitutional amendments or requires the submission of certain statutes to the people for their approval.

trend toward legislation and codification is discernible on the state as well as on the federal level. It may be seen in continuous revision of compiled statutes or codes and in special commissions to study and reform broad areas of the law. From an historical point of view, three milestones have been particularly noteworthy: the promulgation of the Field codes between 1848 and 1865, the organization of the National Conference of Commissioners on Uniform State Laws in 1892, and the creation of the New York State Law Revision Commission in 1934.

Following the American Revolution, the interest in civil law systems prompted curiosity about the French civil code, which was to have a profound influence on the law of Louisiana. Legislative reform was further stimulated by the writings of Jeremy Bentham.[17] But the growth of an organized movement toward codification is directly attributable to the struggle of David Dudley Field of New York.[18] As a result of his efforts, a commission was established in that state in 1847 to reform civil and criminal procedure and to codify the law. By 1850, under Field's leadership, complete codes of procedure had been submitted to the New York legislature, and the code of civil procedure had been adopted. However, at this point the movement lost ground, and in the same year the legislature disbanded the commission. In 1857, Field again succeeded in having the legislature appoint a commission to codify substantive law. Field personally undertook, with two assistants, the drafting of the civil code. By 1865, the commission submitted its final report with the full text of five codes: civil procedure, criminal procedure, penal law, civil law, and political law and procedure. New York adopted only Field's first draft of the code of civil procedure and, in 1881, the code of criminal procedure. The civil code was passed by the legislature, but the governor vetoed it as the result of opposition by leaders of the bar. A code of civil procedure that was an elaboration based on his later draft was adopted between 1876 and 1880.

---

17 Jeremy Bentham (1748–1832) was an English jurist and philosopher. He is remembered for his theory of utilitarianism, in which the morality of actions is measured by their utility or effect on happiness, and for his advocacy of codification as a means of reform of the law.

18 David Dudley Field (1805–1894) was admitted to practice in New York in 1828 after an apprenticeship in a law office. In the years after the Civil War, he was a prominent lawyer, argued several landmark cases before the Supreme Court of the United States, and was elected to the United States House of Representatives to fill a vacancy for a short time. He is most remembered for his role in the codification of law and procedure.

In spite of their relative lack of success in New York, the influence of the Field codes was considerable. Some thirty states adopted or based their codes on the code of civil procedure, which became a model in other jurisdictions and profoundly influenced procedural reform.[19] Sixteen states adopted the penal code and the code of criminal procedure, and five states, including California, adopted and still retain the civil code. Field's failure to secure more widespread adoption may have been due in part to the success of the works of the great nineteenth century text writers, including Kent and Story, in lessening the demand for codification. Perhaps if all of Field's codes had been adopted in New York, widespread adoption in other states would have followed, and the course of history of the law in the United States would have been significantly altered. As it happened, however, the enthusiasm for codification was on the wane, and the movement made little headway from this point. Field's civil code was probably premature. It had been too heroic a task for a single man, even a man of his ability; it was not of the highest quality, and it was often ignored by the courts of the states in which it was in force. It was the need for unification that was next to give impetus to codification.

The desirability of uniformity among the laws of the states was recognized in 1878 at the time of the organization of the American Bar Association, which included as one of its original objectives the promotion of "uniformity of legislation throughout the Union." In 1889, the Association appointed a Committee on Uniform State Laws, and, in 1890, the New York legislature authorized the appointment by the governor of commissioners to confer with representatives of other states on the preparation of uniform laws. Under the leadership of the American Bar Association and the State of New York, the National Conference of Commissioners on Uniform State Laws was organized.[20] Its first meeting was held in 1892, and by 1912, all of the states officially participated in the conference.

---

[19] For an indication of the place of the Field code in the development of the law of procedure, see Chapter 10, infra.

[20] See NCCUSL home, http://www.nccusl.org/Update/. For more on this organization, see Day, The National Conference of Commissioners on Uniform State Laws, 8 U. FLA. L. REV. 276 (1955). Its work is criticized in Patchel, Interest Group Politics, Federalism, and the Uniform Laws Process: Some Lessons from the Uniform Commercial Code, 78 MINN. L. REV. 83 (1993) and in Schwartz & Scott, The Political Economy of Private Legislature, 143 U. PA. L. REV. 595 (1995).

Each state is represented by commissioners, usually three in number, who are appointed by the governor from the bench, the bar, and the law faculties to serve without compensation. The commissioners meet annually for a week to discuss proposed laws, but most of the preliminary work is done in committees, which function much as the committees of a legislature.

The national conference is, however, not a legislative body. The commissioners have no power to enact laws or to obligate their respective states to do so. They can only recommend laws to the legislatures of the states, which are free to adopt their proposals, with or without amendments, or to reject them. Nevertheless, the commissioners have been remarkably successful in furthering the cause of uniformity, particularly in the field of commercial law where the need is perhaps most clear. Uniform acts are promulgated by the commissioners when they have concluded that uniformity is desirable in the subject in question. Model acts are drafted when there is no special need for uniformity but when there is a demand for legislation in a number of states. The commissioners currently recommend about ninety uniform acts, though the conference has promulgated over two hundred and fifty acts in the last century.[21] Many others that were formerly recommended have been withdrawn for a variety of reasons. Only a few of these have been adopted by all states. Less than half have been adopted by more than a majority of the states. Many have been adopted by only a handful or less. The commissioners' most ambitious project has been the Uniform Commercial Code.[22]

A leading institution for reform of the law within a single state has been the New York State Law Revision Commission. Its origins go back to Judge Benjamin N. Cardozo's call for a "Ministry of Justice . . . to watch the law in action, observe the manner of its functioning, and report the changes needed when function is deranged."[23] To this end, the New York legislature in 1934 created the Law Revision Commission as an agency of the legislature to make a continuing study of the decisional and statutory law to discover "defects" and "anachronisms" and to recommend changes to bring the law "into harmony with modern conditions."

---

[21] *See* Annual Report, National Conference of Commissioners on Uniform State Laws (2008).

[22] The code is discussed at Chapter 11, *infra*.

[23] Cardozo, *A Ministry of Justice*, 35 HARV. L REV. 113, 114 (1921).

The commissioners are nine in number, four ex officio members of the legislature and five appointed by the governor, usually from the bar and the law faculties in the state. They are salaried, though not full time, and have the assistance of a permanent full-time staff in addition to consultants who are retained to study particular problems. The work of the commission has thus far been confined primarily to specific problems of private substantive law in such fields as contracts, torts, real property, restitution, corporations, commercial law, and criminal law, and it has avoided questions of political import.[24] While it has been a disappointment to some that the commission's work has largely been directed to the remedying of isolated defects rather than to the reorganization and revision of broader areas of the law, it has fulfilled the limited purposes for which it was conceived. Similar institutions have been created elsewhere, notably in California, where a law revision commission was established in 1953 as a successor to an earlier commission.

Suggested Readings

The Library of Congress maintains a pamphlet by the Parliamentarian of the U.S. House of Representatives, Charles W. Johnson, *How Our Laws Are Made* (2003), at http://thomas.loc.gov/home/lawsmade.toc.html. More extensive discussions can be found in E. Redman, *The Dance of Legislation* (2001). On the role of the courts in statutory interpretation, see the now-classic text, G. Calabresi, *A Common Law for the Age of Statutes* (1982). A casebook with much helpful material is W. Eskridge, P. Frickey & E. Garrett, *Cases and Materials on Legislation: Statutes and the Creation of Public Policy* (4th ed. 2007). Information on state legislatures is tabulated biennially in Council of State Governments, *The Book of the States*, Chapter 3, State Legislative Branch.

---

[24] From 1953 to 1956, the commission undertook a particularly ambitious study of the proposed Uniform Commercial Code, resulting in five volumes of hearing and studies.

SEVEN

Statutes

The judicial attitude toward legislation has undergone substantial change in the United States during the past century. What is the form of statutory law? What are the current techniques of statutory interpretation?

Form of Statute Law

An act of Congress or of a state legislature begins with a title ("An act to . . ."), which sets forth the subject of the statute, followed by an enacting clause ("Be it enacted by . . ."), and sometimes by a preamble or purpose clause, stating the reason or policy behind the enactment. Then comes the main body of the statute. It is frequently more detailed than would be the case in many civil law systems and may contain an extensive list of definitions. This emphasis on detail may be due to a variety of factors: the complexity of the subject matter—to which a pluralistic society, a highly developed economy, and a federal system all contribute; the legislator's desire for specificity born of a fear of restrictive interpretation by the courts; and the lower level of abstraction on which the common-law lawyer operates (in comparison to the civilian lawyer). Furthermore, the pressures of the enactment process often narrow the scope of legislation.

Because of the number and the variety of legislatures in the United States, it is no easy task to keep up with the avalanche of current legislation. Congressional enactments are first officially published in the form of slip laws, unbound pamphlets for each act that become available almost immediately after presidential approval. They are also almost immediately available from the THOMAS service of the Library of Congress,[1] on Lexis and Westlaw, and are promptly published by several unofficial services. At the end of each session of Congress, those statutes enacted during that session are collected in chronological order and published in the *United States Statutes at Large*. Official slip laws are not usually available for state legislation, although state statutes are promptly put on state Web sites of the legislature or the state's secretary of state; on Lexis and Westlaw; and in some states, the publisher of the permanent edition of state statutes issues advance sheets while the legislature is in session.[2] At the end of the session, the statutes enacted during that session are published as session laws, which are also arranged chronologically.

However, the form in which legislation is ordinarily consulted by the lawyer is a compilation of statutes by subject matter. Compilations generally omit repealed and temporary acts, combine and edit the remaining laws as necessary, and arrange them in classified order by subject. The *United States Code* is the official compilation of federal statutes under some fifty title headings. There are also unofficial annotations of the code, of which the *United States Code Annotated* is the most commonly cited. Similar compilations exist for each state under such designations as codes, compilations, consolidations, general statutes, general laws, or revisions of statutes. They generally contain the state constitution as well, but municipal charters, ordinances, and codes are available only in special publications for the particular municipality. The term "code" may be misleading for, with few exceptions, such as the Field codes and the codes of Louisiana, which show the influence of French and Spanish law, these compilations are ordered collections of separately enacted statutes rather than unitary codes, which were enacted as a single intellectual enterprise and which are amended by integrating changes into the original, codified structure. Indeed, except to

---

[1] Since 1995, bills and statutes have been published online at http://thomas.loc.gov/.

[2] The editors of Findlaw.com have arranged a state-by-state library of state materials online, including state legislation. *See* State Resources, www.findlaw.com/11stategov/index.html.

the extent that the compilation has itself been enacted into positive law, the original session laws are in principle the final evidence of the law. Somewhat less than half of the titles of the *United States Code* as well as the compilations of some of the states have been enacted as law by their respective legislative authorities. In practice, however, the compilations are used for the sake of convenience, even where they have not been enacted.

It may seem surprising that in the United States, it is sometimes more difficult to make a thorough nationwide search of statute law than of case law. There is for legislation no current counterpart of the elaborate system of nationwide classification and indexing that exists for judicial decisions. The Shepard's citator system does cover federal and state legislation and includes constitutions, session laws, compiled statutes, city charters, municipal ordinances, and court rules. But while each state compilation has an index that is adequate for that state, there is no comprehensive current index or digest comparable to the case digest in the American Digest System. However, a number of computer systems, including Lexis and Westlaw,[3] contain the United States Code, the federal regulations, and most state legislative material.

Rules and regulations of federal administrative agencies and executive orders of the president are published, as issued, in the daily *Federal Register*, and those that are general, permanent, and currently in force are collected and systematically arranged in the *Code of Federal Regulations*. Unofficial services, including free and subscription databases, duplicate most of these materials. Publication of state administrative rules and regulations is less well developed, and only a few states have systems that compare with the federal system. However, unofficial services in special subjects often collect state as well as federal rules and regulations in a particular field, and more and more can be found online.

Techniques of Interpretation

Although the interpretation of statutes raises some questions peculiar to the American legal system, many of the fundamentals are familiar to most legal systems. To begin with, it is axiomatic that as between the court and

---

[3] *See* Chapter 5, *supra*.

the legislature, the command of the legislature is supreme except, to be sure, on the point of validity of the statute itself. Case law can be and often is altered by statute, but, at least in principle, statutes cannot be altered by court decision. The court's function in dealing with legislation is that of interpretation. As to the nature and limits of this function, however, there is not universal agreement.

On the surface, the simplest approach to interpretation is to look to the common, unspecialized meaning of the words used by the legislature. This approach is sometimes implemented by a durable doctrine known as the "plain meaning rule." Its classical formulation is that where the statute is "clear," "plain," and "unambiguous" on its face, so that taken by itself it is fairly susceptible of only one construction, that construction must be given to it and any inquiry into the purposes, background, or legislative history of the statute is foreclosed. The rigors of this rule have been relaxed by permitting an exception where the result would be "cruel," "monstrous," or "absurd" or sometimes merely "impractical," "unjust," or "unreasonable." With a growing understanding of the difficulties that attend the use of language to express legal rules, there has come a realization that no statute can be so clearly and accurately drawn as to avoid mistake or ambiguity entirely and be applied literally in all situations.

The emphasis upon the common meaning of words as the principal or exclusive basis for interpretation, and in particular upon the plain meaning rule, has largely given way to a search for the "intention of the legislature." This may be true in practice even where, as in the Supreme Court of the United States, judges continue to pay lip service to the rule.

Legislative "intention" may be understood either in the specific sense of the understanding of the legislators themselves as to the meaning of the statutory language or in the general sense of the purpose that the legislature sought to achieve by enactment of the statute. In the first sense, it is often elusive. The number of legislators is large, even in the state legislature; virtually all legislatures are divided into two houses which function separately; the average legislator can have only a minimal knowledge of the fine points of a bill, which are not usually discussed on the floor; and the problem before the court may have been unforeseen and even unforeseeable at the time of enactment. Yet in spite of these difficulties, the legislative history not infrequently discloses that at least some responsible legislators considered the point before the court and had a specific intention as to the language in question.

Even where the existence of a specific intention is the case, use of extrinsic aids to show legislative intention has been opposed for practical reasons by critics who maintain that, "Aside from a few offices in the larger cities, the materials of legislative history are not available to the lawyer who can afford neither the cost of acquisition, the cost of housing, or the cost of repeatedly examining the whole congressional history."[4] Nevertheless, courts have frequently used extrinsic aids to establish legislative intention as a guide to statutory interpretation.[5] The weight given to these aids depends on how reliable they seem as indications of an intention of the legislature as a whole. Because of the importance of the committee system, the views of the members of a single committee may, with some justification, be taken as those of the entire legislature. The report of a committee that has considered the bill or a statement on the floor of the legislature by the member of that committee who is in charge of the bill may be particularly persuasive; changes in successive drafts of the bill and action on proposed amendments may also be considered; but statements of individual legislators made during floor debate rarely show a common understanding and are likely to be the views of only one person. The use of legislative history as a practical matter is largely confined to the interpretation of federal laws because adequate records are not usually available for state legislatures.

When the legislative history of the statute is not available or, if available, does not indicate any specific legislative intention as to the language, the court may turn instead to the more general legislative purpose. The technique of purpose interpretation was applied in English courts over four centuries ago, and the classical statement of the process involves these steps: examination of the law before enactment of the statute; ascertainment of the "mischief or defect" for which the law did not provide; analysis of the legislative remedy; determination of the reason or purpose of the remedy; and application of the statute so as to "suppress the mischief, and advance the remedy."[6] Purpose interpretation does not, therefore, require the use of

---

[4] Justice Jackson, concurring, in Schwegmann Bros. v. Calvert Distillers Corp., 341 U.S. 384, 396 (1951). The force of this objection is surely fading as more legislative materials are made freely available on the Internet.

[5] See generally Kernochan, *Statutory Interpretation: An Outline of Method*, 3 DALHOUSIE L.J. 333 (1976).

[6] This is the formulation reported by Sir Edward Coke in *Heydon's Case*, 3 Coke 7, 76 ENG. REP. 637 (Court of Exchequer 1584).

legislative history and is frequently used in the construction of state statutes when records of legislative history are unavailable. The court may even find a helpful statement of the purpose of enactment set forth in the preamble or purpose clause of the statute itself. However, purpose interpretation is not limited to situations where there is no relevant legislative history, and it is no less effective if the purpose of the enactment is derived from one of the extrinsic aids already mentioned, or, for example, from a presidential message describing the need for legislation.

Regardless of which approach to statutory interpretation a court may adopt, it may embellish its opinion with one or more of the innumerable time-honored maxims of statutory construction.[7] Many of these are based on assumptions as to how words are commonly used. Thus, there is the maxim *expressio unius est exclusio alterius*—the expression of one thing excludes another; the maxim *noscitur a sociis*—the meaning of a word may be determined by reference to the words associated with it; the *ejusdem generis* rule—where general words follow an enumeration they are to be read as limited to things of the same general kind as those specifically mentioned; and the rule that statutes *in pari materia*—that is, statutes on the same subject—are to be construed consistently with each other. Other maxims reflect what are assumed to be broad policies of the law. Among these are the maxims that statutes on other than procedural matters will not be interpreted as retroactive and the maxim that ambiguous penal statutes are to be strictly construed in favor of the accused.[8]

The authority of maxims is weakened by their very number, their generality, and their inconsistency. There is a maxim for almost every purpose, and, for nearly every maxim, an opposite can be found. For example, when a statute is enacted in an area already governed by case law, the prior law is not entirely eradicated but subsists to the extent that it is not displaced by the statute. In fixing the limits of the statute, a court may call upon the familiar rule that such statutes in derogation of the common law are to be narrowly construed, or it may call upon the equally familiar rule that such

---

[7] For an extensive collection of maxims, statutory and otherwise, *see Bouvier's Law Dictionary and Concise Encyclopedia* (F. Rawle, 8th ed. 1914) under "maxims."

[8] This latter rule, sometimes called the rule of lenity, has been abrogated or modified by statute in a number of states. *See* Hall, *Strict or Liberal Construction of Penal Statutes*, 48 Harv. L. Rev. 748 (1935). Still, it retains some force, both as a rule of statutory construction and, under some circumstances, a constitutional obligation.

remedial statutes are to be broadly construed.[9] Nevertheless, maxims cannot be disregarded and may be particularly significant in the interpretation of state statutes when the lack of adequate records makes it more difficult to show legislative intention.

Weight of Prior Interpretations

The interpretation of statutes also raises a few questions that are more peculiar to the American legal system. One of these concerns the role of precedent. Generally, the doctrine of precedent applies as fully to cases interpreting statutes as to other cases. One consequence is that a lower court is bound to follow the interpretation that a higher court has put upon the same statutory language and is not free to interpret the statute directly. The same policies support the use of the doctrine of precedent here as where no statute is concerned. Indeed the doctrine of precedent seems to have additional force where a statute is concerned, and it is generally said that American courts feel more constrained by their prior interpretations of statutes than by their decisions on non-statutory grounds. The notion is that the legislature has, by its silence and inaction in failing to amend the statute, confirmed the prior interpretation even though it may have been erroneous. Quite plainly, this reasoning fails to take account of the many other possible explanations for legislative inaction. It may be more persuasive if there has been a lapse of time during which the prior interpretation has been relied on or if the legislature has reenacted the statute or its relevant language without change following the prior interpretation.

A situation analogous to that of reenactment after court interpretation arises in the case of a "borrowed" statute. In many instances, state statutes have been fashioned after or copied outright from those of other states. Usually the statute has been construed by the courts of the state of its origin at the time of its enactment by the borrowing state. What weight should be given to such out-of-state decisions? Although the courts of one state are not bound by the doctrine of precedent to follow out-of-state decisions, the courts of the borrowing state will usually apply the statute

---

[9] For a list of conflicting maxims, *see* K. Llewellyn, *The Common Law Tradition: Deciding Appeals*, Appendix C (1960).

as it had been construed by the courts in the state of its origin, up to the time that it was borrowed, on the assumption that the legislature intended to introduce not only the statute itself but also the judicial exposition of the statute as well.

Adherence to out-of-state precedent in the interpretation of statutes is of particular significance in the case of uniform laws. Since such statutes are promulgated for the purpose of making uniform the law of the states which adopt them, it is important that their interpretation be uniform. Decisions from other states should therefore be respected even when they came after the date of enactment by the state where the subsequent case has arisen. To implement this policy, each of the uniform acts provides that it shall be interpreted so as "to make uniform the law" among the states which adopt it.

Prior interpretations of a statute by an agency charged with its administration are also given special weight, particularly when the agency has adhered to the interpretation over a period of time. The creation of the agency may have been, at least in part, the result of a need for highly specialized technical knowledge, and the expertise that such a body gains from everyday experience in administering the statute is entitled to respectful consideration, even by the court that reviews its activities.

Judicial Attitudes Toward Legislation

The end result of a judicial exercise in statutory construction may depend not only on which technique of interpretation the court chooses to emphasize but also on its attitude toward legislation in general. For though in principle a statute cannot be altered by judicial decision, in practice it is within the power of the court through interpretation to give free rein to the statute or to hobble it. During much of the nineteenth century, the orthodox judicial attitude toward statutes regarded the legislature as encroaching upon the courts in their role of creating, or at least declaring, the common law. Legislation was regarded as exceptional and was applied strictly and narrowly so as to confine it to the cases which it expressly covered. One observer remarked of the English courts in 1882 that some of their rules of statutory interpretation "cannot well be accounted for except upon the theory that Parliament generally changes the law for the worse, and that the business of the judge is to keep the mischief of its interference within the narrowest possible bounds."[10] Fortunately, this restrictive attitude no longer prevails in the United States, and it can be expected that at the very least a statute will be given a fair and liberal interpretation to cover the entire field that it was intended to cover.[11]

The change in attitude is evidenced by a greater willingness on the part of courts to use statutes as bases of reasoning by analogy. The change was urged by Chief Justice Harlan Fiske Stone in 1936: "The reception which the courts have accorded to statutes presents a curiously illogical chapter in the history of the common law. Notwithstanding their genius for the generation of new law from that already established, the common-law courts have given little recognition to statutes as starting points for judicial law-making comparable to judicial decisions. They have long recognized the supremacy of statutes over judge-made law, but it has been the supremacy of a command to be obeyed according to its letter, to be treated as otherwise of little consequence. The fact that the command involves recognition of a policy by the supreme lawmaking body has seldom been regarded by courts as significant, either as a social datum or as a point of departure for the process of judicial reasoning by which the common law has expanded. . . . I can find in the history and principles of the common law no adequate reason for our failure to treat a statute much more as we treat a judicial precedent, as both a declaration and a source of law, and as a premise for legal reasoning."[12] By 1970, however, the Supreme Court of the United States asserted: "It has always been the duty of the common-law courts to perceive the impact of major legislative innovations and to interweave the new legislative policies with the inherited body of common law principles—many of them deriving from earlier legislative exertions."[13]

There are two classes of cases in which courts traditionally have derived general principles from statutes and have applied them to cases not within their express terms. One of these involves illegal contracts and the other

---

[10] F. POLLOCK, ESSAYS IN JURISPRUDENCE AND ETHICS 85 (1882).

[11] *See* Pound, *Common Law and Legislation*, 21 HARV. L. REV. 383 (1908).

[12] Stone, *The Common Law in the United States*, 50 HARV. L. REV. 4, 12–13(1936).

[13] Moragne v. States Marine Lines, Inc., 398 U.S. 375, 392 (1970) (Harlan, J., holding that wrongful death statutes apply by analogy in maritime law). See the similar views expressed by two distinguished state-court judges in Schaefer, *Precedent and Policy*, 34 U. CHI. L. REV. 3, 18–22 (1966); Traynor, *Statutes Revolving in Common Law Orbits*, 17 CATH. U. L. REV. 401 (1968).

negligence as a matter of law. If a statute forbids certain activity, makes it an offense, and provides a penalty, it does not commonly expressly make void a contract if the making or performance of a contract would violates the statute's terms nor does it usually confer a right of recovery upon one who is injured by the failure of another to comply with the statute. Nevertheless, a court will, with some exceptions, refuse to enforce such a contract, thus giving support to the broad legislative policy behind the statute. A court will also, again subject to some exceptions, allow recovery to an injured party upon a showing that the violation of the statute caused the loss, regardless of whether there was actual fault as is usually required in an action based on negligence where no statute is involved. The violation of the statute is said to be negligence as a matter of law. In addition to these traditional examples, there are now many other cases in which courts have been willing to reason by applying general principles derived from statutes.[14]

Suggested Readings

Changing trends in statutory interpretation are traced in P. Frickey, *From the Big Sleep to the Big Heat: The Revival of Theory in Statutory Interpretation*, 77 Minn. L. Rev. 241 (1992). The history of the background and interpretation of a single statute is set out in E. Levi, *An Introduction to Legal Reasoning* (rev. ed. 1962). More recent is S. Burton, *An Introduction to Law and Legal Reasoning* (2d ed. 1995). For interesting monographs, see G. Calabresi, *A Common Law in the Age of Statutes* (1982) and W. Eskridge, *Dynamic Statutory Interpretation* (1994). A useful casebook is W. Eskridge & P. Frickey, *Cases and Materials on Legislation: Statutes and the Creation of Public Policy* (1988). A current review of the interpretation of statutes is in L. Jellum, *Mastering Statutory Interpretation* (2008).

---

[14] Thus, courts in cases not involving the sale of goods have imposed implied warranties analogous to those imposed by statute on a seller of goods. For example, *see* Cintrone v. Hertz Truck Leasing & Rental Service, 212 A. 2d 769 (N.J. 1965) (lease of truck): Newmark v. Gimbel's Inc., 258 A.2d 697 (N.J. 1967) (furnishing of permanent wave solution).

EIGHT

Secondary Authority

The common law is sometimes supposed to hold "secondary authority," such as treatises, legal periodicals, and encyclopedias, in low esteem. How available and how influential are such materials in the United States? What has been the impact of the Restatement of the Law?

Significance of Secondary Authority

"Secondary authority" is a general term that embraces treatises, articles in legal periodicals, encyclopedia entries, commentary posted on the Internet on law-related sites, and other aids to finding and interpreting such "primary authority" as statutes and cases. Such a work may be useful for its collection of citations; for its organization of the subject matter; for its statement of legal rules; or for its original analysis, criticism, and proposals for improvement. The quality and reliability of secondary authorities varies widely. Although practitioners' writings are not lacking, most of the significant works of secondary authority have emanated from the law faculties.

Secondary authorities are, at most, persuasive. No judge is bound to follow the views of an author in the way that a judge is bound to follow a statute or a case. Practically, however, secondary authority is frequently cited by judges in their opinions. There are some notable instances in which scholars have led the way for the courts to follow: a law review article by two young men on the right of privacy helped to persuade many courts to recognize that right[1]; and one by a distinguished legal historian on the history of the Judiciary Act of 1789 was relied upon by the Supreme Court of the United States in overruling *Swift v. Tyson* in the case of *Erie Railroad Co. v. Tompkins*.[2] However, the effect of secondary authority depends more upon its intrinsic worth and upon the court's esteem for the particular writer than upon any veneration of scholars in general.

The volume of systematic commentary on the law by distinguished authors is not as great as might be expected in view of the large number of lawyers and of university law schools in the United States. The legal encyclopedias are not the work of scholars, and their value lies more in their accessibility than in the quality of their distillations of the law. While there have been some American treatises of the highest quality, such as *Corbin on Contracts, Powell on Real Property, Scott on Trusts, Wigmore on Evidence*, and indeed *Farnsworth on Contracts*, there are many fields of law for which there is no comparable work.[3]

One reason for the scarcity of systematic exegesis is the inherent difficulty of preparing comprehensive treatises in a system that has the dual characteristics of federalism and the common law. Treatises typically contain statements of minority rules as well as majority rules, supported by extensive citations of statutes and of cases culled from the courts of the fifty states and from the federal courts. The prospect of collecting such authority may not appeal to the mature and reflective scholar. A second reason is that much of the effort that might otherwise go into treatises goes into other lines of scholarly endeavor, notably casebooks and articles

---

[1] Brandeis & Warren, *The Right of Privacy*, 4 HARV. L. REV. 193 (1890). Twenty-six years later, Brandeis became a member of the Supreme Court of the United States.

[2] Warren, *New Light on the History of the Federal Judiciary Act of 1789*, 37 HARV. L. REV. 49 (1923), *cited in* Erie Railroad Co. v. Tompkins, 304 U.S. 64. 72–73 (1938). For a typical case in which the Supreme Court of the United States noted that the "great weight of scholarly opinion has been critical of the decision" in an earlier case and then overruled that decision, *see* Continental T.V., Inc. v. GTE Sylvania Inc., 433 U.S. 36, 47–48 (1977).

[3] *Farnsworth on Contracts* was not included on this list in the editions of the present book that Professor Farnsworth wrote or revised, yet it is added in this posthumous edition of the *Introduction* because it certainly deserves inclusion, being cited thousands of times by American judges and remaining an influence around the world.

in legal periodicals. Whereas formerly the professor's lecture notes could serve as the germ of later published treatises, the advent of the case method put an end to the preparation of formal lectures, and the energies of the leading faculties were turned instead to the preparation of casebooks for student use. The introduction of the university law reviews near the turn of the century provided yet another alternative to the writing of treatises, and, since that time, much of the original thought about law in the United States has found expression in these journals, where it is not uncommon for a single article covering a substantial topic to be as long as fifty or one hundred pages.[4] Nevertheless, there can be found in the United States most of the varieties of legal writing that are available elsewhere, along with a few that are indigenous.

Kinds of Secondary Authority

The principal kinds of secondary authority are these:

1. **Dictionaries.** The traditional American law dictionary is Bouvier's *Law Dictionary and Concise Encyclopedia* (F. Rawle ed., 8th ed.1914), in two or three volumes, with a new edition expected in 2010. Popular one-volume works are *Black's Law Dictionary* (B. Garner ed., 9th ed. 2009) and *Ballantine's Law Dictionary* (W. Anderson ed., 3d ed. 1969). The statements of law sometimes appended to the definitions contained in these sources should not, however, be taken as reliable.

2. **Encyclopedias.** There are two popular general encyclopedias, *American Jurisprudence 2d* and *Corpus Juris Secundum*, each in roughly one hundred volumes. Both are well indexed, contain ample citations, and are kept up to date with annual cumulative supplements to each volume. Although they may be useful aids in finding cases, they are concerned mainly with the exposition of the law as it is rather than with critical analysis and are less reliable than the better treatises and texts. The contributions, which are unsigned, are those of the publisher's permanent staff rather than of known scholars.

---

4 Comment on individual cases is left, by and large, to the student editors of the reviews. It should be remembered that the judge's discussion of principles is often extensive, so that need for commentary is less acute than in countries where opinions are more laconic.

3. **Treatises and textbooks.** Treatises and textbooks may be designed to serve several purposes. Some treatises, like those of Corbin, Powell, Wigmore, and Farnsworth, mentioned above, are carefully reasoned and scholarly expositions of a field with explanation of the reasons behind the rules and criticism of the present state of the law. They are equally useful to the scholar and the practitioner. Others, often written by practicing lawyers on specialized topics such as automobile accidents or insurance, are intended primarily for the practitioner whose chief concern is with the present state of the law and who is searching for a case or other authority in a particular field. Treatises of both kinds are usually kept up to date with annual cumulative supplements. Single-volume textbooks, such as E. Farnsworth, *Contracts* (3d ed. 1999) or D. Dobbs et al., *Prosser & Keeton on Torts* (5th ed. 1984), have been written in many fields to serve as introductory works for students as well as practitioners. Occasionally, shorter student editions of major treatises, such as the abridgments of Powell and Scott, have been published. In addition, there are many interesting monographs on particular aspects of the law, such as B. Ackerman, *We the People: Foundations* (1991) and G. Gilmore, The *Death of Contract* (1974).

4. **Casebooks.** While the casebook is chiefly a teaching tool for student use, it should not be ignored as a research work as well. Many casebooks, such as J. Choper, J. Coffee & R. Gilson, *Cases and Materials on Corporations* (7th ed. 2008) and E. Farnsworth, W. Young, C. Sanger, N. Cohen & R. Brooks, *Cases and Materials on Contracts* (7th ed. 2008), contain copious notes and references to leading articles as well as cases. Since they are more frequently revised than many treatises, they may contain more recent material.[5]

5. **Legal periodicals.** The most distinguished American legal periodicals are the university law reviews, which now number several hundred. Traditionally, they are edited by top-ranking students and print student notes and comments as well as signed leading articles and book reviews by professors, lawyers, and judges. The leading articles are apt

---

[5] On the history and influence of casebooks, *see* Farnsworth, *Contracts Scholarship in the Age of Anthology*, 85 MICH. L. REV. 1406 (1987).

to be more original, argumentative, and critical than is the material found in treatises. The quality of the student work is often high and has not infrequently merited citation by the courts. Many reviews stress the local law of their jurisdiction or geographical area. Some emphasize special fields. Thus, the *Tulane Law Review* is devoted to the civil law, comparative law, and admiralty, and many law schools now have separate journals for such subjects as international and comparative law or human rights. Some reviews are edited by faculty rather than students, as is the case for *Law and Contemporary Problems*, published at Duke, and the *Journal of Legal Studies*, published at Chicago. Aside from the university law reviews, there are many journals that are published by bar associations and specialized groups. Examples are the *American Bar Association Journal*, the *Journal of Legal Education*, the *American Journal of International Law*, and the *American Journal of Comparative Law*. A summary of recent developments in various fields is published each year in the *Annual Survey of American Law of the New York University School of Law*. Work published in most English language periodicals in the United States and elsewhere is indexed in the cumulative *Index to Legal Periodicals*, and, beginning with 1980, in the somewhat more comprehensive *Current Law Index*.

6. **Loose-leaf services.** Loose-leaf services, notably those published by Bureau of National Affairs (BNA), Commerce Clearing House (CCH), and Prentice-Hall, enable the lawyer to keep abreast of developments in such rapidly changing fields as environmental law, federal and state taxation, business regulation, and administrative law. Examples are the BNA Environmental Law Reporter, the CCH Standard Federal Tax Reporter, and the Prentice-Hall Corporation services. Each service covers one specific field as completely as possible, including all types of authority together with comment and explanations.

7. **Miscellaneous.** The lawyer who is concerned with the drafting of legal documents may find help in form books, some general and some specialized, that collect standard forms for such documents, both substantive and procedural. Another useful aid for the practitioner is the *Martindale-Hubbell Law Directory*, a multi-volume set that contains a directory of American lawyers and a collection of brief digests of the law of the fifty states and many foreign countries.

Restatements of the Law

No discussion of secondary authority in the United States would be complete without mention of that unique effort at systemization of case law that culminated in the *Restatement of the Law*.[6] When the American Law Institute was organized in 1923, its objectives included "the clarification and simplification of the law." Its founders had concluded that "Two chief defects in American law are its uncertainty and its complexity. These defects cause useless litigation, prevent resort to the courts to enforce just rights, make it often impossible to advise persons of their rights, and when litigation is begun, create delay and expense." They saw in the growing number of decisions a threat to the vitality of the law. It was becoming increasingly difficult for the lawyer working on a case to find, read, and digest the relevant cases of the courts in the relevant state, and when this task yielded up no firm precedent, the lawyer was thrown upon the almost inexhaustible store of cases decided in the courts of other states and in the federal courts. They concluded that what was needed in those areas of the law that had not submitted to legislation was an authority greater than that of any single treatise to bring order into the chaos of case law.

To meet this need, the *Restatement* was prepared under the auspices of the Institute. It covered fields in which case law was dominant, and the effect of varying state statutes was minimal: agency, conflict of laws, contracts, judgments, property, restitution, torts, and trusts. The *Restatement* of each field was drafted by one or more "reporters," eminent law teachers, in collaboration with a group of advisors, including teachers, practitioners, and judges. The results of their combined efforts were then considered and approved by the Council of the Institute and finally by the membership of the institute. The *Restatements* in these fields were published between 1933 and 1944. The *Restatements* have now been revised by the same method and published as the *Restatement (Second)*, *Restatement (Third)* and in a few instances, *Restatement (Revised)*. The *Restatement (Second) of Conflict of Laws*,

---

[6] *See generally* Abrahamson, *Refreshing Institutional Memories: Wisconsin and the American Law Institute*, 1995 WIS. L. REV. 1; Farnsworth, *Ingredients in the Redaction of the Restatement (Second) of Contracts*, 81 COLUM. L. REV. 1 (1981); Goodrich, *The Story of the American Law Institute*, 1951 WASH. U. L.Q. 283 (1951); LEWIS, HISTORY OF THE RESTATEMENT, IN RESTATEMENT IN THE COURTS 1 (perm. ed. 1945); Wechsler, *The Course of the Restatements*, 55 A.B.A. J. 147 (1969).

for example, contains 423 sections, cites upwards of four thousand cases, and took over a decade and a half to prepare. The *Restatement (Third)* is in process and covers some subjects, such as foreign relations law and law governing lawyers, that were not part of the original *Restatement*.

The *Restatements* of each field are divided into sections, each of which commence with a black-letter statement of principles or rules, often with subdivisions. Each section is followed by comments that explain the section's purpose and scope and by illustrations of the section's application. Reporter's notes follow, in which the reporter will cite cases and other authorities and may mention conflicting views.

Although the *Restatement* is intended to be what its name signifies, it is not merely a summary of what has been decided by the courts in the past; on occasions, it has adopted a minority rule on the ground that it is demonstrably better than the majority rule. But neither is the *Restatement* a statement of what the institute would like to see the law become in the future. Rather, it is the considered opinion of some of the country's foremost legal scholars as to the law that would be applied by an enlightened court today. The quality and significance of the *Restatement* is not the same in all of its fields. On the whole, its influence has been considerably greater than that of an ordinary treatise, but it is by no means followed as a code. The *Restatement* is cited by appellate courts at a rate of over four thousand times a year. Citations are collected in volumes entitled *Restatement in the Courts*. The *Restatement* can exercise an important influence toward unification when a new question arises. The *Restatement* has not resulted in a movement for codification, but it was never the intention of its sponsors to aim at codification. The *Restatement* is designed to preserve, not to alter, the common-law practice of expressing and adapting law to social change.

Suggested Readings

The methods of legal research have been quickly changing, owing to the new computer databases. A useful introduction to both the computer platforms and traditional library work is in K. Olson, *Principles of Legal Research* (2009). For a brief, updated survey, see M. Cohen & K. Olson, *Legal Research in a Nutshell* (9th ed. 2007). A standard manual for citation form is *The Bluebook: A Uniform System of Citation* (18th ed. 2008).

II

Organization and Substance

NINE

Classification

Several factors make the classification of American law particularly difficult. Fundamental distinctions can, however, be drawn between law and equity, between substance and procedure, and between public and private law. What are these distinctions and how useful are they in the characterization of legal problems?

The Problem of Classification

Any system of law can be divided into categories according to a more or less rational scheme of classification. The lawyer, perhaps unconsciously, makes a preliminary characterization of a problem as a means of orientation and an essential prelude to analysis and research. Characterization may also have legal consequences as where, for example, it determines which choice of law rule a court will apply. Yet no system of classification can avoid arbitrariness and ambiguity, and several features of American law make classification particularly difficult. First, it has no comprehensive plan of codification from which to derive a scheme of classification. Second, its case-oriented approach is more pragmatic and empirical than theoretical and abstract and does not lend itself to generalization. It is symptomatic that the American lawyer does not see the broad general categories that are perceived by counterparts in civil-law countries.[1] Third, the common methods and techniques that pervade all branches of law tend to inhibit the development of autonomous fields. This is due in part to the absence of special courts, like those found in some civil law countries, for such major branches as public and commercial law.

In spite of these difficulties, there are some well-recognized distinctions that are useful for the purposes of orientation, analysis, and research. They are perpetuated through the content of law school courses and casebooks; through the titles of treatises and the *Restatement*; through the topic headings of digests and encyclopedias; and in some instances, through the purview of statutes. Three broad divisions will first be considered: that between law and equity, that between substance and procedure, and that between public and private law.

Law and Equity

The history of the distinction between law and equity begins in the developing system of law that followed the Norman conquest of England. A plaintiff who wished to have a complaint heard in the king's courts rather than the local courts had to purchase from the office of the chancellor a writ, or royal command, that fitted the facts of his case and required the defendant to appear in court. The variety of writs available, and with it the jurisdiction of the king's courts, expanded until the second half of the thirteenth century when, under pressure from the nobility, the power to issue writs was circumscribed, the jurisdiction of the king's courts was limited, and the flexibility of the law was diminished. Nevertheless, there was a residual power in the king and his council to do justice in special cases, and he began to refer petitions for redress to the chancellor who, as the chief

---

[1] The fragmentation of American law is most acute in the field of private law, where it was encouraged by the multifarious forms of action in the law courts before the procedural reforms of the nineteenth century. Thus, the area of private law known in civil-law countries as "civil law" is thought of by the American lawyer as such separate subjects as contracts, torts, properly, and family law; and the field of torts, for example, is divided into such distinct torts as assault, battery, and trespass. *See* Chapter 11, *infra*.

law member of the council, might give relief as a matter of "grace" or of "conscience" in cases where relief at law was inadequate.

From these beginnings, there grew up for non-criminal cases a supplementary system, known as "equity," in which, by the early fifteenth century, justice was administered through a separate court, the Court of Chancery. The law courts were forced to accept this system after a notorious struggle that ended in the early seventeenth century. Among the distinctive features of a suit in equity as opposed to an action at law were the absence of a jury, a more flexible procedure, and a wider scope of review on appeal. While the law courts were generally restricted to the award of money damages as relief, equity operated on the person of the defendant, and the court could, for example, issue an injunction, forbidding specified acts in order to prevent further injury, or it could decree specific performance, ordering performance of an obligation. A defendant who disobeyed could be punished by fine or imprisonment for contempt of court until compliance. But because these equitable remedies were considered to be extraordinary, they were only available where the remedy at law could be shown to be inadequate, and money damages remained the standard kind of relief.

Equity also came to differ from law in substance as well as procedure, as may be seen from one of its most important creations, the trust. The trust concept grew out of the conveyance of property by the owner (the settlor) to a transferee (the trustee), who was to hold it for the benefit of another (the beneficiary). For the transaction to succeed, some means had to be found to compel the trustee to comply with the terms of the trust. Since equity acted upon the person, it was able to enforce the trustee's fiduciary duties by its sanctions of fine and imprisonment, while at the same time recognizing the legal ownership of the trustee. Out of the beneficiary's equitable rights came the concept of equitable, as distinguished from legal, ownership. Around this new institution, a whole new branch of substantive law was to grow. Today, the express trust is widely used in the United States for both real and personal property, especially income-producing securities, and trust administration has become a task for professionals with the resultant rise of corporate trustees. Private express trusts are relied upon to dispose of most substantial family wealth at death; charitable express trusts are used to create large philanthropic foundations. The trust concept has also proved a useful tool in the hands of the courts: resulting trusts, inferred from the circumstances, are used to carry out the presumed intentions of parties to transactions in property;[2] and constructive trusts, implied as a matter of law, have become an essential device for avoiding unjust enrichment in cases of fraud and mistake.[3]

Equity found its way into most of the colonies in spite of some resistance that stemmed from the close relationship between equity and the crown. It was generally received in the states, was developed by the courts in the early part of the nineteenth century, and was the subject of one of Story's great treatises. Some states had separate systems of courts for law and equity; others had a single system in which a court might sit as either a law court or an equity court, depending on the nature of the case. Both schemes occasioned inconvenience, expense, and delay, as where a party sought relief in the wrong kind of court and had to begin all over again. By the middle of the century, there was a demand for merger of law and equity. New York led the reform by enactment of the Field Code of Civil Procedure in 1848. The code abolished the distinction between a suit in equity and an action at law, substituted a single civil action for the different forms of action previously available, and consolidated the rules of procedure, borrowing heavily from the more liberal equity rules. Law and equity procedure were united in the federal courts in 1938 and have been merged in practically all of the states.

The merger cannot be fully realized, however, because the right to a jury trial under federal and state constitutions generally extends only to cases formerly triable at law and not to those formerly triable in equity. Thus, for historical reasons, the distinction between law and equity must even now be observed for this purpose. Where there are both legal and equitable issues in a jury trial, the legal issues of fact are decided by the jury, while the equitable issues are decided by the judge. Moreover, rights that originated in the equity courts are still referred to as "equitable." They are

---

[2] For example: "A deposits money in a bank in the name of B. In the absence of evidence of a different intention on the part of A, B holds his claim against the bank for the amount of the deposit upon a resulting trust for A." RESTATEMENT (SECOND) OF TRUSTS, Section 440, Illustration 2.

[3] For example: "A, the owner of land, makes a gratuitous conveyance to B. By a mistake in the description in the deed, A transfers not only the tract which he intended to convey but also a second tract which he did not intend to include. B does not know of the mistake and believes that A intended to transfer both tracts. B holds the second tract upon a constructive trust for A." RESTATEMENT OF RESTITUTION, Section 163, Illustration 1.

exercised in much the same way and are subject to most of the same limitations as they were in the courts of equity. The most important restriction is that they are still available only where the legal remedy is inadequate.

It is therefore important to realize that "equity" is not a synonym for "general fairness" or "natural justice." It refers instead to a particular body of rules that originated in a special system of courts. However, these rules have to a considerable extent been assimilated into the appropriate categories of law and are now often regarded as part, for example, of property or contract law. One result has been that law schools no longer give a separate course in equity, though the subject may be dealt with as part of a broader course in remedies. It is true in the United States, as in England, that "if we were to inquire what it is that all these rules have in common and what it is that marks them off from all other rules administered by our courts, we should by way of answer find nothing but this, that these rules were until lately administered, and administered only, by our courts of equity."[4] Certainly for the purposes of this book, the distinction between law and equity is not a helpful basis for classification.

Substance and Procedure

The distinction between substance and procedure is a more fruitful one. Some such distinction is familiar to all legal systems. In the United States, the subject of procedure, or adjective law as it is occasionally called, has taken on special importance, not only because of the creative role accorded the courts in all common-law countries but also because of such indigenous factors as the professional emphasis of law study and the complexities of the federal system. The distinction may be important for a variety of purposes: if a statute concerns a matter of "procedure" rather than "substance," it will be unaffected by constitutional prohibitions against retroactive legislation; if a question is one of "procedure" rather than "substance," a federal court in a diversity case will follow federal law rather than defer to state law under *Erie Railroad Co. v. Tompkins*[5]; if an issue is one of "procedure" rather than "substance," a state court will apply its own law rather than the law of

---

[4] F. MAITLAND, LECTURES ON EQUITY 1–2 (1909), speaking of equity in England.

[5] *See* Chapter 4, *supra*.

some other state whose law would be chosen to govern the primary rights and liabilities.

The line of demarcation is sometimes difficult to fix, and what a court will consider to be "substance" and what it will consider to be "procedure" in a particular case may depend upon the purpose for which the distinction is to be drawn. Thus, a statute of limitations may be regarded as "procedural," as barring a remedy, for one purpose and as "substantive," as terminating a right, for another. Nevertheless, the number of borderline cases is relatively small, and the boundaries of the field of procedure are in the main well established. It is concerned with all aspects of the conduct of legal controversy before the courts, including access to the courts, who may sue and be sued, the form of the action, the availability of countervailing claims, the conditions of maintaining suit, the steps before trial, the method of proof, remedies, the effects of the court's judgment, and appeals.

Procedure includes both criminal and civil procedure. It also encompasses the subject of evidence, which is concerned with the rules relating to proof before a court. Because the significance and intricacy of this field are greatly heightened by the adversary system and the use of the jury, the law of evidence is generally treated as a distinct branch of the law. Finally, the subject of conflict of laws has a very heavy procedural ingredient and, for the sake of convenience, is placed here under the heading of procedure.[6]

Public and Private Law

The division of substantive law into public and private law is, while not uncommon, of more questionable utility than the division of law into substance and procedure.[7] As the Supreme Court of the United States has said, "It is often convenient to describe particular claims as invoking public or private rights, and this handy classification is doubtless valid for some purposes. But usually the real significance and legal consequence of each term

---

[6] The subject of federal jurisdiction, which is concerned with the jurisdiction of the federal courts, is also essentially procedural. It has been discussed in an earlier chapter and will not be repeated here.

[7] The distinction between public and private law should not be confused with that between public and private laws or enactments. *See* Chapter 6, *supra*.

will depend upon its context and the nature of the interests it is invoked to distinguish."[8]

Because there is no special system of courts to handle public law matters, there is rarely an occasion when the distinction is of practical importance in the United States. It has been suggested that public law encompasses those rights that are enforced through the administrative process, while private law is concerned with those that are left to enforcement on private initiative through the law courts.[9] This, however, gives but a narrow compass to public law. Even constitutional law, for example, is part of the everyday work of the ordinary courts in resolving suits between private parties. Perhaps the lawyer tends to think of public law, if he or she thinks of the distinction at all, in the classic sense of a branch of law devoted to the functioning of government and the adjustment of relations between individuals and the government, while private law is occupied with the rights of individuals among themselves. Of course, even this distinction is difficult to apply to the increasing number of situations where the state intervenes or becomes involved in relations between private individuals.

Whatever the merits or nature of the distinction, all lawyers would probably include in public law the fields of constitutional law and administrative law. Also included are labor law, which is primarily concerned with government control over labor relations, and trade regulation, which is primarily concerned with government control over business activity, as well as criminal law, which directly affects the relationship between the individual and the government. The inclusion of tax law may be more controversial because of its strong affinity in practice with private law fields such as corporation and property law.[10]

Private law is more fragmented. What is known in most civil law countries as "civil law" is broken down into contracts, family law, property law, and torts. The laws of negotiable instruments, sales, and secured transactions have only in recent decades been recognized as parts of a whole called "commercial law." And the subjects of agency, corporations, and partnerships

---

[8] Justice Jackson in Garner v. Teamsters Union, 346 U.S. 485, 494 (1953).

[9] *Id.*

[10] The field of international law, by which is meant public international law, is somewhat a branch unto itself and is not discussed here because its substance is less peculiar than that of the other fields to the United States.

can only with some artifice be grouped for the sake of convenience under the heading of business enterprises.[11]

Suggested Readings

The more important areas of American law are illustrated with cases and discussion in G. Fletcher & S. Sheppard, *American Law in a Global Context: The Basics* (2002). A more traditional introduction for students is W. Burnham, *Introduction to the Law and Legal System of the United States* (4th ed. 2006). Two collections of essays by various authors are *An Introduction to the Law of the United States* (A. Levasseur & J. Baker eds., 1992) and *Introduction to the Law of the United States* (D. Clark & T. Ansay eds., 2d ed. 2001).

The most popular book for practitioners that deals with equitable remedies is D. Dobbs, *Handbook on the Law of Remedies: Damages-Equity-Restitution* (2d ed. 1993). A nice history of equity is in G. Watt, *Equity Stirring: The Story of Justice Beyond Law* (2009). The relationship of equity, particularly equitable remedies, to constitutional litigation is illustrated in P. Hoffer, *The Law's Conscience: Equitable Constitutionalism in America* (1990). For criticism of limitations on equitable remedies, see D. Laycock, *The Death of the Irreparable Injury Rule* (1991). Substantive aspects of the field, such as trusts, may be found in the works cited under the appropriate fields of law.

[11] Other fields, such as admiralty or maritime law, bankruptcy, copyrights, insurance, patents, and trusts are discussed under the most appropriate of the topics named. A few, such as comparative law and jurisprudence (as legal philosophy is frequently called) are not sufficiently indigenous to warrant discussion.

TEN

Procedure

The subjects of civil procedure, criminal procedure, evidence, and conflict of laws may be grouped under the general heading of procedure. What factors have influenced their development and contributed to their distinctive characteristics? How is litigation carried on in the United States?

Civil Procedure

SCOPE AND SOURCES

Procedure in non-criminal cases in the United States has been greatly influenced by two factors. First, the adversarial rather than inquisitorial character of litigation has encouraged the opposing lawyers to act as zealous partisans in presenting their cases and has contributed to a tradition of tactical maneuvering and of proprietorship over witnesses and information. It has accorded a relatively passive role to the judge, who in spite of some recent changes that make the judge more active, undertakes no independent investigation and often acts as mere arbiter. Second, the institution of the jury has tended to compress the trial, has given it a dramatic flavor, and has resulted in elaborate rules to separate the functions of the jury from those of the judge and to control the jury. In spite of these similarities among states in approach to procedural problems, each state court system, as well as the federal court system, operates under its own law of civil procedure.

At first, the states adapted their procedural law from that of England, which was compounded of court rules, judicial decisions, custom, and occasional statutes. However, dissatisfaction with the resulting rigidity and formality led reformers to seek more extensive legislation. The contributions of the Field code, enacted in New York in 1848, have already been mentioned,[1] and as other states followed the lead of New York in enacting procedural codes, control over procedure passed to the legislatures. But the codes themselves proved rigid and became increasingly detailed,[2] and pressure built up to return the rule-making function to the courts.

In 1934, Congress was persuaded to give the Supreme Court of the United States the power to make general rules of procedure for the district courts, subject to congressional disapproval. Complete or substantial rule-making power has also been given to the courts in a growing number of states, where it is usually exercised by the highest state court with the assistance of an advisory body such as a judicial council. In 1938, the Supreme Court promulgated the Federal Rules of Civil Procedure, which had been prepared by an advisory committee drawn from the bench and bar. The rules have since been amended many times and are under continuous study by the Judicial Conference of the United States, a group of senior federal judges that is advised by committees of judges, lawyers, and professors. The rules embody many of the most modern ideas on procedure and are not only law for the federal district courts but have been closely copied in over half of the states. Nevertheless, the law of civil procedure is far from uniform.

Procedure varies not only with the jurisdiction but also with the remedy sought by the plaintiff. Most civil actions involve claims for compensatory money damages; many of the civil actions filed in the major trial courts of the country involve damage claims for personal injury.[3] In a

---

[1] *See* Chapter 6, *supra.*

[2] In New York, the successor to the Field code at one time contained upwards of three thousand sections.

[3] A substantial portion of the remainder are family disputes. While business disputes play numerically a minor role, they attract much of the attention of the profession.

few instances, remedies sought by the plaintiff at law were specific rather than compensatory: replevin was available to compel the return of specific items of personal property that had been wrongfully taken and ejectment to recover possession of a specific parcel of real property. These names are still in common use among lawyers, even where there is now only one form of civil action. But aside from such exceptional cases, money damages are the standard remedy unless it is shown that compensatory relief will be inadequate so that equitable relief, such as a decree of specific performance or an injunction, may be granted. The following discussion is of necessity both general and simplified and is limited to the most common sort of case, an action *in personam*—a personal action—for compensatory money damages.[4] The object of such an action is to determine the rights of the parties with respect to the controversy and to impose liability. An action may also be one *in rem*, in which the purpose is not to impose liability upon anyone but to affect the interests of all persons who have or might have a property interest or claim in a thing, or article of property. Or an action may be one *quasi in rem*, to affect the interests of particular persons who are known to have a claim to, or possible interest in, a thing. In addition, federal and state courts are now permitted under special statutes to grant declaratory judgments, declaring the rights of the parties when there is an actual controversy between adversary parties, but other relief would be premature, unnecessary, or ineffective.[5]

CHARACTERISTICS—BEFORE TRIAL

There is a sharp distinction between the proceedings that precede the trial and the trial itself. At the trial, the issues of fact will be heard and determined. In the pre-trial proceedings, these issues must be defined, and the adversaries must be given adequate notice to prevent their surprise at the trial. This is of special importance because the trial, owing to the influence

---

[4] The discussion here assumes that only two parties are involved. Claims by the defendant against the plaintiff, and claims by or against third parties, will not be taken up.

[5] See Chapter 4, *supra*. There are special procedures for the prerogative writs of *certiorari, habeas corpus, mandamus*, prohibition, and *quo warranto*, for summary proceedings, and for some courts of limited jurisdiction. A writ of *habeas corpus*, for example, is available under proper circumstances to a person who has been physically detained by another, whether in a public or private capacity; the writ directs the other person to produce "the body" of the detained person in court for a determination of the legality of the detention.

of the jury system, is normally concentrated in one continuous hearing in open court. Any rulings before trial are made, often after argument between the lawyers, by a judge (who rules without the presence of advice of a jury).

Parties to litigation need not be – but almost invariably are – represented by lawyers who undertake the preparation of the necessary papers and appear in court. The steps taken by the parties in the description that follows are, therefore, ordinarily taken by their lawyers on their client's behalf.

An action is commenced by two writings, a complaint and a summons. The complaint is a statement setting out the nature of the plaintiff's claim and a demand for relief. The summons is a notice informing the defendant that an action is being brought and calling upon the defendant to answer the complaint. In order to meet the constitutional requirement of due process, service of the summons must be by a means that is reasonably designed to give the defendant actual notice. Ordinarily it is delivered to the defendant personally or left with an appropriate person at the defendant's residence or place of business within the geographical jurisdiction of the court. In special cases, service may be accomplished by mail, by publication in a newspaper or in a public place, or by some other means. The defendant then commonly enters an appearance by filing a paper, known as an answer, that is responsive to the complaint. If the defendant does not appear in court by filing an answer or challenging the proceedings otherwise, a default judgment may be entered against the defendant. The plaintiff's complaint, the defendant's answer, and any reply the plaintiff may file comprise the pleadings.[6] In a proper case, the plaintiff may also use provisional remedies to ensure that the action, if successful, will not have been futile because, for instance, the defendant hid assets that might have been used to satisfy a court order directing the defendant to pay the plaintiff. For example, the plaintiff may be able to have the defendant's property seized through an order of attachment and held as security for any judgment or to obtain a temporary injunction or restraining order to prevent the defendant from taking action to frustrate the plaintiff's suit.

---

[6] In the United States, the term "pleading" in civil procedure is limited to the exchange of these written documents before trial and does not include, for example, the lawyer's argument at the trial.

Before the enactment of the procedural codes, the theory of pleading, known as common-law pleading, was that the parties themselves should develop a single precise issue of fact or of law by means of elaborate written pleadings exchanged in advance of trial. One of the innovations of the Field code was to replace this "issue pleading" with "fact pleading," in which the parties were asked only to plead simple statements of the essential facts that they expected to prove at the trial. But there was confusion over the particularity with which facts should be stated, and the Federal Rules of Civil Procedure abandoned "fact pleading" in favor of what has sometimes been called "notice pleading."[7]

Under the rules, the emphasis is less on pleadings than on other more efficient means of obtaining information. The complaint need contain only a short and plain statement of the claim, showing that the plaintiff is entitled to relief; allegations may be general, and the allegations may even be inconsistent. Protection against surprise at trial that might otherwise result from this more general pleading form is afforded by important rights to pre-trial discovery.[8]

Under "fact pleading," the complaint would be more detailed and contain more paragraphs. A party's right to discovery includes rights to depose orally any person with relevant information, to submit written questions to adversaries and require written responses, to inspect relevant tangible evidence such as documents and property, and even to require a mental

---

[7] The Supreme Court has recently attempted to restrict complaints that raise allegations that may only be proven from evidence that is believed by the plaintiff to be available through discovery in the case, tightening the standards in Bell Atlantic Corp. v. Twombly, 550 U.S. 544 (2007). This and later interpretations of the rules of pleading may be altered by the Congress and are unlikely to be accepted in the states.

[8] For example, the sample Complaint for Negligence, as found in Form 11 of the Federal Rules of Civil Procedure, reads:

1. <Statement of Jurisdiction. See Form 7.>
2. On <Date>, at <Place>, the defendant negligently <drove a motor vehicle> against the plaintiff.
3. As a result, the plaintiff was <physically injured, lost wages or income, suffered physical and mental pain, and incurred medical expenses of $<___>>.
Therefore, the plaintiff demands judgment against the defendant for $<___>, plus costs.

FED. R. CIV. P., Appendix, Illustrative Civil Rules Forms, Civil Form 11. Complaint for Negligence, *at* www.uscourts.gov/rules/cvforms2.htm (2009). Material in <brackets> varies according to the facts the plaintiff alleges.

or physical examination of an adversary. While most discovery is at the request of a party, there is a trend in court rules to compel parties to disclose important information—such as the existence of critical evidence or the names of witnesses at the outset of litigation, prior to any request. In addition, the judge may call a pre-trial conference, a hearing at which both sides are present, in order to limit the issues and obtain admissions that will avoid unnecessary proof. Important by-products of the pre-trial conference may be the settlement of many cases without trial, the shortening of trials through concessions, the limitation of issues, and better preparation of all sides for trial.

Pre-trial procedure will occasionally result in a decision by the court that there should be no trial at all. The defendant may attack the legal basis of the plaintiff's case by a motion[9] to dismiss the complaint on the ground that it fails to state a legally sufficient cause of action of claim for relief. This was known in common-law pleading as a demurrer. The judge will grant the defendant's motion only if, assuming the truth of all the allegations of the complaint, the plaintiff would still have no right to relief. Such motions, however, rarely end the litigation. If the complaint is found to be insufficient, the plaintiff will ordinarily be allowed to amend it; if it is found to be sufficient, the defendant will usually interpose an answer that raises an issue of fact. This the defendant may do in two ways, either by denying some or all of the plaintiff's allegations or by alleging additional facts that constitute a defense to the claims the plaintiff made. Under modern pre-trial procedure, however, it is sometimes possible to resolve even an issue of fact before trial. After discovery, the judge may grant a motion for summary judgment in favor of either party if the judge determines, on the basis of affidavits and other documents chronicling the evidence each side intends to present if the case is tried, that there is no genuine issue of fact justifying a trial. The defendant may also make a variety of motions that seek to avoid or delay going to the merits of the controversy. They range from a motion to dismiss the complaint because the court does not have jurisdiction to a motion to require the plaintiff to make the

---

[9] A motion is an application to the court for a ruling, in this case for an order to dismiss. An order is the traditional form for any judicial determination, short of a final judgment disposing of the entire case.

complaint more definite, by making some allegations or claims more specific, or allegations of fact more detailed.

If the plaintiff's complaint has withstood the defendant's tactics, and if the case is not one of the great majority that are settled before the trial, the plaintiff will request the clerk of the court to put the case on a list, called a calendar or docket, to await trial. Because of the number of litigants, the plaintiff may have to wait for a substantial period of time, well over a year in some congested courts, before the case comes to trial.

CHARACTERISTICS—TRIAL

Although modern pre-trial procedure has done much to counter the tradition of surprise and proprietorship over proof, it is still a basic tenet that the parties themselves can most effectively present their own cases and, after each case has been subjected to attack by an adversary, the truth can then be determined by an impartial tribunal. The trial is held before a single judge, who may sit with or without a jury[10] It may last for a matter of hours, days, or even weeks; and particularly in cases heard also by a jury, the trial is customarily a single continuous process without prolonged adjournment. Where the plaintiff seeks compensatory money damages, there is generally a right to jury trial, although this right may be waived. Jurors are not noted for their skill in coping with complex and involved transactions and, for this or for other reasons, both parties may prefer to put their case solely in the hands of a judge.

Even so, in many cases, one party or the other desires the issues to be heard and decided by the jury. In a jury trial, the jurors are selected by lot from a larger group of qualified citizens, a cross section of the community, who have been summoned for jury duty.[11] At common law, jurors numbered twelve, but many states now provide for a smaller number, ranging down to six. Jurors sit for a single case only and are paid a modest amount to cover expenses. They must meet minimum requirements relating to such matters as citizenship, eligibility to vote, age, general health, and impartiality. Prospective jurors are subjected to what is known as a *voir dire* examination

[10] Judges in the United States wear black robes while in court but no wigs or caps. Lawyers wear business suits, and jurors wear more casual but suitable attire.

[11] The trial jury is the *petit* or petty jury, often called simply "the jury," as distinguished from the grand jury, discussed in Chapter 10, *infra*.

on their qualifications, during which a juror may be challenged for cause by either party and excluded by the judge if the juror is not qualified. In addition, each party has a number of peremptory challenges that may be used to exclude a juror without any stated reasons, subject to the limitation that the exclusion may not be based on race or gender. After the jurors have been sworn to try the issues, they are seated in the jury box, and the trial begins. It is the task of the jury, at least in theory, to decide issues of "fact" and that of the judge to decide issues of "law." The dividing line between the two is often a shadowy one, and, for example, whether the jury's decision on an issue of "fact" has been reasonable is itself an issue of "law."

The plaintiff has the initial burden of presenting evidence. First, both parties make opening statements in which they explain their side of the case to the jury so that it will be better able to follow the proof.[12] The plaintiff then proceeds with proof. This is done by the introduction of both oral and written evidence. Documentation may be voluminous in large cases where business records are involved. One consequence of the adversary system is that witnesses are generally called on behalf of the parties themselves and not on behalf of the court. The court may issue subpoena that orders a party who is within the court's territorial jurisdiction to appear and to give testimony or to produce a writing or an object, if the witness will not do so voluntarily. The parties themselves are generally competent to testify.

The first witness for the plaintiff is called to the witness stand for direct examination and takes an oath by which the witness is sworn to tell the truth.[13] The witness's testimony is elicited by questions posed by the plaintiff's lawyer. It is the practice of lawyers in the United States to discuss with their clients' witnesses the witnesses' testimony in advance of trial in order to prevent waste of time and surprise at trial. It is, of course, improper for a lawyer to use this occasion to manipulate a witness's testimony. After direct examination of the witness by the plaintiff's lawyer, the defendant's lawyer is allowed to cross-examine the witness to show additional facts or

---

[12] In some jurisdictions, however, the defendant's opening is not made until after the plaintiff's case is concluded, and the plaintiff rests; after the defendant's opening argument, the defendant calls witnesses and introduces evidence, sometimes offering new witnesses and sometimes recalling witnesses whom the plaintiff had called.

[13] A witness who has religious scruples about taking an oath can make an affirmation.

inconsistencies, or to attack the witness's credibility. Because the witness has been called on behalf of the plaintiff, the right to cross-examine is an important one. There may then be redirect and recross examination until the witness is excused. The judge may also question the witness at any time the witness is on the stand,[14] but the burden of examination is on the lawyers. Other witnesses are then called, and documents and physical objects may be presented. These are subject to the rules of evidence, however; and, for example, the results of the pre-trial procedure, such as depositions and documents, are not necessarily admissible at the trial. After presenting proof, the plaintiff will rest.

At this point, the plaintiff must have introduced enough evidence on all issues as to which the plaintiff has the burden of proof to justify a favorable jury verdict.[15] The defendant may test whether the plaintiff has done so by a motion for judgment as a matter of law.[16] The issue raised is only whether a reasonable jury could, on the basis of the plaintiff's evidence, reach a verdict for the plaintiff. This is therefore regarded as an issue of "law" rather than one of "fact," and the judge alone rules upon the motion. If it is granted, the dismissal ends the trial and operates as a judgment on the merits for the defendant. If it is denied, the defendant must proceed with proof.

The defendant will present evidence in the same manner as did the plaintiff. This time, the plaintiff will have the right of cross-examination of the defendant's witnesses. At the conclusion of the defendant's case, the plaintiff may offer proof in rebuttal of the evidence introduced by the defense. At the close of all the evidence, either party may move for a directed verdict on the ground that a reasonable jury could only return a verdict in favor of the moving party. This motion is also considered to raise a question of "law" rather than one of "fact." If the judge grants the motion, the trial will end, and judgment will be entered for the moving party. Under modern practice, the judge no longer actually goes through

---

[14] The judge in some jurisdiction will pose specific questions to a witness at the written request of jurors.

[15] The allocation of the burden of proof is therefore a matter of no small importance. The various meanings of the term "burden of proof" are discussed in *McCormick on Evidence* in Chapter 36 (J. Strong et al., 4th ed. 1999). For a brief discussion of the effect of presumptions, *see id.* 521–29.

[16] This is sometimes known as a motion that the plaintiff be nonsuited or that a verdict be directed for the defendant.

the formality of directing the jury to bring in the appropriate verdict. If the judge denies the motion, the trial will proceed to its conclusion.

Both parties will then make their closing arguments to the jury. In some jurisdictions, the plaintiff's closing is first, followed by the defendant's closing, then by the plaintiff's rebuttal. In others, the defendant's closing is first, followed by the plaintiff's closing. Arguments must be confined to the evidence that has been presented. Each side will attempt, by analysis of the proof, to persuade the jury that it should decide the case in its favor.

The judge will then charge the jury by instructing it in the rules of law under which it is to reach its decision. Before closing argument, both sides may submit to the judge instructions that they propose that the judge give, and the judge will then disclose to them the instructions that will be given so that they can frame their arguments accordingly. In some jurisdictions, however, the charge is given before the closing argument.

The authority of the judge was reduced during the nineteenth century as a result of confidence in the average juror's abilities and of unpleasant recollections of arbitrary and absolute judges who were supposed to have represented crown control during colonial times. The narrower role of the judge has resulted in a wider one for the jury and, indirectly, for the lawyers. One symptom of this is the rule in a number of states that the charge must not contain any comment on the weight of the evidence or the credibility of the witnesses but must be confined to the rules of law to be applied. In some states, the judge is not even permitted to summarize the evidence, and, in some, the judge may not charge the jury orally but must do so in writing. These limitations have been much criticized by the organized bar, however, and the trend is now toward an expansion of the judge's role. Where the trial has been without a jury, there is, of course, no charge to make because the judge determines the contested issues of facts.

After the charge, the jurors retire to the jury room where they deliberate in secret for a matter of hours and sometimes days, until they reach their verdict. In a civil case, the jury must be persuaded "by a preponderance of the evidence," or in other words that the existence of the contested fact is more probable than not. Historically, the verdict of the jurors had to be unanimous, but this rule has often been altered by constitution or statute. In some jurisdictions, however, a jury may render a verdict that is less than a unanimous verdict only with the prior consent of the parties. The "hung" jury—one unable to reach a decision by the required majority—is nevertheless highly unusual. The jury may be polled by asking each juror in open court whether he or she agrees with the verdict, in order to make certain that the required number of jurors consent. No record is kept of their deliberations, and rules severely restrict jurors from later testifying to impeach their own verdict. The jury's verdict may be simply a general one, a finding for one side with an assessment of damages (if there are any); or the jury may be required to answer specific questions of fact put to it by the judge.[17] In some places, the verdict is given orally. In others, a written verdict is returned, and the jury gives oral assent when it is read in court. After receiving the verdict, the judge discharges the jury, and the trial is ended. If there has been no jury the judge makes findings of fact and conclusions of law. The judge may also write an opinion.

After the jury verdict, the losing party may move for a new trial on a variety of grounds, including prejudicial error by the judge in ruling on the admissibility of evidence or in instructing the jury, or a verdict that is against the weight of the evidence. If the judge concludes that the damages awarded by the jury are unreasonably high, the judge may by an order known as *remittitur* subtract an appropriate amount and order a new trial if the change is not accepted by the parties. If the judge, at least in most state courts, determines that the jury erred in awarding damages that are too low, the judge may award more damages as *additur*.[18] The losing party may also make a motion for judgment as a matter of law in order to permit the judge to give a favorable judgment on the merits, when the judge had denied an earlier motion for such a judgment.[19] The grounds of the earlier and the later motions are the same. The judge may be more willing to grant a motion to give judgment as a matter of law after the jury has reached its verdict because, should the granting of the motion be reversed on appeal, there is then a verdict upon which the appellate court can enter judgment, and it will save the time and expense of a new trial. The judge will also have had more time to deliberate before passing on a motion for judgment notwithstanding the verdict.

---

[17] Traditionally, the answers to specific questions were given in the form of a special verdict, as distinguished from a general verdict. Today a more common procedure is to ask the jury for a general verdict together with the answers to questions known as interrogatories.

[18] *Additur* is not allowed in federal courts. *See* Dimick v. Schiedt, 293 U.S. 474 (1935).

[19] This is sometimes called a motion for judgment notwithstanding the verdict (*non obstante veredicto*).

Finally, assuming that all motions made after the verdict was rendered have been denied, judgment will be entered on the verdict. The judgment will ordinarily require the losing party to pay the costs of the successful party. These include such fees as those paid to the court by the successful party but generally do not include lawyers' fees.[20] If the losing party refuses to pay a money judgment, a number of procedures are available by way of execution. For example, that party's property may be seized by a court officer and sold at a public sale to pay the judgment.[21]

CHARACTERISTICS—APPEAL

After the trial, a party may appeal from the judgment, claiming error on the part of the trial judge or in the trial proceedings, which prevented a fair and lawful trial. The party who appeals is called the appellant, petitioner, or plaintiff-in-error; the other party is the appellee, respondent, or defendant-in-error. During the appeal, execution of judgment can be suspended upon the posting of a bond by the appellant. Ordinarily the appellant must have taken appropriate steps during the trial, by making or opposing a motion, by raising an objection, or otherwise to bring the matter to the attention of the judge. By the end of the trial, the judge will have ruled on a variety of such contested points—motions attacking pleadings, objections to the admission or exclusion of evidence, motions for a directed verdict, and so on. The appeal will usually be based on one or more of these rulings. Whether the losing party may appeal from interlocutory rulings that are not finally dispositive of the case varies from state to state.

There is no new trial, no jury, and no witnesses in the appellate court. The judges' knowledge of the case is derived solely from the record, a stenographic transcript of the proceedings in the lower court that shows the actions at trial that the appellant asserts were errors. The appellate court is aided by detailed written briefs prepared by the parties in support of their cases. When the question on appeal is of importance beyond the immediate parties themselves, the court may also have before it a brief *amicus curiae*—a

[20] For a reaffirmation of the general rule that costs do not include attorneys' fees, *see* Alyeska Pipeline Service Co. v. Wilderness Society, 421 U.S. 240 (1975). This rule has been modified by statute, however, in important instances.

[21] This officer in the state courts is a sheriff, a county official, and in the federal courts is a United States marshal.

brief by a "friend of the court" such as the government or an interested private group. Oral proceedings are limited to questions of "law," and the parties will urge upon the court those precedents and other authorities that they regard as controlling. The court will not intrude upon the province of the jury as trier of issues of "fact," but it may determine that the jury exceeded the bounds of reasonableness in reaching its verdict if this issue had been raised by a proper motion before the trial judge. The appellate court will be reluctant to reach such a conclusion, however, in cases in which the judge and jury had the opportunity of observing key witnesses when they testified.

The decision of the appellate court, usually accompanied by a written opinion, may not be handed down for weeks or even months, while the judges study the briefs and confer among themselves. If the court concludes its review and finds that there was no error, or if there was error that was "harmless" and probably did not affect the outcome, it will affirm the judgment below. If the court finds reversible error, it will reverse the judgment and remand the case either for entry of judgment for the appellant or for a new hearing or trial, depending on the circumstances. If the case is remanded, the lower court is bound to follow the instructions of the appellate court. The costs of the appeal, which again fall short of actual expenses, are borne by the losing party, and the expense of appeals tends to limit the number of litigants who seek review.

Suggested Readings

Treatises include J. Friedenthal, M. Kane & A. Miller, *Civil Procedure* (4th ed. 2005); F. James, G. Hazard & J. Leubsdorf, *Civil Procedure* (4th ed. 1992); and M. Green, *Basic Civil Procedure* (2d ed. 1979). The Federal Rules of Civil Procedure are discussed in C. Wright, *The Law of Federal Courts* (4th ed. 1983) and are available online in several free sites, such as the Legal Information Institute, LII: Federal Rules of Civil Procedure, www.law.cornell.edu/rules/frcp/ (2009). Multi-volume works on federal procedure are J. Moore, *Federal Practice* (2d ed. loose leaf) and C. Wright & A. Miller et al., *Federal Practice and Procedure* (1969–). A multi-volume work on the procedure of a single state is J. Weinstein, H. Korn & A. Miller, *New York Civil Practice* (loose leaf), condensed as Weinstein, Korn & Miller *CPLR Manual* (D. Ferstendig, ed., loose leaf). Some aspects of procedure are dealt with in the *Restatement (Second) of Judgments* (1982). Others are dealt with in the

American Law Institute's Complex Litigation Project (1993), which recommends changes to improve the efficiency and fairness with which the American legal system handles large-scale civil litigation.

See G. Fletcher & S. Sheppard, *American Law in a Global Context: The Basics,* Chapter 26.

Criminal Procedure

SCOPE AND SOURCES

The law of criminal procedure has been affected, to a much greater extent than that of civil procedure, by both federal and state constitutions. In detail, it is largely statutory in form and varies considerably from one jurisdiction to the next. Field's code of criminal procedure was a less influential force for unifying rules across states than was his code of civil procedure,[22] and the Federal Rules of Criminal Procedure promulgated by the Supreme Court of the United States have had less impact on the states than have the Federal Rules of Civil Procedure. The main purposes of the proceedings are the determination of who has committed a crime and the assessment of punishment for it, though in sentencing, account may be taken of whether the accused has made restitution. The following discussion concerns a typical prosecution; petty offenses are tried by a more summary procedure.

CHARACTERISTICS

Criminal procedure in America is essentially accusatorial, with the prosecutor taking the leading role, rather than inquisitorial, with the judge taking the leading role. The trial of criminal cases reflects the adversary nature of the judicial process and confidence in the capacities of lay jurors. On the one side stands the prosecutor, an elected official or a political appointee, whose extraordinary powers and discretion are one of the chief characteristics of the administration of criminal justice in the United States. On the other stands the person accused of a crime, one who is protected against abuses on the part of the prosecutor and the police by a defense

---

[22] *See* Chapter 6, *supra* for a discussion of the Field codes.

counsel who may call upon extraordinary constitutional safeguards that may require the reversal of a conviction for the most technical departures from the requirements of the due process of law.[23] Between them stand judges and jurors, as impartial arbiters.

The first official step in most criminal cases is the arrest by a police officer of the person suspected of the crime. The suspect must, without unnecessary delay, be brought before a judicial officer, known as a magistrate, who will conduct the preliminary examination, which is termed a first appearance or preliminary hearing in different jurisdictions. This is an informal public hearing to determine whether the evidence is sufficient to warrant holding the suspect. If the proceeding is not dismissed at this stage, the magistrate will fix bail as security for the suspect's return after release from custody. The preliminary hearing is not inquisitorial, and it is not the practice for the magistrate to interrogate the suspect. The preparation of the prosecution's case is left entirely to the prosecutor. There is sometimes a tendency for the police to prolong the period between arrest and preliminary examination in order to interrogate the suspect before the suspect has seen a lawyer. Improper threats, pain, or pressure by the police that is intended to elicit a confession during this questioning is popularly known as the "third degree," and it is not only forbidden, but any evidence thus procured is inadmissible. The suspect has, however, the constitutional privileges of refusing to answer questions and of representation by a lawyer, and any information divulged by the suspect before being reminded of these privileges (and any acquired if these rights are not respected) is likewise inadmissible.[24]

Formal accusation, designed to inform the accused of the charges, may be made in many states by either indictment or information. An indictment

[23] As a matter of constitutional law, the Supreme Court of the United States has held that evidence obtained by an unreasonable search and seizure or a coerced confession is inadmissible in both the federal and state courts. Such evidence is known as the "fruit of the poisonous tree." A conviction obtained as a result of such evidence or confession will be reversed. Other types of illegally obtained evidence are also inadmissible in the federal and some of the state courts. The controversial subject of evidence gained by wiretapping is the subject of a federal statute and also of statutes in some states.

[24] The right to counsel during questioning was established in Miranda v. Arizona, 384 U.S. 436 (1966).

is an accusation framed by the prosecutor and authorized by a grand jury.[25] A grand jury is a panel that normally hears only the evidence for the prosecution and authorizes an indictment if the evidence is found to sufficiently justify sending the matter on to trial. In many jurisdictions, indictment by a grand jury has given way to a simpler procedure in which a formal accusation, known as an information, is filed by the prosecutor.

The indictment or information is followed by arraignment before the trial judge, the formal reading of the charge to the accused in open court followed by an oral plea of "guilty" or "not guilty." Generally, if the accused pleads not guilty at this stage, the defendant need not indicate the nature of the defense to be raised on which the plea is based. The accused may also object at the arraignment on a variety of grounds to the legal sufficiency of the accusation. Or the accused may plead guilty to a lesser offense than that charged. And in some jurisdictions, the accused may plead *nolo contendere* (I do not wish to contend), which authorizes judgment and sentence just as a plea of guilty would but which may not be considered an admission of guilt and used against the accused in other criminal or civil proceedings. Pleas of guilty are entered in the great majority of cases. Many are obtained by concessions from the prosecutor to accept the plea of guilty to a lesser offense than charged or to recommend leniency in the sentence. If, however, the plea is not guilty, both sides prepare for trial. Pre-trial discovery procedure is much more limited than in civil cases.

Trial is commonly before a judge sitting with a jury, though in most jurisdictions, the defendant may agree to waive the constitutional right to jury trial. Not only are trials of criminal cases nearly always open to the public, but the case may be the subject of almost unrestricted comment by news media before and during trial. Although freedom of the press may

---

25   In some states, the grand jury may be composed of as many as twenty-three members, as opposed to the twelve-member trial or petty jury. It is empowered to compel witnesses to attend and testify under oath, and for this reason the prosecutor may prefer to proceed by indictment rather than by information. The suspect is not present, and the proceedings are secret, in part to protect the reputation of the suspect should the grand jury decide not to indict and in part to prevent premature disclosure of the prosecution's case to the suspect. The grand jury's vote need not be unanimous. Traditionally, it has also had broad authority to investigate on its own initiative, and it may be empowered to make its own independent accusation in the form of a presentment.

help to ensure a fair trial, the possible effect upon the jury of prejudicial reports poses a serious and unresolved problem, which is of growing concern to the bench and bar. The procedure at trial does not differ greatly from that of a civil action.[26] The defendant is competent to take the witness stand and testify, as might any other witness. But the defendant cannot be compelled to do so,[27] and failure to testify creates no presumption against the defendant and may not be commented upon by the prosecution. The presentation of evidence in open court, first for the prosecution then for the defense, is followed by arguments for both sides: the judge's charge to the jury, its deliberation and verdict of guilty or not guilty, and the judgment of the court. All evidence is presented in open court. There is no file or *dossier* prepared before trial for the private use of judge or jury. As in civil actions, witnesses are interrogated one at a time and do not confront each other, and it is the practice of each side to question its witnesses in advance of trial. The jury will be instructed that they must acquit unless they are convinced of guilt "beyond a reasonable doubt," and their verdict generally must be unanimous.

After judgment, if the accused is convicted, sentence is imposed within limits set by statute, usually by the judge but sometimes by the jury. It may, depending upon the gravity of the offense, consist of a fine, imprisonment, or, at least in most states, death.[28] The defendant may appeal from a conviction and, if the appellate court reverses, it may in some circumstances order a new trial. But because of constitutional protections of the defendant against double jeopardy, the prosecution may not seek reversal of an acquittal. Only a few American jurisdictions, however,

---

[26] The defendant is ordinarily represented by a lawyer. A lawyer in private practice may take or refuse the case of an accused person without regard to a belief in the client's innocence. The Constitution has been construed to require that a lawyer be furnished to an indigent defendant charged with an offense other than a minor one in either a state or a federal court. During the trial, the lawyer and the accused are permitted to sit and to speak freely. The prosecutor sits on the same level as the defense and wears a business suit, as does the defense lawyer.

[27] The Fifth Amendment to the federal Constitution provides that, "No person . . . shall be compelled in any criminal case to be a witness against himself . . . ," and many state constitutions contain similar provisions. In spite of this language, the so-called "privilege against self-incrimination" extends to all judicial or official hearings, inquiries, or investigations where a person is called upon formally to give testimony.

[28] *See* Chapter 12, *infra* for a discussion of sentencing.

have enacted statutes that give the convicted defendant who has served part of a sentence the right to damages upon a later finding of not guilty. But while the small minority of cases which go to trial attract the public's attention, the overwhelming majority of criminal proceedings are disposed of without trial, largely by dismissal on preliminary examination and by plea of guilty on arraignment.

Suggested Readings

A useful source is the *Uniform Rules of Criminal Procedure* (1987), promulgated by the National Conference of Commissioners on Uniform State Laws. The American Law Institute has published a *Model Code of Pre-Arraignment Procedure* (1975), including commentary by the reporters. Treatises include W. LaFave, J. Israel & N. King, *Criminal Procedure* (4th ed. 2004) and C. Whitebread & C. Slobogin, *Criminal Procedure: An Analysis of Cases and Concepts* (5th ed. 2007).

See G. Fletcher & S. Sheppard, *American Law in a Global Context: The Basics, Introduction* and Chapters 27 through 29.

Evidence

SCOPE AND SOURCES

The law of evidence deals with such matters as the kinds of judicial proof, or the forms of evidence that may be admitted in court; the competency of witnesses to testify in general; the form and extent of questions allowed during the examination of witnesses; the reasons for the admission or exclusion of evidence in a given cause of action; privileges by a given witness against testimony; burdens of proof required of the plaintiff or prosecutor to win; and presumptions, or the conditions under which a fact may be assumed to be true. The law of evidence was traditionally found in judicial decisions and varied from one jurisdiction to another. Today, however, the field of evidence shows considerable uniformity as the result of the adoption in 1975 of the Federal Rules of Evidence and the promulgation at about the same time of the Uniform Rules of Evidence. The two sets of rules are similar, and most states now have rules of evidence based on them.

With some exceptions, the law of evidence in criminal cases is fundamentally the same as in civil cases.[29]

CHARACTERISTICS

Like the rest of the law of procedure, the law of evidence bears the stamp both of the adversary character of litigation and of the institution of the jury. In keeping with the contentious nature of the proceeding, the initiative is on the parties rather than the judge, both to develop the evidence and police its admission. They bear the sole responsibility for producing the proof, and decisions on issues of fact are based exclusively on evidence brought forth in open court. Some facts, however, may be such common knowledge that the court will take judicial notice of them, without proof.

Traditionally, testimony is elicited by the examining lawyer from the witness, question by question, and documents are submitted into evidence in the court, item by item. The practice as to documents is changing, however, particularly in large cases where quantities of business records are involved. The tradition enables the other party to make prompt objection, often when the question is asked or when the item is proffered, if the evidence is to be excluded from the consideration of the jury. Failure to do so is ordinarily a waiver of the objection. Although the aggrieved party may appeal an erroneous ruling, the trial judge is accorded considerable discretion, and the appellate court will reverse only if it concludes that there is a substantial probability that an improper ruling influenced the verdict or finding below.

Another result of the adversary nature of the proceeding has been that traditionally each witness is called on behalf of one of the parties, rather than on behalf of the court and is subject to cross-examination by the opposing party's lawyer. The parties are expected to produce not only their own lay witnesses but also their own expert witnesses, including, for example, medical doctors, scientists and engineers, handwriting and

---

[29] Compare, however, the burden of persuasion to prove a civil claim "by a preponderance of evidence" in civil cases with the higher burden to prove a criminal charge "beyond a reasonable doubt." *See* "Criminal Procedure," *supra.*

ballistics specialists, and experts in foreign law.[30] The result is not infrequently a battle of experts in which each adversary is represented by a battery of paid specialists, selected, at least in part, because their testimony will be favorable to the side that selects them. Each specialist is required to submit to cross-examination by the opposing party. Dissatisfaction with this system has begun to produce change. Thus, one of the purposes of the pre-trial conference may be to limit the number of expert witnesses, and the court is often allowed to appoint neutral experts in addition to those called by the parties.

A second factor, the central role of the jury in both criminal and civil trials, has also had a pervasive influence on the law in this field. The common law's highly refined rules of evidence developed largely in order to control the jury, and the rules devised for the jury system have affected all trials. Although in practice, a judge may be more likely to admit questionable evidence when sitting without a jury, in principle, the same rules apply to both jury and nonjury trials.

A particularly important result of the jury system is that, beyond the exclusion of irrelevant evidence, there are some rules that exclude relevant evidence on the ground that its value is outweighed by the danger that the jury may give it too much weight. This policy is at the root of that most notorious of all exclusionary rules of evidence, the hearsay rule. This rule, which is subject to many exceptions, generally excludes evidence of any statement made out of court if the statement is offered for the purpose of proving whatever the statement asserts. Accordingly, a witness will not be allowed to prove the occurrence of an event by testifying that someone else said that the event took place.[31] The conventional justification of the rule is that the judge or juror, who comes to the trial with no prior knowledge

---

[30] With few exceptions, any person, including a party to the action, is generally competent to testify as a lay witness. Lay witnesses are, within the bounds of reason, required to state "facts," that is, to describe what they observed, rather than give "opinions." The jury is expected to draw its own inferences of the meaning to give these reports of their observations.

[31] For example, Witness C will not be permitted to testify that C overheard, in a restaurant, Person A say to Person B that B committed a crime in order to prove that B committed the crime at issue in a trial. But the rule does not prevent Witness C from testifying that A said that B committed the crime in order to prove that A actually made such a statement and so is liable to B for defamation.

of the facts, can form a reliable impression of the truthfulness of a witness by observing the witness's demeanor while testifying, particularly under cross-examination. Because the out-of-court statement was made out of the sight of judge and jurors at a time when there was no opportunity to cross-examine its author, hearsay evidence is thought to be of doubtful reliability as well as being made beyond the assessment of the jurors. Instead of receiving the evidence and leaving its evaluation to the jurors, it is excluded lest they give it too much credence. The hearsay rule operates to exclude written as well as oral statements made out of court and thus has contributed to the tradition of oral testimony in open court.

Although the present tendency is clearly toward relaxation of the exclusionary rules,[32] efforts have been directed at reformation of the rules rather than at a fundamental shift in the methods of proof. It is only fair to admit that litigation in the United States is, and will probably remain, appreciably more costly and time consuming because of its adversary nature and its jury tradition.

Suggested Readings

Treatises include J. Weinstein & M. Berger, *Weinstein's Evidence Manual: A Guide To The Federal Rules Of Evidence Based on Weinstein's Federal Evidence* (2008); *McCormick on Evidence* (J. Strong et al., 4th ed. 1999); M. Graham, *Handbook of Federal Evidence* (3d ed. 1991), and C. Mueller & L. Kirkpatrick, *Evidence* (1995). The classic multi-volume work on evidence is J. Wigmore, *Evidence in Trials at Common Law* (1940 -), which influenced its successor, *The New Wigmore: A Treatise on Evidence* (2008-). A more recent multi-volume work is J. Weinstein & M. Berger, *Weinstein's Evidence: Commentary on Rules of Evidence for the United States Courts and Magistrates* (loose leaf).

[32] There are other rules that exclude evidence for reasons not only of the dubiousness of certain evidence but also as a matter of public policy. Thus, one spouse cannot be forced to testify against the other spouse. And the fact a person repaired a condition on a property from which another is injured may not be used to prove the condition was unreasonably unsafe.

Conflict of Laws

SCOPE AND SOURCES

The subject matter of conflict of laws, as private international law is known in the United States, consists primarily of jurisdiction, enforcement of foreign (including out-of-state) judgments, and choice of law. Conflict of laws is especially important in the United States because each of the fifty states treats the other states as a foreign jurisdiction. Because there was no developed law in this field in England at the time of the Revolution, American judges and writers drew at first upon works of civil law authors.[33] Subsequent development was largely at the hands of the courts, and each state now has its own conflict-of-laws rules, found for the most part in cases and to a lesser extent in statutes, including some uniform laws. As was mentioned earlier, these rules are binding on the federal courts in diversity cases. There are also several notable clauses of the federal Constitution that affect conflict of laws, as well as occasional federal statutes and, in the international sphere, treaties.

CHARACTERISTICS

The subject is of great importance in interstate as well as in international situations, and the states and federal courts have generally applied the same rules to both. Although the American people are highly mobile and business is conducted in disregard of state boundaries, each state has its own local law and, to a marked degree, its own sovereignty. Because of this, conflicts arise with far greater frequency than in most other countries, and the subject is characterized by more refinement and detail than it is elsewhere. The authors of the Constitution, sensitive to the possibility of chaos, included a number of provisions relating to conflict of laws, and the constitutional cast of the subject is perhaps its most striking feature.

Under the Constitution, the federal government itself is given limited powers in this sphere, including the treaty power and the power to legislate in specified areas. But the most important constitutional provisions are those that restrict the states. Of these, two are of special significance: first,

---

[33] *See* note in Chapter 1, *supra*, for mention of Justice Story's treatise on conflict of laws, the first on this subject in the English language.

the Due Process Clause of the Fourteenth Amendment, which provides that no state shall "deprive any person of life, liberty, or property, without due process of law;"[34] and second, the Full Faith and Credit Clause, which requires that each state must give "Full Faith and Credit" to the "public Acts, Records, and judicial Proceedings of every other State." As to these restrictions, which affect chiefly the law of jurisdiction and the enforcement of foreign judgments, the Supreme Court of the United States has the final voice.

The earliest bases for personal jurisdiction recognized by American courts were the party's consent to jurisdiction and the party's physical presence within the area of the forum's jurisdiction. In addition, many other bases for personal jurisdiction have now been developed by statute, including the party's domicile in the state, doing business in the state, doing an act within the state, and even doing an act outside the state that has consequences within the state. Jurisdictional rules are subject, however, to the due process clause. The procedure provided in the state—both for the notice of a claim to be given to the party that the claim is against and for an opportunity for that party to be heard in defending against that claim—must satisfy the tests of reasonableness and "fair play and substantial justice" that the Supreme Court has laid down under that clause. Otherwise, a judgment of a court that employed the insufficient procedure will be void.[35]

Once a judgment has been rendered, the Constitution also affects its enforceability in other states. Under the Full Faith and Credit Clause, as implemented by statute, the court of one state is bound to recognize a valid and final judgment of a court of another state. The rule also applies as between state and federal courts. If, however, the court that rendered the judgment had no jurisdiction, so that the judgment would not be valid even in the state of rendition, the clause does not require its enforcement in any other state. The requirement of full faith and credit extends only to judgments of American courts and not to judgments rendered in foreign countries, which are enforceable only under the doctrine of comity,

---

[34] The Fifth Amendment, which applies to the federal government, contains substantially the same language.

[35] A court that has jurisdiction may nevertheless decline to exercise its jurisdiction under the doctrine of *forum non conveniens* if the forum is seriously inappropriate or inconvenient to the parties and witnesses, and an appropriate forum is available.

without compulsion. American courts have, however, been very liberal in enforcing such judgments as well.

Rules relating to choice of law are less affected by the Constitution. A state may violate the due process clause if it applies its own law to a state of facts that is not sufficiently connected with that state to make it reasonable to apply its law, but the full faith and credit clause has had little impact upon choice-of-law rules. For the most part, these are found in case law and show close kinship to those of civil law countries.

Suggested Readings

An authoritative source is the *Restatement (Second) of Conflict of Laws* (1971). Treatises include R. Leflar, L. McDougal & R. Felix, *American Conflicts Law* (5th ed. 2001); E. Scoles & P. Hay, *Conflict of Laws* (4th ed. 2004); and R. Weintraub, *Commentary on the Conflict of Laws* (3d ed. 1986). A shorter work is L. Brilmayer, *Conflict of Laws* (1995).

ELEVEN

Private Law

Private law in the United States, in spite of its fragmentation, can be grouped, for the sake of convenience, under six major headings: contracts, torts, property, family law, commercial law, and business enterprises. What do these fields encompass and what are their principal characteristics?

Contracts

SCOPE AND SOURCES

The law of contracts is concerned primarily with the enforcement of promissory obligations. Contractual liability may be based on consent given in the form of an express promise or of a promise implied in fact from the acts of the parties. Furthermore, in some circumstances, a court will impose liability on a person for restitution in order to avoid unjust enrichment despite lack of consent by that person.[1]

---

[1] For example, a doctor who renders emergency treatment to an unconscious person is entitled to restitution. This is often described as liability in "quasi-contract" and may be said, somewhat misleadingly, to rest on a "promise implied in law."

The subject matter of contract law includes the capacity of the parties to enter a contract, formalities required in an effective contract, offer and acceptance, consideration, mistake and misrepresentation, duress and unconscionability in the making of the contract, unenforceability on grounds of public policy, interpretation and construction of the terms, performance and conditions of performance, frustration of purpose and impracticability of performance, discharge of duties, rights of assignees and contract beneficiaries, and remedies for breach or partial breach. It has, to a considerable extent, preserved its unitary quality, resisting fundamental distinctions between different classes of contracts according to either the subject of the agreement or the nature of the parties. Accordingly, with some important exceptions, its general principles are applicable to agreements on such varied subjects as employment, sale of goods or land, and insurance and to such diverse parties as individuals, business organizations, and governmental entities.[2]

Contract law is largely state rather than federal law, but it usually differs only in detail from one state to another. Although it is still primarily case law, an increasing number of statutes deal with particular problems. The Uniform Commercial Code, for example, contains important provisions on the formation of contracts for the sale of goods. And by the Tucker Act of 1887, as amended, one of the most significant of the federal statutes in the field, the United States government has waived its sovereign immunity in contract actions by consenting to suit in the federal courts. Some rules laid down by statute, and by case law as well, are mandatory (i.e., compulsory) and cannot be avoided by the parties, while others are suppletory (*i.e.*, interpretative)[3] and can be varied by agreement.

CHARACTERISTICS

A contract may be defined as a promise for the breach of which the law gives a remedy,[4] though the word "contract" may also be used to refer to the agreement of the parties itself or to the document that the

---

[2] Among the notable exceptions to this generalization are some special rules of the Uniform Commercial Code that apply only to "merchants" (*see infra*) and some special statutes that apply only to "consumer" transactions.

[3] It is fashionable to call these "default rules," borrowing from computer terminology, because they apply in default of any provision made to the contrary.

[4] This is essentially the definition of the *Restatement (Second) of Contracts* Section 1.

parties executed. Not all promises are enforceable, and several criteria must be met before the law will give a remedy for breach of a promise. Two of the most fundamental of these are the requirement of a writing that will memorialize, and later be used to prove, some types of contracts (though not all contracts require a writing) and the requirement of consideration, which is a condition of all enforceable contracts.

The requirement of a writing is imposed by the statutes of frauds, derived from the English Statute of Frauds of 1677, which have been enacted throughout the United States. Typically, they provide that, with some exceptions, specified kinds of contracts are unenforceable unless evidenced by a writing.[5] The most common kinds of contracts covered by these statutes are contracts between merchants to sell goods,[6] contracts to sell land, contracts of suretyship, and contracts not to be performed within a year.[7] Many agreements, such as most contracts to furnish services or to sell personal property, are not included, and such oral contracts are enforceable even though there is no writing. But despite the repeal of most of the English Statute of Frauds in 1954, there has been no widespread movement for complete abolition of the statute in the United States.

Apart from any requirement of a writing, a promise is not generally enforceable in the United States unless it is supported by consideration.[8] Consideration is something (*e.g.*, a promise by the promisee or an act such as a payment or a service) for which the promisor has bargained and that the promisor expects to receive in exchange for the promisor's promise.[9]

---

[5] They do not, however, require that the contract itself be written and do not, therefore, exclude evidence of oral statements once a writing has been produced that satisfies the minimum requirements of the statute. Still, the parol evidence rule, may operate to severely limit evidence of prior or contemporary oral, or even written, statements where the contract is embodied in a writing which purports to be complete.

[6] A writing is not required, however, for contracts subject to the United Nations Convention on Contracts for the International Sale of Goods. *See* Chapter 11, Commercial Law, *infra*. The revision of Article 2 of the Uniform Commercial Code is expected to eliminate the statute's application for contracts for the sale of goods.

[7] Contracts in which one of the promises is a promise to enter into a marriage are also subject to the statute and must be written to be enforced.

[8] Historically, a promisor could make a binding written promise without consideration by affixing a wax seal to the writing, but the seal became an empty formality, and its effectiveness has been largely eliminated by state statutes.

[9] The terms "promisor" and "promisee" in a contract can be confusing. If two parties enter a contract based on acts each will do in the future, each is making a promise. Therefore, as to

But a gratuitous promise, a promise to do something for nothing in return (including a promise to pay for goods or services which have already been furnished at the time the promise is made), is not supported by consideration. A gratuitous promise may, however, become binding if the promisee relies on it under a principle often referred to as "promissory estoppel."

Fortunately, there are only a few instances of business promises in which the requirement of consideration is not met. One of the most troublesome involves the "firm offer" (*i.e.*, an irrevocable offer). The traditional rule in the United States is that an offeror can revoke the offer at any time before its acceptance, and a promise by the offeror not to revoke is not generally effective unless supported by consideration. A common device for holding the offeror to such a promise is the payment to the offeror of a nominal sum, for example one dollar,[10] as consideration for what is then known as an "option." (The payment is made by the offeree.) Under the Uniform Commercial Code, an offeror can make an irrevocable offer to buy or sell goods simply by putting it in a signed writing that states that it is irrevocable. Furthermore, a number of courts have held that, in some circumstances, an offer becomes irrevocable when the offeree relies on it. As this suggests, the tendency has been to attempt to remedy the deficiencies of the doctrine of consideration rather than to discard the doctrine altogether.

In the United States, contract documents, like statutes, are characteristically detailed and prolix. Those prepared by lawyers are often compounded of standard clauses, popularly known as "boilerplate," taken from other agreements kept on file or from form books. Even when a lawyer is not directly involved, the parties may use or incorporate by reference a standard printed form that has been drafted by a lawyer, perhaps for a particular enterprise, perhaps for an association of enterprises, or perhaps for sale to the general public. This attention to detail may be due to a number of causes, including the standardization of routine transactions, the frequent involvement of lawyers in all stages of exceptional transactions, the inclination to use language that has been tested in previous controversies, and the

---

either promise, the person making a promise is a promisor, and the other party is the promisee. In this way, both parties to the contract are promisors and both are promisees; which is which depends on which promise is under discussion. In contrast, an "offeror" is the person who makes an offer to the "offeree," and these terms are unchanged if the offer is accepted.

[10]   Traditionally, the doctrine of consideration has not insisted upon adequacy or fairness in the exchange.

desire to avoid uncertainty when the law of more than one state is involved. All of these add to the general disposition of the case-oriented American lawyer to provide expressly for specific disputes that have arisen in the past or which might be foreseen in the future.[11]

In recent decades, courts and legislatures have become increasingly concerned with the abuse of bargaining power and the imposition of unfair terms. Common examples involve the use of "contracts of adhesion," such as tickets, property leases, and retail sales contracts that are forced upon the weaker party with all of the terms written by the stronger party. Courts began, under the guise of interpreting the contracts, to favor the weaker party. The Uniform Commercial Code empowers courts to deal with the problem directly by refusing to enforce a contract or term that the court determined to be "unconscionable." Although the code provision is directed only at contracts for the sale of goods, the principle has been extended to all contracts. Furthermore, legislatures have enacted statutes aimed at specific abuses, particularly in contracts with consumers. Nevertheless, in spite of the erosion of the doctrine of freedom of contract in many areas, the doctrine is still the rule rather than the exception.

Suggested Readings

The Restatement (Second) of Contracts (1981) is authoritative. For one-volume works, *see* E. Farnsworth, *Contracts* (4th ed. 2004). A multi-volume treatise is E. Farnsworth, *Contracts* (1990–), and a nice summary designed for readers from other legal systems is E. Farnsworth, *United States Contact Law* (1999). Two classic multi-volume treatises, both in the process of revision, are A. Corbin, *Contracts* (J. Perillo, rev. ed. 1993–) and S. Williston, *A Treatise on the Law of Contracts* (R. Lord, 4th ed. 1990–). For other perspectives, *see* J. Calamari & J. Perillo, *The Law of Contracts* (3d ed. 1987); J. Murray, *Contracts* (3d ed. 1990). A shorter introduction is M. Chirelstein, *Concepts And Case Analysis in the Law of Contracts* (2006). On equitable remedies, see E. Yorio, *Contract Enforcement: Specific Performance and Injunction* (1989). Three collections of readings are *Perspectives on Contract Law* (R. Barnett ed., 1995), *Foundations of Contract Law* (R. Craswell & A. Schwartz eds., 1994), and *A Contract*

---

[11] *See* Langebein, *Comparative Civil Procedure and the Style of Complex Contracts*, 35 Am. J. Comp. L. 381 (1987).

Anthology (P. Linzer, 2d ed. 1995). Three provocative short books on contracts are C. Fried, *Contract as Promise* (1981), G. Gilmore, *The Death of Contract* (1974), and I. MacNeil, *The New Social Contract* (1981). On economic aspects, see two collections of readings – *Readings in the Economics of Contract Law* (V. Goldberg ed., 1989) and *The Economics of Contract Law* (A. Kronman & R. Posner eds., 1979). An outstanding history of the rise of contract law in England is A. Simpson, *A History of the Common Law of Contract: The Rise of Assumpsit* (1987).

A multi-volume work on restitution is G. Palmer, *The Law of Restitution* (1995), which has an annual update. D. Dobbs, *The Law of Remedies: Damages-Equity-Restitution* (2d ed. 1993) has a shorter treatment of restitution. Revision of the *Restatement of Restitution* (1937) was discontinued after two tentative drafts. Sources in related fields, including insurance and suretyship, are listed below under Commercial Law.

See G. Fletcher & S. Sheppard, *American Law in a Global Context: The Basics*, Introduction and Chapters 17 through 21.

Torts

SCOPE AND SOURCES

The field of torts embraces a group of civil wrongs, other than breach of contract, that interfere with person, property, reputation, or commercial or social advantage.[12] While an act such as an assault may sometimes be both a crime punishable by the state in a criminal prosecution and also a tort actionable by the victim in a suit for damages, the criminal prosecution and the damage action are separate and unrelated proceedings. The essential purpose of the law of torts is compensatory and, though punitive damages may occasionally be awarded, its function is distinct from that of

---

[12] Tort, or the noncontractual wrong with a private cause of action for resulting injury, is roughly equivalent to the civil claim for delict in legal systems more influenced by Roman law. In the United States, torts include both intentional torts and negligence, and so they would include most actions that would be brought in either delict or quasi-delict, and there is no effect on the right of action for a private plaintiff if a criminal prosecution had occurred (though a party cannot recover in a private action and also have received full compensation for the same harm through criminal restitution).

criminal law. Conversely, criminal law is essentially punitive, and an injured party is not awarded compensation in the criminal proceeding.

Tort law is chiefly state rather than federal law, and so what is a tort and what remedies may be had for a tort both vary somewhat throughout the country. Although it is predominantly case law rather than statutory law,[13] a variety of statutes deal with special problems. Common examples are wrongful death acts and survival statutes governing rights upon the death of the injured party[14] and statutes substituting a system of comparative negligence for that of contributory negligence. One of the more significant federal statutes is the Federal Tort Claims Act of 1946, by which the United States has, with some exceptions, waived its sovereign immunity from liability for the torts of its employees so that recovery may now be had in a suit against the United States in the federal courts but without a jury, in circumstances where it would be liable if it were a private person.

CHARACTERISTICS

The field of torts can be divided into three broad categories, depending on whether liability is based on intent, is based on negligence, or is based on an absolute or strict duty that may be breached without regard to either intent or negligence.

The intentional torts that cause interference with person or property include the classical torts that were adopted from English law with relatively few changes: assault, battery, conversion, false imprisonment, and trespass. An unreasonable interference, whether intentional or negligent, with another's use or enjoyment of land may also amount to a private nuisance, and such cases involving, for example, the creation of fumes or noise by one land-owner to the detriment of neighbors, have often been considered appropriate for equitable relief by way of injunction.[15] Intentional torts where the invasion is of less tangible interest have undergone considerable judicial

---

[13] There are, of course, many statutes that require a course of conduct in a specialized circumstance, such as setting safety requirements to protect workers in a woodworking mill, and violation of such a statute may be used to show negligence as a matter of law.

[14] Wrongful death acts were enacted to reverse the prior case-law rule that no action could be founded upon the death of a human being. Survival statutes were enacted to change the prior case-law rule that personal tort actions did not survive the death of either the plaintiff or the defendant.

[15] Abatement of the nuisance by self-help, without court action, may also be permissible.

development in recent decades; they include infliction of mental anguish, injurious falsehood, interference with contractual relations, malicious prosecution, misrepresentation, and invasion of the right of privacy, a tort of relatively modern origin.[16] However, the vast bulk of tort litigation concerns claims for personal injuries based on negligence or strict liability.[17]

Negligence is economically a more significant basis for tort liability than is intent. The jury, which is almost always impaneled in an action in tort for damages that reaches trial, plays a central role in negligence cases. In a negligence case, the jury will be instructed to decide whether the defendant's conduct met the standard of care expected of a reasonable person under similar circumstances. If the jury finds that the defendant failed to conform to this standard, and as a result of that failure the plaintiff suffered measurable injury, then the jury is to allow the plaintiff to recover the amount of the injury attributable to the defendant's failure. The jury not only determines liability but also fixes damages.[18] These may be apportioned so that the plaintiff's award is reduced according to the plaintiff's portion of fault in the injury. This was not always so, and the United States was long the last major stronghold of the common law doctrine of contributory negligence, but that doctrine has now been replaced by a system of comparative negligence in most states.[19]

---

[16] On the origin of this tort, see Chapter 8, supra.

[17] Compensatory damages in such cases may include allowance for medical expenses, pain and suffering, and loss of income and earning power, but not attorneys' fees. However, these cases are often handled by the lawyer for the plaintiff on a contingent fee basis under which the lawyer's fee is fixed as a percentage of the recovery.

[18] In the 1963 and subsequent editions, Professor Farnsworth wrote in the text above, "But since the jury's verdict is, within wide limits, conclusive on this issue, there is little to prevent it from imposing nearly absolute liability, regardless of fault, upon a defendant who, because of ability to pay or to insure, can in the jurors' eyes best bear the loss." He qualified this statement with the note, "Although jurors' attitudes are undoubtedly influenced by the likelihood of insurance, evidence of liability insurance is not admissible in a negligence suit." This edition has demoted these comments, mainly because appellate courts are now more willing to reduce or vacate jury awards than they were in 1963 and also because recent social science data suggests that juror sympathy for a poor plaintiff against a rich defendant plays less of a role in the verdict than was once assumed. See N. VIDMAR, MEDICAL MALPRACTICE AND THE AMERICAN JURY (1997).

[19] Under the doctrine of contributory negligence, even where the defendant has been negligent, the defendant may avoid all liability by proving that the plaintiff's negligence contributed to the loss. Since the relative degrees of fault of the two parties are immaterial, in theory there are only two alternatives: complete recovery if only the defendant was negligent, and no recovery if neither party was negligent or if the plaintiff was negligent

Strict liability was at first imposed in connection with abnormally dangerous things and activities, such as the keeping of explosives.[20] Its modern significance, however, is largely as a basis for the liability of manufacturers and other sellers of defective products. Strict liability has generally replaced negligence as the principal basis for product liability. Jury verdicts in product liability cases involving personal injury resulting from defectively designed or manufactured products may run millions of dollars.[21]

The adequacy of traditional tort doctrines to cope with personal injury claims in an industrialized society has been the subject of considerable controversy. The first significant departure from orthodox tort law came with the enactment in every state of workers' compensation statutes to cover personal injuries sustained by employees covered by statute in the course of their employment. The advantage to the employee is that if the accident is within the scope of the statute, the liability of the employer is absolute without regard to negligence on the part of either employer or employee. In return, workers' compensation is the employee's exclusive remedy against the employer. The employee loses the opportunity to sue the employer for negligence and to seek a large verdict from a sympathetic jury and must take, instead, a much smaller amount of compensation that is determined under a statutory formula. The employer is aided by a system of compulsory and usually private liability insurance for which the employer alone pays, usually transferring any additional cost to the consumer. The system is administered by a state administrative agency.

A second significant departure from orthodox tort law came with the enactment during the 1970s in roughly half the states of no-fault automobile accident compensation laws.[22] Although these laws vary considerably

---

in any degree. In practice, however, these extreme results are tempered by the jury's power not only to determine whether the parties were negligent but also to decide what damages, if any, are to be awarded. The jury might therefore ignore the doctrine of contributory negligence by allowing recovery and then taking account of the plaintiff's negligence in calculating damages.

20 The seminal case was Rylands v. Fletcher, [1868] L.R. 3 H.L. 330, which involved damage due to a flood caused by water from a reservoir built on the defendant's land.

21 In an attempt to rationalize and make uniform product liability law, a Model Uniform Product Liability Act was promulgated in 1979, and the American Law Institute is restating the subject.

22 The concept of no-fault insurance gained attention after publication of R. Keeton & J. O'Connell, *Basic Protection for the Traffic Victim: A Blueprint for Reforming Automobile Insurance* (1965).

from state to state, they rely on a requirement that each motorist procure insurance covering economic loss, up to a fixed level, to motorist, and passengers. Typically, the motorist is given immunity in tort to the extent of an injured individual's no-fault benefits. Persons protected by the system are barred, at least to the extent of their protection, from claiming compensation from a motorist who has injured them, regardless of whether the motorist was at fault. Each no-fault system provides for a threshold, however, so that the fault system returns if damages reach a certain level or if a specified kind of injury occurs.

Suggested Readings

The *Restatement (Second) of Torts* (1965–77) contains an orderly compilation of generally prevailing rules. It has been supplemented by volumes of the *Restatement (Third) of Torts: Products Liability* (1994–). The standard treatises are *Prosser & Keeton on Torts* (W. Keeton, 5th ed. 1984) and the multi-volume F. Harper, F. James & O. Gray, *The Law of Torts* (2d ed. 1986). A nice one-volume book is D. Dobbs, *The Law of Torts* (2005). Selected readings are contained *in Foundations of Tort Law* (S. Levmore & C. Sharkey eds., 2009). For economic analysis, see S. Shavell, *Economic Analysis of Accident Law* (1987) and the classic G. Calabresi, *The Costs of Accidents: A Legal and Economic Analysis* (1970). Excellent narratives of the cases in many torts courses is in R. Rabin & S. Sugarman, *Torts Stories* (2003). The essential history of the field in the United States is G. White, *Tort Law in America: An Intellectual History* (2003).

See G. Fletcher & S. Sheppard, *American Law in a Global Context: The Basics*, Introduction and Chapters 22 through 25.

Property

SCOPE AND SOURCES

The roots of American property law are in the feudal land law of medieval England. Accordingly, it distinguishes between real property, which historically consisted chiefly of feudally important estates in land, and personal property, which consisted of most other assets, tangible and intangible.[23] The distinction persisted even after England had evolved into a commercial nation and personal property had taken on much greater importance, but there has been a tendency in the United States toward its gradual elimination. For example, the rules of intestate succession are now largely the same for real and personal property. But since commercial dealings in personal property are embraced by the distinct field of commercial law, property law is still concerned primarily with real property. It includes the kinds of interests one may have and types of ownership that may be created in property; conveyances of property from one owner to another, mortgages and other claims to another's property; gifts, transfers, and other *inter vivos* transfers of interests in property; the transfer of property after the owner's death, through wills and intestate succession; the creation and management of trusts over property; and restrictions on the use of property.

Property law in the United States is a matter of peculiarly local concern, and its variations from state to state are more substantial than is the case, for example, for contracts or torts. In several areas in the United States that were once under the rule of Spain or France, the influence of the civil law can still be detected, and eight states now recognize what is known as community property, in which husband and wife have a variety of common ownership that is derived from the civil law. Each state has a substantial collection of statutes relating to property, most notably on matters of intestate succession. Some are uniform acts adopted in a number of states, and others have been borrowed from sister states. Rarely, however, do these statutes form a well-organized and integrated whole. Federal legislation, dealing with such diverse subjects as protection of the environment and the accommodation of disabled persons, also affects the work of the property lawyer.

CHARACTERISTICS

The elaborate scheme of interests in land that distinguished English land law at the time of the Revolution was received almost in its entirety into

---

[23] Personal property now includes such intangibles as contract rights, including bank deposits and corporate stock, and industrial property, including patents and copyrights. It also includes rights, often called "entitlements," under such government programs as the social security programs.

the laws of the young U.S. states.[24] The first great division among these interests demarcates those legal interests that confer or may confer upon the holder of the interest the actual right of ownership with a right of possession of the land. These are then divided into possessory estates or interests, under which the holder has the present right to possession and future or nonpossessory estates or interests, under which the holder may or will come into possession at some future time. Possessory interests, in turn, are classified according to duration[25] and future interests according to the probability or certainty of the holder coming into possession and the conditions under which possession is gained or lost.[26] There are rights of possession that confer no ownership, the most important of which is the leasehold, a nonfreehold estate similar to freehold for a term of years, though leases are defined largely by the conditions under which they terminate, by a date certain, by a failure of renewal during a term in succession, by a failure of termination during a term in succession, or until the landlord or tenant give notice of termination.[27] There are also present, nonpossessory interests, such as easements and franchises, which consist only of limitations on the rights of another to the use and enjoyment of land. Last, there are interests that may be divided among people at the same time, or cotenancies.[28] The common law has shown itself capable of remarkable abstraction in dealing with interests in land. Ownership is viewed as projected in time and may be divided according to the needs of the owner and the ingenuity of the lawyer, with the result that all persons who have estates, whether

---

[24] The English concept of tenure, under which all land was held ultimately from the king, had almost no influence in practice in the United States.

[25] Examples are a fee simple absolute, which has a potentially infinite duration; a life estate, which has a duration fixed by the life or lives of one or more persons; and an estate for years, which is fixed in terms of years, months, weeks, or days.

[26] For example, the unconditional future interest left in the holder of an estate in fee simple absolute, after the holder has granted a life estate to another, is described as a "reversion."

[27] These are the lease for a term of years, periodic tenancy (or year to year, or month to month, or week to week tenancy), and tenancy at will. A further form of tenancy is created by a tenant in possession with no lease, which is tenancy by sufferance of the landlord.

[28] The three cotenancies are tenancy in common, which allows people to have different interests in the property from one another and each share is alienable; joint tenancy, which gives each tenant the same share in all regards and leaves the last living tenant holding the whole interest; and tenancy by the entireties, which is a form of joint tenancy between spouses.

possessory or future, are present owners of vested interests in the land.[29] The common law balances the rights of the owners with the interests of other present and future owners by giving wide latitude for an owner to control property with only a few limits in tort to prevent one owner's use of property to interfere with other owners' uses of theirs, and the owner may limit the future use of land through the grant of easements, covenants and restrictions, leases and licenses, trusts, and future interests, but even these are subject to loss under rules, such as the doctrine of adverse possession, which allows loss of ownership through the long possession by others of one's property, or the doctrines furthering alienability of property, which forbid most efforts to control land longer than three generations.[30]

The most significant departure from English property law after the Revolution related to assurance of title. The standard instrument of land transfer in America is the deed, a writing that was historically made under seal that passes title to the property it describes through the act of delivery of the deed. It sometimes contains a provision by which the transferor agrees to compensate the transferee for loss resulting from defective title. In England, the transferee got further assurance by examination of the original deeds, which were passed on with the land. A different system, that of public recordation, came into use in the colonies and subsequently spread throughout the United States. State recording acts require that all conveyances be promptly recorded in a local public office so that the prospective transferee may rely, with some safety, upon an examination, usually by a local expert, of the resulting public records. The penalty for failure to record is loss of priority to other competing interests, a matter on which the details of state statutes differ considerably. Now very common, the assurance from recordation is supplemented by a system of private title

---

[29] Therefore, for example, the holder of the reversion mentioned in the preceding footnote is free to dispose of the reversion as the holder might dispose of any property, either during life or at death and then transfer the right to possession at some future time, even though the person who had transferred the reversion may die before the death of the life tenant, whose death makes the reversion a possessory interest.

[30] Perhaps the most famous common-law rule is the Rule Against Perpetuities, which prevents the owner of lands from conveying land to so many sequential future interests following one another (O grants to A for life then to B for life then to B's youngest child for life then to B's youngest grandchild for life, etc.) that the owner would require the land to pass to members of generations the owner could never know or assess. Such grants are void as too remote in their "vesting" or determination of who, exactly, owns the future interest.

insurance in which the title insurer, after a search of the records, agrees to indemnify the insured for loss due to defective title. Such insurance is usually required for land purchased with bank financing. An alternative to recordation, known as title registration or the Torrens system,[31] exists to some degree in a minority of states. Expansion of title registration seems unlikely, however, in the face of growth of title insurance based on recordation.

In recent decades, the attention of the American property lawyer has turned increasingly from land transfer to two other areas: first, the transmission of wealth on death; and second, restrictions on the use and enjoyment of land. The importance of the first of these areas has been enhanced by the taxation of estates on death at both the federal and state level. The lawyer who counsels clients with significant wealth must take account not only of the law of wills and of probate but also of the law of taxation and of trusts, and great sophistication may be required in crafting a suitable estate plan. The importance of the second area has increased as the increasing complexities of urban living have been met by expanded governmental regulation on the federal, state, and local levels. Under its power, known as the police power, to provide for the public welfare, government may establish planning agencies, restrict the use of land through zoning, impose minimum structural and sanitary standards, and impose requirements to protect the environment.[32] Under its power of condemnation or eminent domain, it may also acquire private property for public uses, subject to the requirements of federal and state constitutions which include the payment of just compensation.[33] Difficult questions arise as to whether governmental action is a "taking" for which it must pay compensation and, if it is not, whether it is a valid exercise of the police power. In a nation where the

---

[31] Under this system, the title itself, rather than the conveyance evidencing the transferor title, is registered through a formal proceeding that results in a conclusive determination of title followed by issuance by the state of a certificate of title, which is then kept up to date by notation of later interests. The system was named after Sir Robert Torrens, an Australian who introduced it there in the middle of the nineteenth century. It has since spread to most of the common-law world outside the United States, including England.

[32] More on environmental law is discussed in Chapter 12, *infra*.

[33] The Fifth Amendment to the Constitution prohibits the federal government from taking private property for public use without just compensation. The same limitation has been applied to the states under the Due Process Clause of the Fourteenth Amendment.

great majority of families own their own housing, such issues are of vital importance.

An additional area of property—intellectual property—is of particular federal and international significance and has grown increasingly prominent for students and practitioners as well. Intellectual property is the law of patents, copyright, and trademark.[34] As the global movement of goods and services increases and as the Internet eases the movement of ideas and information from one place to another with great scale and speed, the recognition of property in ideas has grown increasingly significant. In recent years, great debates have been driven by technological change, over the extent of copyright and of its limits in fair use, over the role of patents in animals and genetic structures used in humans as well as other living beings, and the protections of trademarks moving among states and nations. In the United States, patent, trademark, and copyright are largely matters of federal law, though state law could be the basis of copyright until 1978, when state copyright was nearly eliminated by federal law. [35] Though the registration of these interests is administrative, they are usually enforced by private causes of action for infringement.[36] The United States participates in an array of treaties to integrate its standards with other countries, including the World Trade Organization Agreement on Trade Related Aspects of Intellectual Property Rights, or TRIPS.

Suggested Readings

The *Restatement (Second) of Property* (1936–44) is being revised by the *Restatement (Third) of Property* on a topic-by-topic basis, and the volume on donative transfers is expected to be concluded in 2010. Treatises include R. Boyer, H. Hovenkamp & S. Kurtz, *The Law of Property* (4th ed. 1991); J. Cribbet & C. Johnson, *Principles of the Law of Property* (3d ed. 1989); and R. Cunningham, W. Stoebuck & D. Whitman, *The Law of Property* (2d ed. 1993). A short book is C. Moynihan & S. Kurtz,

---

[34]   There is an interesting question of whether intellectual property is more a matter of public law or private law, but it might be best to see it as both. *See* S. SELL, PRIVATE POWER, PUBLIC LAW: THE GLOBALIZATION OF INTELLECTUAL PROPERTY RIGHTS (2003).

[35]   Trademarks and patents are registered with the U.S. Patent and Trademark Office, *at* www. uspto.gov. Copyrights are registerable at the Copyright Office, www.copyright.gov/.

[36]   *See* Chapter 12, *infra*.

Introduction to the Law of Real Property (3d ed. 2002). R. Powell, *The Law of Real Property* (P. Rohan ed., loose leaf) and *Thompson on Real Property* (D. Thomas ed., 1994) are multi-volume treatises that are routinely updated. *Perspectives on Property Law* (R. Ellickson, C. Rose & B. Ackerman, 2d ed. 1995) is a collection of readings. Future interests are dealt with in L. Simes, *Handbook of the Law of Future Interests* (2d ed. 1966) and T. Bergin & P. Haskell, *Preface to Estates in Land and Future Interests* (2d ed. 1984). On mortgages, see G. Nelson & D. Whitman, *Real Estate Finance Law* (3d ed. 1993). On wills and intestate succession, a basic introduction is provided by the ABA. See *American Bar Association, American Bar Association Guide to Wills and Estates* (3d ed. 2009). On personal property, see R. Brown, *The Law of Personal Property* (W. Raushenbush, 3d ed. 1975). The history of property is nicely explored in A. Simpson, *A History of Land Law* (1986). The constitutional parameters of property law are discussed in J. Ely, *The Guardian of Every Other Right* (3d ed. 2007). The best general history of the ideas of property in the United States is G. Alexander, *Commodity and Propriety: Competing Visions of Property in the American Legal Thought* (1999).

The *Restatement (Second) of Trusts* (1959) is authoritative in its field. An excellent introduction is P. Petit, *Equity and the Law of Trusts* (11th ed. 2009). A classic multi-volume work is A. Scott & W. Fratcher, *The Law of Trusts* (4th ed. 1987–88), which is cumulatively supplemented on a biennial scheme.

There are rich materials on intellectual property, including the statutes, treaties, and regulations of the offices mentioned in the notes to this section. For a good overview of the U.S. law of trademark, see L. Tancs, *Understanding Trademark Law: A Beginner's Guide* (2009). On the debate on the proper extent of copyright and patent, see L. Lessig, *The Future of Ideas: The Fate of the Commons in a Connected World* (2002). For a treatise, see R. Shechter & J. Thomas, *Intellectual Property: The Law of Copyrights, Patents and Trademarks* (2003). For a comparative view of copyright, see E. Adeney, *The Moral Rights of Authors and Performers: An International and Comparative Analysis* (2006). Multi-volume treatises on trademarks include J. Gilson, *Trademark Protection and Practice* (loose leaf) and J. McCarthy, *Trademarks and Unfair Competition* (3d ed. loose leaf). Multi-volume works on patents include D. Chisum, *Patents* (loose leaf), E. Lipscomb, *Walker on Patents* (3d ed. 1984), and P. Rosenberg, *Patent Law Fundamentals* (loose leaf). Multi-volume works on copyright include P. Goldstein, *Copyright: Principles, Law and Practice* (1989) and M. Nimmer & D. Nimmer, *Nimmer on Copyright* (loose leaf).

See G. Fletcher & S. Sheppard, *American Law in a Global Context: The Basics*, Introduction and Chapters 15 though 19.

Family Law

SCOPE AND SOURCES

Family law, or domestic relations law as it is sometimes called, is concerned with the relationships between husband and wife and between parent and child, with the rights and duties that spring from these relationships by operation of law or contract, and with the status of married persons, other family members, and especially children. It is affected by the growing statutory regulation of family life in such areas as divorce and property distribution, child custody and support, termination of parental rights, child neglect and abuse, and adoption.[37] And it is concerned with some problems that affect persons outside the family unit, including contraception, abortion, and rights of unmarried cohabitants.[38] It is traditionally state law, though federal legislation in such fields as taxation, immigration, and social welfare may have significant impact and important problems have arisen under the federal Constitution in recent years. Strongly influenced by English law during colonial times, U.S. family law has everywhere been greatly altered by legislation and varies substantially from one state to another, though some uniformity has been achieved in limited areas through the adoption of uniform laws. In a number of jurisdictions, it is administered by a separate family or domestic relations court and staffed with personnel who are specially trained in family problems. The discussion here is confined to the marital relationships and does not deal, for example, with child custody or child care.

CHARACTERISTICS

Marriage in the United States is fundamentally a relationship created by mutual consent of the spouses. All states provide by statute for the issuance of marriage licenses, and most require a formal ceremony at which consent is solemnized before a member of the clergy or a public official.[39]

---

[37] *See*, for example, the universally adopted Uniform Child Custody Jurisdiction Act and the Uniform Premarital Agreement Act.

[38] A landmark case on the rights of unmarried cohabitants is Marvin v. Marvin, 557 P.2d 106 (Cal. 1976).

[39] Proxy or absentee marriages are not usual in the United States.

Common restrictions on capacity to marry relate to the age of the parties, the degree of any blood relationship between them, and their mental capacity. A restriction can sometimes be circumvented by going to another state that has no such restriction, for a marriage that is valid in the state of celebration will ordinarily be recognized as valid by other states. A significant exception to this recognition has arisen in the states that have, with Congressional approval, refused to recognize marriages allowed in several states between spouses of the same gender.[40]

The marital relationship may be ruptured in two main ways: by annulment, a court determination that no valid marriage ever existed between the parties; and by divorce, a court decree dissolving the marital relationship, generally leaving the parties free to remarry. Divorce is much more common. In colonial times, divorce was generally by legislative act. After the Revolution, statutes were ultimately enacted in all states substituting judicial divorce on widely varying grounds. All of these grounds required a showing of some serious fault, typically desertion, cruelty, or adultery on the part of the other spouse. By the twentieth century, the pressure for easier divorce had led to collusive divorce actions, in which the spouses cooperated in establishing the required fault and to out-of-state or "migratory" divorces, in which one or both spouses went to another jurisdiction in which divorces were more liberally granted.[41] The result was a movement in many states to liberalize the grounds of divorce by dispensing with a showing of fault. The more moderate of the new divorce laws permit divorce by mutual consent, as in New York, which has added "living apart for two years" as a ground. The more extreme laws permit divorce at the instance of one spouse, as in California, where it is enough if one

---

[40]   The Defense of Marriage Act, 28 U.S.C. § 1738C, was passed in 1996, declaring that no state need recognize a same-sex marriage authorized in another state, although there are continuing questions of the act's constitutionality as well as recurrent arguments for its repeal. Massachusetts became the first state to recognize marriages between spouses of the same gender, in Goodridge v. Dept. of Public Health, 798 N.E.2d 941 (Mass. 2003). Several other states have since done so.

[41]   The Supreme Court of the United States has held that domicile of either spouse alone is an adequate jurisdictional basis to entitle the divorce decree to full faith and credit. If the defendant has appeared in the divorce action, the court's own finding as to domicile cannot later be attacked, and every state must recognize the divorce. A few states, of which Nevada was the most notorious, commercialized migratory divorces by liberalizing grounds and relaxing requirements for domicile.

spouse shows "irreconcilable differences, which have caused the irremedi-able breakdown of the marriage." As divorce became more common, states attempted to reduce its use by requiring delays in proceedings to prevent hasty dissolution, by providing facilities for marital counseling and concili-ation, by minimizing the adversary character of the proceedings, and by some states' introduction of "covenant" marriages, which are more difficult to end. Even so, for many reasons rooted in its society and economy as well as its laws, the divorce rate in the United States remains the highest in the world.

The law has increasingly turned its attention to dealing with the rights of the spouses rather than preserving their relationship. Under English law, a married woman was subject to a variety of legal disabilities growing out of the view that husband and wife were one person, and that authority was in the husband. For example, all of the wife's personal property as well as control of her real property went to the husband on marriage. Beginning in the nineteenth century, enactment of married women's property acts throughout the United States resulted in the emancipation of the wife by conferring upon her the right to her separate property, lifting her pro-cedural disabilities, making explicit her power to contract, and, in some states, giving her the right of action for injury even as against her husband. This system of separate property still tended to favor the husband on divorce, however, and in most states, courts now have a broad power, varying in extent from state to state, to apportion all property of both spouses upon divorce. In eight states, spouses are subject to a system of community property.

Of comparable importance is the obligation of support.[42] A spouse may obtain a separate maintenance decree during the life of the marriage, and this obligation of support has been secured against avoidance by flight through universal enactment of the Uniform Reciprocal Enforcement of Support Act. Upon divorce, the support obligation may be replaced by an agreed-upon lump settlement or by a court decree ordering periodic payments of alimony. Alimony, which may be awarded both during and after the divorce litigation, is usually justified on alternative theories: either

---

[42] Although this obligation has traditionally been viewed as that of the husband to support the wife, it is now regarded as that of one spouse to support the other. Both parents now have an obligation to support a child.

that it is in substitution for the support obligation, or that it is in settlement for the dissolution of the marital partnership.[43] It is some indication of the inadequacy of legal procedures in meeting the fundamental problems of the marital relationship that in contested divorce cases it is usually the issue of support and not that of maintaining the relationship itself that is at the heart of the dispute.

Suggested Readings

There is a dearth of written text in this area. H. Clark, *The Law of Domestic Relations in the United States* (2d ed. 1998) is a treatise. A short book is H. Krause, *Family Law in a Nutshell* (2d ed. 1986). The history of marriage in law is considered in J. Witte, *From Sacrament to Contract: Marriage, Law, and the Western Tradition* (1997). Marriage has received considerable scrutiny in recent years by social scientists. See A. Cherlin, *The Marriage-Go-Round: The State of Marriage and the Family in America Today* (2009); and P. Amato et al., *Alone Together: How Marriage in America is Changing* (2009).

Commercial Law

SCOPE AND SOURCES

The concept of "commercial law," or "commercial transactions" as it is sometimes called, as a distinct field is relatively recent in the United States. The practicing lawyer may still think of law practice as "commercial" to the extent that it involves any aspects of business, including even taxation, but the advent of the Uniform Commercial Code has given a narrower ambit to the term "commercial." The subjects included are sale of goods, leases of goods, negotiable instruments (including promissory notes, drafts or bills of exchange, and checks), bank deposits and collections, electronic funds transfers, letters of credit, documents of title (including bills of lading and warehouse receipts), investment securities (including stocks and bonds),

---

[43]   Theories of alimony vary widely from state to state. Some states consider fault in the computation of alimony, but increasingly courts look to other factors such as the length of the marriage; the relative earnings of the spouses; and the age, health, status, amount and source of income, vocational skills, employability, and needs of each of the parties.

bulk transfers, and secured transactions (including assignments of accounts receivable as well as security interests in goods).

Commercial law in this sense is largely a matter of state law because, though Congress has the power to enact legislation concerning interstate commerce, it has been reluctant to exercise that power in this sphere of private law. Traditional exceptions are bankruptcy law and admiralty, or maritime, law.[44] A more recent exception is the United Nations Convention on Contracts for the International Sale of Goods, which was ratified by the United States effective in 1988 and is now federal law governing such contracts.[45]

The reluctance of Congress to enact legislation in this field is due in part to the success of the National Conference of Commissioners on Uniform State Laws in promoting uniformity through voluntary adoption of uniform laws. The Negotiable Instrument Law, patterned after the English Bills of Exchange Act, was proposed in 1896 and adopted by all the states by 1924. The Uniform Sales Act, based in part on the English Sale of Goods Act, was recommended in 1906 and eventually adopted by about two-thirds of the states. A succession of uniform laws followed.[46]

At the end of the Second World War, the commissioners, together with the American Law Institute, undertook a joint project to draft a comprehensive and modern Uniform Commercial Code to replace the older uniform laws. It was proposed in final form in 1957, and by 1967 it had been adopted in almost every state.[47] The code contained four hundred sections, divided into nine articles,[48] and filled over seven hundred pages with

[44] The Constitution gave Congress the power to establish "uniform laws on the subject of bankruptcies throughout the United States." The federal statute is known as the Bankruptcy Code. There are also assorted state laws concerning the rights of creditors against distressed debtors. Admiralty law is, for the most part, case law as laid down by the federal courts supplemented by a few federal statutes. Problems of federal jurisdiction form a peculiarly significant part of American admiralty law.

[45] The ratification by the United States imposed a requirement of reciprocity so that the convention is applicable to a given contract for the sale of goods only if the other party to the sale has its place of business in another country that has adopted the convention.

[46] One of these, the Uniform Bills of Lading Act, was enacted by Congress as the Federal Bills of Lading, or Pomerene, Act and still governs bills of lading in interstate and foreign commerce.

[47] Louisiana, the sole exception, later adopted much of the code.

[48] The code's substantive "articles" correspond roughly to the "books" of a civil law code. These articles are divided into "parts," which correspond to "titles," and these are divided into "sections," which correspond to "articles."

its elaborate comments. It had taken dozens of drafters and advisors over a decade to prepare and represented the most modern thinking in its field. After several decades, however, the process of revision began and continues.[49]

Although the code unites into one statute such previously separate fields as sales and negotiable instruments,[50] it omits a number of subjects that are sometimes regarded as part of commercial law in other countries. Several of these (insurance is an example) have been omitted because of the difficulty of unification on so grand a scale. Others, such as bankruptcy law and admiralty law, have been left out because they are within federal rather than state jurisdiction. Still others, such as corporations and partnerships, are not included because the American lawyer sees no close affinity between them and the other topics in the code. Furthermore, even on matters within the code's area of concern, the lawyer may have to look outside its provisions to federal and state laws on taxation, trade regulation, banking restrictions, and the like.

CHARACTERISTICS

Commercial law in the United States lacks two of the characteristics that distinguished the law merchant during the middle ages and that have been retained in some civil law countries. First, the separate commercial courts that once existed in England had declined in influence by the seventeenth century and never took root in the colonies; commercial matters have always been heard by the ordinary law courts in the United States. To a limited extent, the functions of special commercial tribunals are performed by well-established bodies, notably the American Arbitration Association, that offer facilities for commercial arbitration. Second, the medieval conception of merchants as a distinct class for whom commercial law was specifically designed also disappeared from English law before it had a

---

[49] The articles on negotiable instruments, bank deposits and collections, letters of credit, investment securities, and secured transactions have been revised; revision of the article on sale of goods is underway; and a second revision of the article on secured transactions has begun. New articles on leases of goods and on electronic fund transfers have been added, and deletion of the article on bulk transfers has been proposed.

[50] Courses entitled "commercial law" or "commercial transactions" have replaced separate courses in such subjects as sales and negotiable instruments in many American law schools.

chance to influence American law, and the concepts of "merchant" and "commercial act," found in many civil-law countries, are only indirectly part of the American legal tradition. Bankruptcy, for example, is available to all persons and not just to merchants. The Uniform Commercial Code does include a definition of "merchant" in its article on the sale of goods and provides some special rules that apply to such persons because of their expertise, but the code as a whole applies to both merchants and nonmerchants, and, with these few exceptions, applies to both alike.

At the same time, American commercial law produced some important developments of its own. In the field of negotiable instruments, the almost universal habits of making significant payments by check resulted in an elaborate body of case and statutory law that is systematized by the code.[51] And the flexibility of American commercial law is nowhere more evident than in its recognition and development of new legal devices to secure the extension of credit required for the distribution of goods ranging from automobiles to shoes, on both the wholesale and retail level. The most important single contribution of the code is in consolidating, simplifying, and modernizing the law of such secured transactions in personal property.

On the whole, however, the code, like the uniform laws that preceded it, represents no drastic upheaval in concepts and doctrines but rather an effort to order the law and to bring it into harmony with current commercial practices. This is a continuing process, such as when contracts the UCC embraced are now contracts entered by the electronic mailing of an offer and an acceptance. Nor does it make a complete break with the past, for it provides that the "principles of law and equity, including the law merchant. . . . shall supplement its provisions" unless they are "displaced by the particular provisions" of the code.[52] The drafters of the code have also tried to allow for future change. In some instances, they have purposely failed to provide for a problem in order to leave room for

[51] The Federal Reserve Board has, however, promulgated important regulations applicable to the collection of checks, invading a field previously left largely to the states.

[52] This use of prior law to decide "omitted cases" is characteristic of a number of American statutes, including the earlier uniform laws, that have in the main, codified existing case law.

further development on a state-by-state basis[53]; in others, the code provisions expressly admit of change by the development of usages. In these ways, it is hoped that the code can minimize the pressure for periodic revision.

Suggested Readings

The essential work is the *Uniform Commercial Code* (Official Text with Comments) itself. Up-to-date versions are available in selections of commercial statutes compiled by commercial publishers for student use. Cases involving the code are collected in a Uniform Commercial Code Reporting Service, with accompanying Case Digest. The most widely used text is J. White & R. Summers, *Uniform Commercial Code* (3d ed. 1998). A multi-volume treatise is T. Crandall, M. Herbert & L. Lawrence, *Uniform Commercial Code* (loose leaf). A classic two-volume work on secured transactions is G. Gilmore, *Security Interests in Personal Property* (1965), but it is dated because it was written before the revisions of Article 9. A one-volume work is R. Henson, *Secured Transactions Under the Uniform Commercial Code* (2d ed. 1979). The predicates to the UCC are nicely chronicled in Leon Trakman, *The Law Merchant: The Evolution of Commercial Law* (1983).

A text on bankruptcy is D. Epstein, S. Nickles & J. White, *Bankruptcy* (1993), and a shorter work is *American Bar Association Guide to Credit and Bankruptcy* (2d ed. 2009). A text on insurance is R. Keeton & A. Widiss, *Insurance Law* (2d ed. 1988). The *Restatement (Third) of Suretyship* is an authoritative source for that subject. Two texts on admiralty law are G. Gilmore & C. Black, *The Law of Admiralty* (2d ed. 1975) and T. Schoenbaum, *Admiralty and Maritime Law* (1987).

Business Enterprises

SCOPE AND SOURCES

By far, the most common form for the more than thirty million business enterprises in the United States is the individual proprietorship, followed by

---

[53]   For example, the regulation of sales on credit to consumers in order to protect them from overreaching by sellers and financial institutions, is purposely left largely untouched by the code and is now the subject of special state statutes.

the corporation and then the partnership, either general or limited.[54] Nevertheless, business corporations dominate the economy and employ most of the labor force. In keeping with the fragmentation of American private law, what is here treated as the law of business enterprises, or business organizations, is commonly regarded neither as part of a comprehensive body of commercial law nor as a unit in itself but rather as such separate fields as agency; partnerships; and, most important, corporations.

Business enterprises are almost invariably organized under state law,[55] and incorporation has historically been regarded as founded upon a state grant.[56] When, after the Civil War, it became an established principle of constitutional law that no state could exclude a corporation incorporated in another state from engaging in interstate commerce within its territory, large corporations began to seek out the most favorable state of incorporation, and some of the smaller states tailored their corporation laws to attract them. Delaware has been the most successful and leads all other states by a wide margin as the state of incorporation for large corporations. Differences among most state corporation laws are significant in several aspects, notably the degree of independence of directors from owners allowed under the law—states varying, for instance, in the rights of shareholders to get money out of the corporation by the declaration of dividends, partial liquidations, and share purchases and redemptions. Still, the same results can be reached in most states even though procedures may vary. In part, this similarity among state corporations laws has come from the complete

---

[54] Less used forms of unincorporated business enterprise are the joint stock company or joint stock association, in which ownership interests are represented by shares of stock, and the Massachusetts or business trust, in which the business is managed by trustees for the benefit of members. An informal undertaking to carry out a particular venture and dissolve upon its completion may be regarded as a joint venture, with most of the characteristics of a partnership. Most jurisdictions distinguish between business and nonprofit corporations with a separate statute for each. Municipalities, such as cities, towns, and villages are commonly organized as municipal corporations under special state statutes. Corporations are also used by the federal and state governments as public entities to carry on some kinds of governmental activity.

[55] Some banking institutions, however, may be federally chartered, and there are a few other exceptions.

[56] Until the beginning of the nineteenth century, a corporation could only be formed pursuant to a special act of a state legislature, but by the end of the Civil War, general state incorporation laws had been widely enacted, and by the end of the century, use of special legislature charters had been almost entirely abolished.

or partial adoption in most states of the American Bar Association's Model Business Corporation Act. There has been no substantial demand for federal control over the formation of corporations. Case law doctrines have contributed to uniformity and, in spite of the large statutory ingredient, the courts have played a major role in such important and expanding areas of corporation law as the fiduciary duties owed by directors, officers, and shareholders. In addition, the corporate papers—such as the charter, by-laws, and resolutions of the shareholders and board of directors—are of great importance.

There is considerably more uniformity in the field of partnerships as a result of the widespread adoption of the Uniform Partnership Act and the Uniform Limited Partnership Act.[57] The law of agency is to be found largely in judicial decisions.

During the twentieth century, the activities of business enterprises were increasingly affected by federal law. Congress, under the commerce power, has regulated the interstate distribution and trading of securities by enacting such statutes as the Securities Act of 1933 and the Securities and Exchange Act of 1934, which are administered by the Securities and Exchange Commission.[58] Taxation, trade regulation, and the regulation of particular industries have greatly affected business enterprises. The rules and decisions of the agencies that administer these laws are also an important source of law to the lawyer engaged in practice in this field.

CHARACTERISTICS

The corporation is the only one of the three principal forms of business enterprise that has traditionally been regarded for most legal purposes

---

[57]   A 1994 version of the Uniform Partnership Act, and its various amendments, has been proposed to replace the original 1914 version. In most states, a 1976 version of the Uniform Limited Partnership Act has replaced the original 1916 version. Important differences persist between states following different versions of the act, particularly over how a partnership may be sued in a forum other than its primary place of business.

[58]   The commission is not empowered to decide whether a particular security may be issued to the public but only to require full disclosure so that prospective investors can make an informed decision for themselves. Most states also have their own statutes regulating the sale of securities, which are popularly known as "blue sky laws." The economic crisis of 2008 has led to considerable discussion of the regulation of equities and markets, and the scope of both federal and state laws in this area is likely to increase, particularly to better coordinate them with the laws of other countries.

as an entity separate and apart from the persons who compose it. There are similarities among proprietorships, partnerships, and corporations, but important differences distinguish them. A corporation may, of course, deal in property, make contracts, and sue and be sued – all in its corporate name, and one's risk as a shareholder is limited to one's investment. It is true that modern statutes have departed from the older strict view that a partnership is an aggregate rather than an entity so that a partnership may have these and other characteristics of an entity.[59] And under special statutes, a limited partnership may be created in which the risk of the limited or special partners, who take no part in management, is restricted to their capital contributions, although unlimited liability remains in the management group of partners.[60] A further development of the partnership has been the authorization of limited liability partnerships, which allow partners the tax benefits of a partnership but the limitation on all owner liability, in the manner that has been accorded to shareholders of a corporation.[61] But the corporation is the only one of these three forms in which existence may be perpetual,[62] in which ownership interests are readily transferable by the sale of stock, in which management is centralized in a board of directors, and which is treated as an entity for most federal and state tax purposes. Formation of a corporation to obtain these advantages involves formality and expense that are foreign to either of the other types of business enterprise. No formalities attend the creation of an individual proprietorship or even of a general partnership, which is viewed as a voluntary personal relationship arising from agreement among partners.[63]

Most states have a single statute that applies generally to all business corporations regardless of size or distribution of ownership. Nevertheless, corporations vary greatly in structure, and one of the current problems

---

[59] There is also no upper limit to the number of partners in the United States.

[60] The limited partnership was first introduced in New York in 1822 by a statute patterned after the French Code de Commerce which authorizes the *société en commandite*. Today, the tax advantages of the limited partnership have led to its popularity as a "tax shelter."

[61] The revised Uniform Partnership Act (1997) adopted the LLP, although by that time several states had already authorized the form.

[62] An individual proprietorship terminates with the death of the proprietor, and a partnership is technically dissolved by the death or withdrawal of a general partner.

[63] Statutes may require the filing of the name of an individual proprietorship or partnership. Since a limited partnership is purely a creature of statute, it must be organized in accordance with the formalities prescribed by statute.

of corporate law is how best to take account of the obvious differences between the large publicly held, or "public "corporation and the small closely held, or "close" corporation.[64] Although the law developed, for the most part, with the economically dominant public corporation in mind, there is now a trend to give special statutory treatment to close corporations, either by provisions scattered throughout the general corporation law or by a special part of that law.

One of the chief characteristics of the American corporation is the separation of management from ownership. Although authority to make fundamental changes in character or organization, as by merger, dissolution, or amendment of the corporate charter remains in the shareholders as owners of the corporation, the management of the corporation is entrusted to a separate group, the board of directors. The corporate officers—commonly a president, vice president, secretary, and treasurer—are appointed by the board of directors, as agents of the corporation charged with execution of the board's policies. The powers of the board of directors are derived from statute rather than from a contract among shareholders and can be modified by agreement only within statutory limits. Typically, the board controls such matters as products, prices, labor relations, financing, and dividends, though the trend is for the board to monitor the decisions of the officers rather than to make decisions itself. The directors are elected by the shareholders as their representatives and may in extreme cases be removed by them for cause.[65] They owe a fiduciary duty to all shareholders to act for the good of the corporation and not for their personal gain, and they may be held accountable by even a minority interest for abuse of this duty.[66] The scope of these fiduciary duties was tested in the wave of corporate mergers and acquisitions during the 1980s. But directors are not agents of

---

[64] Corporations that are wholly owned by one person are common.

[65] Directors may or may not be officers, and in most jurisdictions, directors need not be shareholders. Although directors who are not also officers are sometimes not compensated beyond their expenses, the trend is toward paying directors salaries, a fee for each meeting attended, or equity in the corporation.

[66] Although a shareholder is sometimes barred from suit in his or her own name to enforce corporate rights, a shareholder may, subject to some limitations, maintain what is known as a shareholder derivative suit, equitable in nature, on behalf of the corporation if the directors wrongfully fail to enforce a corporate claim against persons either within or without the corporation. In some instances, a shareholder may also bring a direct individual suit in his or her own name against the corporation to enforce the shareholder's own interest.

the shareholders, and they are not subject to the demands of a majority of shareholders. Control of the board through election of directors can give effective control of the management of the corporation, and the election of directors is the principal function of the shareholders' annual meeting.

Shareholder control is difficult, however, in public corporations because of the dispersion of ownership, although this dispersion has been diminished somewhat by the rise of large institutional shareholders.[67] The only practical way to exercise shareholder voting power and to meet substantial quorum requirements for shareholders' annual meetings is by proxy voting, through agents who are present to vote the shares of absent owners. This device favors perpetuation of existing management, which proposes its own nominees for directors. However, shares of American corporations are registered on the corporate books,[68] and shareholders who seek to overthrow management are entitled to inspect the stock book and obtain a list of names and addresses of all shareholders in order to solicit proxy votes in a "proxy fight." Solicitation of proxies in most major corporations is subject to the rules of the Securities and Exchange Commission, which also requires detailed financial statements that shareholders may use to evaluate management.[69]

Suggested Readings

Basic texts are F. Gevurtz, *Corporation Law* (2000) and J. Cox & T. Hazen, *Corporations* (2003). Two short introductions are W. Klein & J. Coffee, *Business Organization and*

---

[67] Roughly half of all American households own stock or mutual fund shares. A corporation may have well over ten million shareholders.

[68] Shares of stock may be of various classes with different dividend and voting rights and may be either common or preferred. They evidence an ownership interest, often called an "equity," because of the equitable nature of the shareholder's derivative suit, and must be distinguished from debt securities such as bonds. While bonds are typically issued in bearer form, shares of stock are not. Transfer of investment securities, debt as well as equity, is governed by the Uniform Commercial Code, which replaced the Uniform Stock Transfer Act.

[69] While, except for the regulated industries, the government does not formally prescribe auditing and accounting standards, the commission has had considerable influence in raising these standards in public corporations to a very high level. There is, however, no individual or group that supervises the management of the corporation on the shareholders' behalf.

Finance: Legal and Economic Principles (8th ed. 2002) and the briefer B. Manning & J. Hanks, *Legal Capital* (3d ed. 1990). *Foundations of Corporate Law* (R. Romano, ed., 1993) is a collection of readings. A useful multi-volume work is the *Model Business Corporation Act Annotated* (3d ed. loose leaf). *Fletcher's Cyclopedia of the Law of Private Corporations* (perm. ed.) consists of many periodically revised volumes. Closely held corporations are dealt with in F. O'Neal & R. Thompson, *Close Corporations: Law and Practice* (3d ed. loose leaf).

The role of corporate officers has been under great scrutiny of late. See J. Coffee, *Gatekeepers: The Role of the Professions and Corporate Governance* (2006) and S. Brainbridge, *The New Corporate Governance in Theory and Practice* (2008). Many reforms of the corporate law have lately emerged, such as K. Greenfield, *The Failure of Corporate Law: Fundamental Flaws and Progressive Possibilities* (2007) and C. Milhaupt & K. Pistor, *Law & Capitalism: What Corporate Crises Reveal About Legal Systems and Economic Development Around the World* (2008). After much controversy, the American Law Institute published its *Principles of Corporate Governance: Analysis and Recommendations* (1994).

The standard treatise on the regulation of securities is L. Loss & J. Seligman, *Securities Regulation* (2001). Shorter works are L. Loss & J. Seligman, *Fundamentals of Securities Regulation* (5th ed. 2003) and T. Hazen, *The Law of Securities Regulation* (2006). The American Law Institute has a proposed *Federal Securities Code* (1980) with commentary.

Sources of partnership law include the Uniform Partnership Act, the Uniform Limited Partnership Act, and the Revised Limited Partnership Act. The authoritative work on agency is the *Restatement (Second) of Agency* (1958). Treatises include H. Reuschlein & W. Gregory, *The Law of Agency and Partnership* (3d ed. 2001) and A. Bromberg & L. Ribstein, *Partnership* (loose leaf).

TWELVE

Public Law

The principal fields of public law in the United States are constitutional law, administrative law, trade regulation, labor law, criminal law, and environmental law. What is their purview, how have they developed, and what are their distinctive features?

Constitutional Law

SCOPE AND SOURCES

The study of constitutional law, as that term is used in the United States, is chiefly the study of those decisions of the Supreme Court of the United States that have interpreted the federal Constitution. It includes some questions of constitutional interpretation that the Court has declined to decide on the merits on the ground that they are "political questions" for the executive or legislative to resolve and therefore not justiciable. But it excludes the large number of Supreme Court decisions that turn on other than constitutional grounds. Although each of the states has its own written constitution, "constitutional law" is ordinarily taken to mean federal rather than state constitutional law.

The primary source in this field is, of course, the text of the Constitution itself, the oldest written national constitution now in use.[1] Less than eight thousand words in length, it sought to reconcile the need for an effective national government with the desire to avoid a concentration of power that would threaten a return of the tyranny that had been overthrown. It has been able to survive two centuries with relatively little amendment because important terms such as "commerce," "necessary and proper," "due process," and "full faith and credit" are sufficiently laconic to allow for adaptation. In Chief Justice John Marshall's words, the nature of a constitution requires "that only its great outlines should be marked, its important objects designated, and the minor ingredients which compose these objects be deduced from the nature of the objects themselves . . . We must never forget, that it is a constitution we are expounding."[2]

CHARACTERISTICS

One of the cardinal limitations on the Court's power of judicial review of federal and state legislation on constitutional grounds is that it will decide only a ripened controversy in which the results are of immediate consequence to the parties and will not render advisory opinions or entertain nonadversary proceedings.[3] One writer has called it the "central paradox" of the jurisdiction and function of the Supreme Court that "its special role is to resolve questions of general importance transcending the interests of the litigants and yet it will do so only where necessary to adjudicate a conventional legal dispute between the parties."[4] Among the other significant restraints that the Court usually imposes upon itself are "never to anticipate a question of constitutional law in advance of the necessity of deciding it" and "never to formulate a rule of constitutional law broader than is required by the precise facts to which it is to be applied."[5] If the Court can fairly base

---

[1] Among the aids in its interpretation are the records of the Constitutional Convention, collected by M. Farrand and a series of essays entitled THE FEDERALIST PAPERS, written by three of its framers, Alexander Hamilton, James Madison, and John Jay during the contest over its ratification in New York. But the Court in construing the Constitution has not usually felt bound by the intention of its framers in the way it would if it were construing a statute.

[2] McCulloch v. Maryland. 17 U.S. (4 Wheat.) 316, 407 (1819).

[3] See Chapter 4, supra.

[4] P. FREUND, THE SUPREME COURT OF THE UNITED STATES 16 (1961).

[5] Justice Matthews in Liverpool, New York & Philadelphia S.S. Co. v. Commissioners of Emigration, 113 U.S. 33, 39 (1885).

its decision on some ground other than on a constitutional one, it will do so; if it can dismiss an appeal taken on a constitutional ground from a state court by finding that the judgment rested on an independent ground under state law, it will do so. All in all, the mechanics of judicial review tend to bring constitutional issues before the Court, not at times of its own choosing, but at times determined by aggrieved litigants and by history. Most of these issues can be grouped under two main headings: maintenance of the federal system and preservation of individual rights.

The major problems under the first heading arise under the commerce clause. To ensure a single, free national market, the framers of the Constitution entrusted to Congress the power "To regulate Commerce with foreign Nations, and among the several States, and with the Indian tribes."[6] Congress was slow to exercise this power until an industrial society emerged after the Civil War, and it was not until the late 1930s, when the New Deal legislation enacted during the administration of President Franklin Delano Roosevelt was challenged, that the Court departed from earlier doctrine and finally gave the clause the broad reading that it has today. The commerce power, along with the taxing and spending powers, has given Congress its present wide role in national economic life. Under its authority to regulate business and labor when engaged in production for interstate commerce, Congress has laid the foundations of such burgeoning fields as trade regulation and labor law.

In addition to the positive aspect of the commerce clause as a source of federal power, the clause has a negative aspect, as a limitation on state power. It is, of course, clear that a state statute must yield if it conflicts with a federal statute enacted under the clause, and an act of Congress that "occupies" a particular field supersedes all state legislation in that field. But beyond this, it was early established that even in the absence of a federal statute, state legislation was unconstitutional if it improperly burdened or discriminated against interstate commerce. The clause is thus an important limitation upon exercise by the states of their tax and police powers, both of which may have an impact upon interstate commerce. But although it has been second only to the Fourteenth Amendment as a basis of judicial

---

6 The Articles of Confederation had given Congress no power over interstate or foreign commerce, and each of the thirteen original states had been free to erect trade barriers at the expense of its neighbors. *See* Chapter 1, *supra*.

review of the exercise of state power, no precise line can be drawn between proper and improper state legislation affecting interstate commerce.

The second main heading, preservation of individual rights, derives chiefly from the amendments to the Constitution. The Bill of Rights, embodied in the first ten amendments ratified in 1791, secures the rights of the individual against the federal government. Of even greater significance are the protections created in the nineteenth century that the federal Constitution affords the individual against the states.[7] The chief source of these is the Fourteenth Amendment, the most important of three amendments to the Constitution adopted soon after the Civil War and originally intended to abolish slavery and ensure the freedom of African descendents in the United States. Its principal clauses provide that no state shall "deprive any person of life, liberty, or property, without due process of law" and that no state shall "deny to any person within its jurisdiction the equal protection of the laws." "Due process of law," now the most prestigious of constitutional doctrines, was originally regarded principally as a guaranty of fair procedure. By the end of the nineteenth century, however, the Supreme Court had expanded the concept to impose a restriction on the substantive reasonableness of legislation enacted by the states under their police power, as their power to provide for the public welfare is called. The Court entered a period in which the chief use of the Due Process Clause was to strike down state statutes as unconstitutional invasions of property and contract rights, including those of corporations as well as individuals.[8]

Since the late 1930s, however, these cases have declined in significance in the face of the use of the Due Process Clause for the protection of civil liberties. The Court has now made clear that the most fundamental, although not all, of the more detailed protections afforded against the federal government by the Bill of Rights are to be read into the more laconic Due Process Clause of the Fourteenth Amendment and therefore apply against the states. The protections of freedom of speech, assembly, press, and religious worship, the prohibition of establishment of a state religion, and some of the procedural safeguards for criminal cases are among those which have been held to be incorporated. It was from the Due Process Clause that

---

[7]   There are also, to be sure, protections in all the state constitutions.

[8]   The Court had also determined that corporations were "persons" entitled to the protections of the Fourteenth Amendment.

the Court derived the fundamental right of privacy that served as the basis for its controversial 1973 decision that struck down a state statute proscribing the abortion of a human fetus except when necessary to save the mother's life.[9] Under the Equal Protection Clause, the Court has extended the rights of minority groups by forbidding racial segregation by the states in public schools and other public facilities. The landmark case came in 1954, when the Court held that racially segregated state school systems violated the constitutional guarantee of equal protection.[10] It should be noted, however, that the Constitution protects the individual against governmental action only and not usually against the acts of private individuals.

Of recurrent concern in the late twentieth century was the power of the Constitution over the federal executive, the willingness of the courts to enforce such powers, and the compliance of the officials with that enforcement. One of the great moments of the U.S. Constitution came in the decision of the Supreme Court to order a president of the United States to comply with a trial court order to produce evidence, an order that President Richard Nixon honored though it would lead to his resignation from office.[11] Since that time, the Court has asserted successfully the constitutional authority to regulate presidential elections and the constitutional limits of the confinement of prisoners, even against intense pressure to the contrary.[12]

Suggested Readings

The National Archives maintains a Web site with images of the United States Constitution and the official transcripts of it at http://archives.gov/exhibits/charters/. Treatises include J. Nowak & R. Rotunda, *Handbook on Constitutional*

---

[9] Roe v. Wade, 410 U.S. 113 (1973), finding that the right of privacy, which is not explicitly mentioned, "is broad enough to encompass a woman's decision whether or not to terminate her pregnancy."

[10] Brown v. Board of Education, 347 U.S. 483 (1954), striking down as applied to education the "separate but equal" principle, under which black persons could be provided separate facilities as long as they were equal to those provided to white persons.

[11] United States v. Nixon, 418 U.S. 683 (1974).

[12] *See* Bush v. Gore, 531 U.S. 98 (2000) and Hamdan v. Rumsfeld, 548 U.S. 557 (2006).

Law (7th ed. 2004), also in a multi-volume edition. A more ambitious and idiosyncratic work is L. Tribe, *American Constitutional Law* (2d ed. 1988). For a brief treatment intended for students, see D. Ritchie, *Our Constitution* (2006). The U.S. Constitution has inspired many classic monographs to explain and interpret it, and some of the most important in U.S. law schools include E. Corwin, *The "Higher Law" Background of American Constitutional Law* (2008); A. Bickel, *The Least Dangerous Branch* (1962); H. Wechsler, *Principles, Politics, and Fundamental Law* (1961); J. Ely, *Democracy and Distrust: A Theory of Judicial Review* (1980); L. Henkin, *The Age of Rights* (1989); M. Supperstone, J. Goudie & P. Walker, *Judicial Review* (3d ed. 2005); C. Sunstein, *The Partial Constitution* (1993); and B. Ackerman, *We the People: Foundations* (1993). For a multi-volume collection of the constitutions of the United States and the states, see *Constitutions of the United States: National and State* (loose leaf), prepared by the Legislative Drafting Research Fund of Columbia University. On state constitutional law, see T. Marks & J. Cooper, *State Constitutional Law in a Nutshell* (2003) and J. Shaman, *Equality and Liberty in the Golden Age of State Constitutional Law* (2008).

See G. Fletcher & S. Sheppard, *American Law in a Global Context: The Basics*, Introduction and Chapters 5 through 14.

Administrative Law

SCOPE AND SOURCES

Administrative law is concerned with the powers and procedures of those organs of government, other than legislatures and courts, that affect private interests either by rule or by decision.[13] Although administrative law is thought to have commenced with the judicial oversight of English commissioners who built canals to drain fields in the seventeenth century,[14] the common law in this area was hardly robust, and it has grown considerably in the United States in the years following the Second World War. It is heavily procedural in its emphasis and does not include the substantive law created by administrative agencies. It deals chiefly, though not

---

[13] Such an organ of government, commonly called an agency, may also be known by such names as administrator, authority, board, bureau, commission, department, division, or office.

[14] *See* Rooke's Case, 5 Coke 99b (1598).

exclusively, with the discharge by public officials of functions related to rule making and adjudication[15] and focuses on the oversight of administrators by the courts. Although administrative agencies abound on the state and local levels, the federal agencies have the widest impact and are the easiest to describe.

The administrative process on the federal level goes back as far as 1789, but its modern origins date from the establishment in 1887 of the Interstate Commerce Commission to deal with the problems of the railroad industry.[16] The commission set the pattern for those independent regulatory agencies—functioning outside of the executive departments and regulating some aspect of private activity—that are the most distinctive species of administrative body in the United States. Federal administrative agencies of all kinds multiplied rapidly under New Deal legislation enacted in the 1930s during the administration of President Roosevelt.[17] There are now hundreds of federal agencies, with such diverse concerns as airlines, nuclear energy, banking, farm prices, immigration, labor relations, old age pensions, and the environment.[18]

Administrative law is comprised of constitutional law, statutes, case law, and agency rules and decisions. On the constitutional level, the effect of the Due Process Clause upon administrative procedure is of chief importance. Much of the framework for the national government is statutory, provided largely by the federal Administrative Procedure Act of 1946, which sought to regularize administrative procedure and to clarify the scope of judicial review of administrative action. The act was amended in 1966 by the

[15] Increasingly, important elements of administrative law relate to the making or withdrawal of government grants, such as subsidies or loans. Government contracts provide another major area of administration and law.

[16] For a brief historical introduction, see K. Davis & R. Pierce, *Administrative Law Treatise* (4th ed. 2002).

[17] The most important of these are the "regulatory agencies." Some of the better-known examples are the Federal Trade Commission, the National Labor Relations Board, and the Securities and Exchange Commission, all of which are discussed elsewhere in this book. The Interstate Commerce Commission was abolished in 1995, and its functions are now under the much less famous Surface Transportation Board.

[18] Some of the most important of these, in contrast to the regulatory agencies, are engaged mainly in dispensing benefits. An important example is the Social Security Administration, which administers benefits for some fifty million Americans. *See* http://www.ssa.gov/history/briefhistory3.html.

Freedom of Information Act.[19] Case law also plays a surprisingly large role, due in part to the general nature of many of the constitutional and statutory directives. Because there is no separate system of courts that dispense administrative law, the judicially developed principles of administrative law are similar to those of other fields.

CHARACTERISTICS

Because American government is not a parliamentary democracy, the heads of government agencies have no formal political connection to Congress. They are appointees of the president, usually of the president in office at any given time.[20] Indeed, the American concept of "separation of powers" heightens the distinctions between the chief executive, the legislature, and the courts. The power to review acts of governmental agencies is, however, entrusted to the courts, and much of administrative law is concerned with this review.

Agency procedures may be formal or informal. The vast bulk of decisions are reached by informal proceedings with nothing resembling a formal hearing. As for the small fraction of cases where formal proceedings are heard, the variety of agencies and the scope of their activities defy both general description and uniform regulation. Although the Administrative Procedure Act lays down general guidelines of procedure on matters common to most agencies, no comprehensive and detailed procedural code has been deemed feasible. Nevertheless, the dominant theme of the Due Process Clause of the federal Constitution runs throughout administrative procedure.[21] The chief requirements of procedural due process are notice to a person whose interests might be affected by a rule and an opportunity for that person to have a fair hearing before the burden of a rule or ruling becomes final. It is difficult to generalize, and the rules in this area have evolved largely on an *ad hoc* basis through case law, against the

---

[19] In 1964, the Administrative Conference Act created an Administrative Conference, with nearly a hundred members. It has had limited success in prompting Congress to act on its many useful volumes of recommendations and reports.

[20] Departments are usually led by a secretary, and agencies are usually headed by an administrator, who is usually appointed by the president who is in office, and these appointees' terms are usually at the "pleasure" of the president, and they are expected to be replaced when a new president is elected. Commissions, boards, and some agencies, however, are led by presidential appointees of fixed terms, and their appointments are designed to continue into and perhaps through the terms of later presidents.

[21] State and local administrative agencies are affected by due process requirements in state constitutions as well.

background of vague constitutional and statutory requirements. Hearings are commonly held before agency employees known as administrative law judges, whose initial findings are subject to the final decision of the agency. Notice to the person affected is characteristically brief, and its contents are less important than the pleadings in court procedure. The procedure and rules of evidence for court hearings are not applicable, and the emphasis on written evidence is great. A person affected by a proposed rule may also have the opportunity to present pertinent information and opinion, but not ordinarily in a trial-like hearing.

Of the relatively small number of cases that go to formal administrative proceedings, a much smaller number is subjected to judicial review. Nevertheless, the judicial control of administrative actions is one of the most significant topics of American administrative law. Because no special system of courts handles administrative matters, judicial review is carried out within the framework created for conventional litigation in the regular courts. Most federal regulatory statutes specifically authorize review of particular actions of the agency charged with their administration.[22] Review is commonly appellate in nature, before a federal court of appeals on the record below; less often it is by an original action in a federal district court. Furthermore, there is a general statutory authorization of review in the Federal Administrative Procedure Act[23] as well as nonstatutory review in some cases.[24] Review may also be possible under other circumstances, as when agency action requires court enforcement. A variety of doctrines tend to limit review of administrative adjudication to those who are immediately affected by a final order in a ripe controversy and have exhausted their administrative remedies. Full review can generally be had on the "law," but the "facts" will ordinarily be reviewed only to the extent of determining whether the administrative finding is supported by "substantial evidence," a scope of review similar to that applied to a finding of fact by a jury.

During the 1970s, rule making began to emerge as the dominant form of regulation by agencies. As a result, the Supreme Court was called upon to decide the extent to which Congress can delegate to agencies the power to promulgate legislative rules that resolve fundamental issues of policy.

---

[22] This is also true of many state statutes.

[23] There is a similar provision in the Model State Administrative Procedure Act.

[24] This may be, among other ways, by injunction or declaratory judgment, or by the prerogative writs, which include *mandamus, habeas corpus,* and prohibition.

The decade of the 1980s saw important challenges to the constitutionality of congressional delegation to agencies of broad policy-making power. In a controversial decision concerning judicial review of an agency's interpretation of statutory provisions delegating regulatory power to it, the Supreme Court concluded that if "Congress has not directly addressed the precise question at issue," the reviewing court must affirm the agency's interpretation if it is "reasonable."[25]

Administrative agencies, in spite of their considerable independence, are also subject to some control by the legislative and executive branches. Although there is no general provision for congressional review of administrative rules and regulations,[26] Congress has not hesitated to intervene in agency affairs through its control over agency budgets and through investigation by congressional committees. The president has the power, subject to the consent of the Senate, to appoint agency heads, but the presidential power of removal of many of these before the end of a fixed term is severely circumscribed. The president also controls the agencies' requests to Congress for funds and has limited powers of reorganization of administrative agencies.[27] Criticism has also been directed at the combination in the same agency of the functions of legislating, investigating, initiating proceedings, and judging. This has been met in part by the division of functions within the agencies themselves and through increased independence for the officers who preside over hearings.[28]

Suggested Readings

A multi-volume treatise is K. Davis & R. Pierce, *Administrative Law Treatise* (4th ed. 2002). One-volume texts include A. Aman & W. Mayton, *Administrative Law* (2d ed. 2001) and R. Pierce, S. Shapiro & P. Verkuil, *Administrative Law and Process*

---

[25]   Chevron U.S.A. v. Natural Resources Defense Council, 467 U.S. 837, 843 (1984).

[26]   Some states have general procedures of this kind, and Congress has made selective use of review in special circumstances.

[27]   On the effects of pressure to "deregulate," *see* Trade Regulation in this chapter, *infra*.

[28]   In one notable instance, that of the National Labor Relations Board, the function of initiating proceedings has been completely separated from the agency by the creation of an independent office of General Counsel with final authority to investigate and prosecute unfair labor practices.

(5th ed. 2008). A book designed for readers from other legal systems is P. Strauss, *An Introduction to Administrative Justice in the United States* (1989). *Administrative Law Stories* (P. Strauss ed., 2006) is a collection of quite helpful stories of the major cases in the field. A description of federal administrative agencies is contained in *The United States Government Manual*, published annually.

Trade Regulation

SCOPE AND SOURCES

The field of trade regulation in U.S. law includes both the law of anti-trust, which is designed to encourage competition through the prevention of monopolization and the limitation of restraints of trade; and the law of unfair competition, which requires that competition meet acceptable standards of fairness.[29] Although these are more often considered property, trade regulation is sometimes defined to include the law of trademarks and trade names as well as the primarily statutory law of patents and copy-rights.[30] Although some regulation of trade was affected by case law before modern legislation, the principal sources today are federal, and to a lesser extent state,[31] statutes. Among the most significant of these are the three major antitrust statutes enacted by Congress for the purpose of promoting competition in interstate commerce.

The first and most important was the Sherman Antitrust Act, enacted in 1890 during the period of industrial expansion and concentration of economic power which followed the Civil War.[32] It prohibits, in general

---

[29] International trade regulation is beyond the scope of this section, but it includes the regulation of international trade through corporate and investment laws, food and goods standards, tariffs, prohibitions, and other regulations of goods and services at the border. For an excellent overview of this important field and the U.S. participation in the World Trade Organization, *see* M. TREBILCOCK & R. HOWSE, THE REGULATION OF INTERNATIONAL TRADE (3rd ed. 2005).

[30] *See* Chapter 11, *supra*.

[31] State statutes include fair trade acts, widely enacted under an enabling clause in the federal antitrust laws, to permit "vertical" resale price-fixing agreements. Although antitrust statutes have also been enacted by most states, they have been effective in only a few.

[32] The antitrust laws were named after the nineteenth-century "trust," a closely knit business combination, composed of many corporations in a single industry such as oil or sugar and held together by a trust agreement under unified management by a board of trustees.

terms, unreasonable restraints of trade and monopolization. The Clayton Act, which followed in 1914, is somewhat more specific. With some exceptions, it first prohibits exclusive dealing, tying arrangements,[33] and similar restrictions on the distribution of goods; second, price discrimination, on differentiation, between purchasers, as well as certain related discriminatory practices[34]; and third, acquisition by one corporation of the stock or assets of another corporation—where the effect of any of these "may be substantially to lessen competition or tend to create a monopoly." While the Sherman Act condemns only existing evils, the Clayton Act requires merely a reasonable probability that these evils will result. The third major statute, the Federal Trade Commission Act, also enacted in 1914, is directed generally at "unfair methods of competition." It created the Federal Trade Commission, which is empowered to enforce the act.[35] Together, these three statutes affect the "horizontal" relationships of a business with its competitors, the "vertical" relationships of a business with its suppliers and customers, and, in some cases, the internal corporate relationship within the business enterprise itself.

Because virtually all of American business is privately owned and managed, the maintenance and control of competition is of the greatest importance. In some fields, however, Congress has departed from the ideal of free competition. Thus, there are limited exemptions from the antitrust laws for such industries as aviation, communications, railroads, trucking, and shipping, all of which are closely supervised by special regulatory agencies,[36] as well as a few, such as sports leagues, that are somewhat self regulating but still potentially subject to Congressional and administrative

---

[33] An exclusive dealing arrangement is one in which one firm is allowed to obtain the product of another on the condition that it will not deal in the competing products of third parties. A tying arrangement involves a sale or lease of a product on condition that some other product be purchased with it.

[34] This second prohibition is contained in the Robinson-Patman Act of 1936, which amends and is now a part of the Clayton Act.

[35] The Federal Trade Commission Act also has jurisdiction over such unfair trade practices as false and misleading advertising and over misbranding and related practices in connection with food, drugs, and cosmetics.

[36] Although this is still true, in recent decades there has been political pressure to "deregulate" and rely on "competitive market forces." An early example is the Airline Deregulation Act of 1978, which reduced regulation of commercial airlines.

oversight. Also exempted in most of their activities are labor unions and agricultural cooperatives, which have peculiar problems.

CHARACTERISTICS

A major characteristic of the field of antitrust is that many of the statutory provisions, particularly those of the Sherman Act, are couched in broader and more general terms than is customary for legislation in the United States. This calculated imprecision has given a decisive role to the judiciary, which has been responsible for interpreting the statutes and adapting them to the changing patterns of production and distribution that have evolved since their passage. Rather than lay down precise and inflexible rules, the courts have employed a general "rule of reason," or standard of reasonableness, in implementing the Sherman Act. Its application has varied from time to time and from industry to industry, according to the circumstances as judges have struggled with economic data and other considerations in order to accomplish the less-than-precise objectives of the governing statutes. There is thus no absolute limit to the size of a business enterprise. Size alone, or even dominance, is not of itself condemned, although these are among the circumstances to be evaluated. The courts are in agreement, however, that some practices, such as "horizontal" arrangements among competitors to affect prices or divide markets, are so offensive as to be unreasonable *per se* (in themselves). Doctrines more similar to *per se* rules than to a "rule of reason" are also applied to exclusive dealing and tying arrangements under the Clayton Act and to most forms of price discrimination. As might be expected, there has been considerable controversy over the proper domain of the rule of reason and of *per se* unreasonableness under all the antitrust statutes.

Another of the salient features of the antitrust laws is the unique panoply of remedies available for their enforcement. The government may proceed against suspected violations in three principal ways. The first is by a civil proceeding of an equitable nature brought by the Justice Department to enjoin violations of the Sherman and Clayton Acts. The second is by a criminal prosecution also brought by the Justice Department for a more limited class of *per se* violations, largely under the Sherman Act. And the third is by administrative proceedings brought by the Federal Trade Commission under the Clayton and Federal Trade Commission Acts and leading to a cease-and-desist order by the Commission, which is appealable to a federal court of appeals and carries a fine as the sanction for violation.

In a majority of civil proceedings, a settlement is negotiated between the defendant and the government before trial, and a consent decree setting forth the obligations of the defendant is entered by the court.[37]

In 1974, the Clayton Act was amended to provide for publication in the Federal Register of any proposal for a consent judgment and to require that any materials that the United States considers determinative in formulating the proposal be made available to the public. Whether entered with consent or not, the decree may be broadly phrased to end violations and to prevent future resumptions and may even require dissolution of an offending enterprise or divestiture of its holdings. Remedies are also given to private parties, the most important being the treble damage action under the Sherman and Clayton Acts, in which the aggrieved party may be awarded three times the amount of damages proved. In addition, the rights of private parties may be enforced on their behalf by states' attorneys general.[38] Trademark, copyright, and patent rights are enforced exclusively by private civil suits.[39] Complaints by private parties are also responsible for many of the actions brought by the government under the antitrust laws and by the Federal Trade Commission to prevent unfair trade practices.

One of the criticisms of the U.S. trade laws has been the overlapping of functions of the Justice Department and the Federal Trade Commission, notably under the Clayton Act.[40] While in general they do not conduct simultaneous proceedings and seek to avoid conflict, their approach to antitrust problems will not always be the same; the Justice Department, as an arm of the executive, more closely reflects the view of the administration than does the independent commission. Because of the fluidity of the law, both have considerable discretion, and both have substantially influenced

---

[37]   One inducement to the defendant is that consent decrees are exceptions to the general rule of the Clayton Act that a judgment or decree establishing a violation of the antitrust laws in a proceeding brought by the government is *prima facie* evidence of violation in a later civil suit by a private party.

[38]   The Antitrust Improvements Act of 1976 amended the Clayton Act to give states' attorneys general the right to bring a civil action in the name of the state, as *parens patriae* (literally, parent of the people), on behalf of persons residing in the state for monetary relief for violations of the Sherman Act.

[39]   *See* Chapter 11, Intellectual Property, *supra*.

[40]   Violations of the Sherman Act, under the jurisdiction of the Justice Department, may also amount to violations of the Federal Trade Commission Act, under the jurisdiction of the FTC.

its development. Their enforcement has, on the whole, been effective in preserving competition, notwithstanding the role played by large firms in the American economy.

Suggested Readings

Multi-volume treatises include P. Areeda & D. Turner, *Antitrust Law: An Analysis of Antitrust Principles and Their Application* (1978–) and L. Altman, *Callman on Unfair Competition, Trademarks and Monopolies* (4th ed. loose leaf). One-volume texts include H. Hovenkamp, *Federal Antitrust Policy* (3d ed. 2005); L. Sullivan & W. Grimes, *The Law of Antitrust: An Integrated Handbook* (2006). An influential but controversial treatment is R. Posner, *Antitrust Law* (2d ed. 2001). There is also a one-volume *Restatement (Third) of Unfair Competition* (1995). Economic models current in antitrust theory are depicted in *Handbook of Antitrust Economics* (P. Buccirossi ed., 2008).

Employment and Labor Law

SCOPE AND SOURCES

Labor law, in its broadest sense, is the law that affects working persons by virtue of their employment relationship, a relationship that in the United States is ordinarily with a private employer. It can be divided into two major branches, which are often referred to as employment law and labor law.

Employment law deals with the welfare of workers as individuals. It includes such common state statutes as those establishing workers' compensation, prescribing wage and hour standards, preventing harmful child labor, and proscribing discrimination in employment on the grounds of race, religion, or national origin. There is a federal wage and hour law, the Fair Labor Standards Act of 1938, which along with later statutes and amendments provide federal standards for minimum wages, maximum hours beyond which additional compensation for overtime is payable, the assurance of parental leave for childbirth, some regulation of health care and other benefits, and the prohibition of child labor. There is a federal contributory social security system that provides an old age retirement annuity, payments to survivors, and related benefits. Unemployment insurance is provided in all states by a cooperative federal-state plan. Recent decades have seen particularly significant federal enactments designed to assure safe and healthful working conditions,[41] to facilitate and improve employee pension plans,[42] and to prohibit discrimination on grounds of race, religion, sex, national origin, or age.[43]

Labor law, in its more specific sense, deals with disputes arising out of the activities of organized labor. Its modern development began in the 1930s. Prior to that time, the law of labor relations was largely case law, based on precedent and traditional principles and generally favorable to employers, who were able to obtain court injunctions forbidding many forms of union activity. In reaction to judicial excesses, the role of the courts was severely circumscribed by statute.

The Norris-LaGuardia Act of 1932 so curtailed the power of the federal courts to issue injunctions in labor disputes that is now almost impossible for an employer to get an injunction against peaceful labor activity.[44] The first comprehensive labor relations statute came soon afterwards with the enactment in 1935 of the National Labor Relations Act, commonly known as the Wagner Act, to promote collective bargaining between employers and unions.[45] It assured employees of the right to organize and to bargain collectively and proscribed a list of unfair labor practices by employers, including discrimination against employees because of their union activity and refusal to bargain with an authorized collective bargaining agent.

---

[41] *See* the Occupational Safely and Health Act of 1970.

[42] *See* the Employee Retirement Income Security Act of 1974 and the Multiemployer Pension Plan Amendments Act of 1980.

[43] *See* Title VII of the Civil Rights Act of 1964 and the Age Discrimination in Employment Act of 1967.

[44] Within a few years, many of the states had enacted similar anti-injunction statutes.

[45] The National Industrial Recovery Act of 1933 had recognized the right of employees to bargain collectively, but that statute was held unconstitutional by a unanimous vote in Schechter Poultry Corp. v. United States, 295 U.S. 495 (1935). The Schechter case is notable as a rare case in which the Supreme Court invalidated an attempted congressional delegation of law-making power to an administration agency. The constitutionality of the Wagner Act as a valid exercise of the commerce power was upheld by a five to four decision in National Labor Relations Board v. Jones & Laughlin Steel Corp., 301 U.S. 1 (1937). A minority of states also have labor relations laws, which are generally applicable only to small businesses that have no substantial impact on commerce and therefore do not come under federal legislation.

It created the National Labor Relations Board and gave it two tasks: first, to conduct elections in which employees can, if they choose, select representatives for bargaining purposes; and second, to hear and determine charges of unfair labor practices, subject to review by a federal court of appeals. The board may also seek a court injunction against such practices. In 1947, a climate of public opinion less favorable to labor resulted in the enactment over a presidential veto of the Labor Management Relations Act, popularly known as the Taft-Hartley Act. Among its most important provisions were those establishing for the first time unfair labor practices on behalf of unions, including coercion and certain secondary labor activities in which pressures are applied beyond the immediate parties to a labor dispute. It also limited agreements between an employer and a union requiring or encouraging employees to be members of the union.[46] The Supreme Court has interpreted it both as authorizing the federal courts to fashion a body of federal law for enforcement of collective bargaining agreements[47] and as empowering those courts to enjoin strikes in breach of such agreements.[48] The most recent major enactment is the Labor-Management Reporting and Disclosure Act of 1959, also known as the Landrum-Griffin Act, which amends the two earlier enactments in various respects and provides for the regulation of internal union affairs to ensure honesty and fairness to individual members.

CHARACTERISTICS

In the decades following the first modern labor legislation, union membership grew to include over one-third of the nonagricultural workforce. Although membership has now declined to roughly half of that, leaving most industrial enterprises without union representation, many of the characteristics of American labor law can be ascribed to the distinctive

---

[46] The "closed shop," in which union membership is required before a worker can be employed, is prohibited. The "union shop"—in which a worker must join the union after being hired—is generally permissible under federal law but may be prohibited under "right-to-work" laws enacted in a minority of states under express provision of federal law that a stricter state law may supersede a federal law in this regard.

[47] Textile Workers Union v. Lincoln Mills, 353 U.S. 448 (1957).

[48] Boys Markets v. Retail Clerks Local 770, 398 U.S. 235 (1970).

features of organized labor.[49] One of the most significant of these is its lack of political orientation. Organized labor's chief goals have been better wages and working conditions rather than general social reform, and while organized labor has not hesitated to support specific legislation and particular candidates, it has neither maintained its own political party nor permanently allied itself with either of the two major parties. Organized labor has achieved its objectives primarily through collectively negotiated agreements with employers rather than by comprehensive legislation. These agreements both supplement minimum statutory benefits relating to wages, hours, and pensions, and add benefits that have no counterparts in case law or statute, such as paid vacations, sick leave, seniority, severance pay, and employee participation in the settlement of grievances. The peculiar significance of the collective bargaining agreement is symptomatic of the overall importance of voluntary private procedures for settlement of labor problems in the United States.

The labor relations laws themselves provide no significant governmental machinery for the settlement of disputes over employment conditions. They attempt only to compel bargaining in good faith between management and the elected union representatives of an appropriate bargaining unit of workers. Under the principle of majority rule, the representatives chosen by the majority are the exclusive bargaining agents for the entire unit. If the union is unable to negotiate a satisfactory collective bargaining agreement, the workers are free to strike on the termination of any prior collective bargaining agreement, and it is this weapon that makes the bargaining process effective.[50] In order to avoid and shorten strikes, both

[49] Organized labor shows the pluralism that is so often characteristic of American institutions. While most union members belong to unions that are affiliated with the American Federation of Labor–Congress of Industrial Organizations (AFL-CIO), power is lodged in the many international unions which represent particular crafts and industries. Their local chapters are composed of employees in a particular geographical area or perhaps even a single factory, and it is the international union and not the federation, the AFL-CIO, with which the individual worker deals.

[50] The percentage of hours lost annually because of strikes is nevertheless very small, usually well under one-quarter of one percent. The Taft-Hartley Act limits the right to strike in those rare cases where the strike would be a threat to the national health or safety, by providing for an eighty-day injunction, to be obtained by the government, on the expiration of which the workers are again free to strike. Even here, the main reliance is on informal procedures. There are also limitations on the right of railroad and airlines employees to

federal and state governments provide mediation and conciliation facilities, but they cannot force terms upon the parties.[51] Whether a strike is
had or not, the end result of bargaining is a lengthy and detailed collective
bargaining agreement between the employer and the union for a period,
commonly of two years, during which the union ordinarily agrees not to
strike. One of the key provisions will detail the procedures for the private
settlement of grievances and is especially desirable because of the absence
of special labor courts. Should one of the parties refuse to observe an arbitration agreement, a court will order its specific performance, but it is a
rare instance in which this extreme sanction is necessary. For the most
part, though the collective bargaining agreement is a legally enforceable
contract, its enforcement is entrusted to private agencies, with very limited
reliance upon the courts.

Suggested Readings

Texts include R. Gorman, *Basic Text on Labor Law* (2004) and C. Morris et al.,
The Developing Labor Law (2d ed. 1983). On employment law, see H. Lewis &
E. Norman, *Player, Employment Discrimination Law and Practice* (2004). A useful
introduction is in the *American Bar Association Guide to Workplace Law: Everything
Every Employer and Employee Needs to Know About the Law & Hiring, Firing,
Discrimination,. . .Maternity Leave, & Other Workplace Issues* (2d ed. 2006).

Tax Law

SCOPE AND SOURCES

Both federal and state governments tax the individuals and enterprises subject to their jurisdiction, and within certain constitutional limits, each is
relatively independent of the other. The principal source of federal revenue

---

strike under the Railway Labor Act. Strikes by federal government employees are prohibited by federal statute; state and municipal employees have been regularly held to lack the
right to strike, and a number of states have provisions as well.

[51] Arbitration is rarely used to fix contract terms, and federal law makes no provision for
compulsory arbitration of labor disputes in private industry.

is the individual income tax, which accounts for about one-half of the total. The payroll tax, used to support the social security system, has grown substantially in recent years and is now the second biggest source of federal revenue, at more than a third of the total. The corporate income tax makes up about a tenth of the total. Other federal taxes include excise taxes, gift taxes, and estate taxes, but these are relatively small sources of revenue. State and local authorities raise revenue chiefly through taxes on sales, income, property, and the severance of natural resources. While state and local revenue have grown considerably in recent years, it is still much less than federal revenue.[52]

The federal income taxes, both individual and corporate, are of special importance because of their effects on both personal and business conduct. Their great complexities invite attempts at tax avoidance, and tax considerations often determine the shape of a transaction. Nevertheless, the federal income tax is a creature of this century. In 1895, the Supreme Court of the United States held that a federal tax on income was unconstitutional,[53] and it was not until 1913, when the Sixteenth Amendment to the Constitution became effective, that Congress was empowered "to lay and collect taxes on incomes." Although a progressive income tax on individuals was used in the 1930s during the New Deal to help reduce the extremes of wealth and poverty, as late as 1939, only one out of every twenty-five Americans of working age was a federal income taxpayer. All this changed with the Second World War, when the income tax became the dominant instrument for raising federal revenue, and today some one hundred and forty million individual income tax returns are filed annually.

The primary source of the law of federal income taxation is currently the Internal Revenue Code of 1986,[54] which with its amendments

---

[52]   In 2009, for example, federal revenues were approximately $1.1 trillion, the revenues of state governments about $345 billion, and of local governments $35 billion.

[53]   The Court's decision was based on a provision in the Constitution which forbade the federal government to levy a "direct" tax, unless apportioned among the states according to population. Pollack v. Farmers' Loan & Trust Co., 157 U.S. 429 (1895), *upheld on rehearing*, 158 U.S. 601 (1895).

[54]   A version of the IRC that is relied on by the Internal Revenue Service is provided by the Legal Information Institute of Cornell University. *See* http://www.law.cornell.edu/uscode/html/uscode26/usc_sup_01_26.html.

contains all of the currently applicable federal revenue provisions except those relating to customs duties. Tax law is thus fundamentally statutory, though some of its areas have been greatly influenced by judicially developed doctrines. Treasury Regulations, promulgated by authority of the Secretary of the Treasury, lay down additional detailed rules, intended to interpret, to implement, and to fill gaps in the code. They are valid, however, only to the extent that they are not inconsistent with the code. The most significant of the other administrative pronouncements are the published rulings of the Internal Revenue Service on stated sets of facts usually involving a problem common to a number of taxpayers.[55]

CHARACTERISTICS

Primary responsibility in the administration of the tax laws is with the U.S. Internal Revenue Service, which is headed by the Commissioner of Internal Revenue and is under the supervision of the Secretary of the Treasury. Persons with gross income of more than a statutory amount[56] and all corporations are required to file income tax returns. Current collection of tax during the year the income is obtained is accomplished by the withholding of individual income tax on wages and salaries and the periodic payment by some individual and corporate taxpayers of an estimated tax on other forms of income. Most disputes involving claimed deficiencies in the payment of taxes or claimed refunds for overpayment are settled informally at the administrative level. Taxpayers' appeals from deficiencies asserted by the commissioner are heard by the tax court of the United States. In the alternative, the taxpayer may pay the asserted deficiency and sue for a refund in a federal district court or the United States Court of Claims, which has jurisdiction over refund suits.[57] Nonpayment of income tax may also be punishable by civil penalties, collected along with the deficiency, and in some cases by criminal sanctions imposed in a separate proceeding.

---

[55] Both treasury regulations and current rulings of the Internal Revenue Service are binding upon officials of the service, and even the latter are often persuasive in court.

[56] The amount is higher for married couples that file as a couple than for single individuals.

[57] Appeals from the tax court and the district courts are heard by the federal courts of appeals and may go to the Supreme Court on certiorari.

The federal income tax, both individual and corporate, is essentially nonschedular, that is the rates are the same for all kinds of income. There are, however, a few kinds of income that are wholly or partly tax exempt. Favorable treatment of gains from the sale of capital assets, such as real property or shares of stock, was eliminated by the 1986 act. Income tax rates for individuals increase progressively to a maximum that was significantly reduced by the 1986 act. Income tax rates for corporations are different and in practice are the same for all but small family-owned companies. The individual income tax is distinguished by the wide variety of deductions that are allowed, including, for example, charitable contributions, expenses in the production of income, interest on home mortgages, and state and local taxes. These deductions, together with exemptions, result in a very significant lessening of the amount of taxable income to which the rates apply. The intricacy of the subject matter, the frequent changes in the scope and value of deductions and tax accounting methods, together with what are perceived as high rates of income taxation and the erosion of tax shelters or deductions for many payers, have contributed to the rise of the specialized segment of the bar that advises chiefly on tax matters. The law of federal income taxation is now studied in separate courses in law school by the overwhelming majority of students.

Suggested Readings

A good summary introduction is M. Chirelstein, *Federal Income Taxation* (11th ed. 2009). One-volume texts include Joshua D. Rosenberg & Dominic Daher, *The Law of Federal Income Taxation* (2008) and D. Kah et al., *Corporate Income Taxation* (6th ed. 2009). B. Bittker et al., *Federal Taxation of Income, Estates and Gifts* (1981) is an extensive multi-volume treatise. J. Mertens, *Law of Federal Income Taxation* (loose leaf) provides encyclopedic coverage of the subjects in many volumes. Commerce Clearing House and Prentice-Hall both publish widely used federal tax services. Treatises on particular parts of the federal tax system include B. Bittker & J. Eustice, *Federal Income Taxation of Corporations and Shareholders* (5th ed. 1987); Z. Cavitch, *Tax Planning for Corporations and Shareholders* (2d ed. loose leaf); C. Lowndes, R. Kramer & J. McCord, *Federal Estate and Gift Taxes* (3d ed. 1974); and R. Stephens, *Federal Estate and Gift Taxation* (6th ed. 1991). A useful though controversial primer on tax policy is C. Steuerle, *Contemporary U.S. Tax Policy* (2008).

Criminal Law

SCOPE AND SOURCES

Although American criminal law was derived from that of England at a time when criminal law was largely case law, its basis is now statutory. Each state has its own penal statutes defining both major crimes (felonies) and minor ones (misdemeanors) as well as innumerable petty offenses. Naturally, criminal homicides, rape, and theft are defined similarly from one state to the next, reflecting a common ancestry in English case law and the tendency of American legislatures to copy penal law innovations enacted by the leading states. There are important variations, however, in the coverage of even these most important crimes. For example, about half of the states have now defined rape to include one spouse's rape of the other, a change of the common-law rule. Differences among the states are most noticeable in the severity with which different crimes are viewed and in sentencing policy. In many states, liberal use is made of such alternatives to imprisonment as probation, fines, and conditional releases. In other states, however, jail sentences are a common response to even such lesser crimes as petty larceny and simple drug possession. At the extreme, over half of the states, as well as the United States, have authorized the death penalty for some murders and other serious offenses, a penalty that the Supreme Court has found constitutionally permissible if controlled by proper procedures. As of 2009, fifteen states do not have the death penalty.

While criminal law is predominantly a state concern and the great majority of convictions are by the state courts, the federal government is also active in many aspects of this field. Although the Constitution grants Congress no general legislative authority over penal law, from the earliest days, criminal sanctions have been accepted as a proper way of securing obedience to federal law. The major thrust of federal criminal law is to provide for national investigation and prosecution of crimes with an interstate character.[58] Transporting stolen vehicles across state lines, fraudulent use of the mails, major drug offenses, and organized crime racketeering are principal federal targets. In addition, of course, federal law defines national

---

[58]   The Federal Bureau of Investigation (FBI) handles investigations, and the offices of the United States attorneys handle prosecutions.

security offenses and protects federal officials and institutions. Finally, an important and complex branch of federal criminal law, tracing back to the days immediately following the Civil War, makes criminal infringements of another's civil rights.

CHARACTERISTICS

Until recently, the criminal codes of the various states were in shocking disarray, depending heavily on traditional common-law formulas that were often left unstated. Although sixteen states adopted Field's penal code proposed in 1865, that code was largely a compilation of existing law.[59] To help remedy the situation, the American Law Institute sponsored the Model Penal Code, which was approved in 1962 after a decade of work. It represented a fundamental reconsideration of the subject and, though it was not expected to unify criminal law in the United States, it did prompt and influence the revision of penal laws in two-thirds of the states.

The modern codes that follow the Model Penal Code are organized in general and special parts. The general part deals with principles of liability and exculpation (e.g., requirements of culpability, causation, and the effects of ignorance or mistake), of justification (e.g., defense of one's self or one's property), and of responsibility (e.g., effect of mental disease or defect). The special part contains definitions and gradations of specific crimes. Crimes are functionally organized according to the interest sought to be protected and the evils sought to be averted (e.g., offenses involving danger to the person, offenses against property, and offenses against public order and decency).

The most important improvement accomplished by the Model Penal Code is the treatment of the requirements of culpability. Four kinds of culpability—purpose, knowledge, recklessness, and negligence—are defined. These definitions are used consistently in formulating specific offenses. For example, "reckless" killing is manslaughter. Furthermore, under the Model Penal Code, a person is not ordinarily guilty of a crime "unless he acted purposely, knowingly, recklessly or negligently, as the law may require, with respect to each material element of the offense,"[60] The code thus insists that

---

[59]   *See* Chapter 6, *supra*, for discussion of the Field codes.

[60]   The code leaves it open to the legislature to add strict liability (or absolute liability) as, for example, with respect to a mistake in the age of the victim when the age is material in a sexual offense.

some culpability is required for a commission of a crime but recognizes that the type of culpability may vary not only from crime to crime but from one element of a crime to another.[61] These formulations have now replaced the traditional judicially developed formulations of the required *mens rea* (guilty mind) in about half the states.[62]

An example of the Model Penal Code's special part can be seen in its treatment of homicide. Homicides are divided into three categories: murder, manslaughter, and negligent homicide. An earlier American innovation, having two degrees of murder, with first degree murder requiring a "deliberate and premeditated" killing, is abandoned in favor of a single category of murder based on intent or extreme recklessness. The Model Code employs a new criterion and reduces a murder to manslaughter if the killing is committed "under the influence of extreme mental or emotional disturbance for which there is reasonable explanation or excuse . . . determined from the viewpoint of a person in the actor's situation under the circumstances as he believes them to be." This test replaces the common-law focus on a heat of passion following adequate provocation.

While the Model Penal Code's treatment of homicide and other specific crimes has been influential in the state revision process, it has had less influence in the field of sentencing.[63] The code attempted to rationalize the then-prevailing system of indeterminate sentences. Under that system, the judge had broad discretion in sentencing and might impose a lengthy maximum prison term, but the prisoner was often granted early release on parole by a parole board appointed by the executive. The system came under sharp attack, however, and the trend at present is toward more determinate sentences, with less discretion in the judge and no possibility of early release by a parole board. Sentencing guidelines are used by the federal courts and in a number of states.

---

61 The Model Penal Code provides that a person may not be responsible for criminal conduct as a result of mental disease or defect. The test is whether the accused, "as a result of mental disease or defect [lacked] substantial capacity to appreciate the criminality of his conduct or to conform his conduct to the requirements of the law." This test was intended to replace the traditional test, taken from nineteenth-century English law, of whether one had the capacity to know what one was doing and to know that it was wrong.

62 A crime is often defined as the combination of an *actus reus* with *mens rea*, or the guilty act with a guilty mind, or more prosaicly, the external manifestation of a criminal action made with the psychological state defined by statute as the basis for criminal liability for such an action.

63 The Model Penal Code takes no position on the abolition of the death penalty.

Suggested Readings

Basic treatises include W. LaFave, *Criminal Law* (4th ed. 1986). Discussion of the Model Penal Code can be found in *Model Penal Code and Commentaries* (1980, 1985). For historical background, see L. Friedman, *Crime and Punishment in American History* (1993). Interesting works from a comparative perspective include G. Fletcher, *Rethinking Criminal Law* (2d ed. 2000) and G. Fletcher, *The Grammar of Criminal Law* (2007). A critical and explanatory study of the increasing use of science in the creation of criminal law is in N. Farahany, *The Impact of Behavioral Sciences on Criminal Law* (2009).

Environmental Law

SCOPE AND SOURCES

The environmental law of the United States is in part derived from the English common law of property, which is still the basis for state-law actions for nuisance, trespass, and certain other causes of action such as negligence and the maintenance of water wells. Even so, the bulk of the field is the result of a series of ambitious statutes to regulate threats to the environment and to wildlife and to human health, passed by Congress, initially in the 1970s, with coordinate statutes enacted by the state legislatures, each of which are further elaborated by regulations by federal and state agencies. In many instances, these statutes correspond to international treaty commitments of the United States.

Environmental law encompasses a great number of forms of regulation and causes of action, including at its widest scope, laws regulating the use of public waters and lands, creating national parks, regulating hazards from chemical and noise in the workplace, and regulating the production and management of food. Yet the central concern of environmental law has been, for the last thirty years, the regulation of pollution and materials or activities that cause pollution, as well as the protection of wildlife and habitat. Recent years have led to a greater concern for global risks to the environment, particularly in the ability of the oceans to sustain life and the effects of human activity on the planet's atmosphere and temperature.

CHARACTERISTICS

Common-law causes of action for pollution or negligent use of chemicals depend on proof of specific harm to the individual bringing the action, such as entry onto the land of a landowner or injury to livestock or an individual person from chemical contacts. These actions for nuisance, trespass, or negligence are generally governed by state law and are largely unaffected by the statutory environmental law.

The major federal statutes are intended to inhibit activity that would degrade the natural or human environment and regulate the use of toxic chemicals and production of toxic wastes; the use of pesticides; the creation, transportation, storage, and disposal of hazardous waste; the management of solid wastes generally; the introduction of chemicals, waste, and heated water to waterways; and the introduction of gases or particulates in the atmosphere, including regulating the allowed emissions of automobiles and trucks. Other statutes regulate the taking of endangered species and interference with their habitats as well as regulate major federal projects that might have a significant impact on the environment. The statutes provide for enforcement of these statutes by federal agencies, such as the Environmental Protection Agency, Army Corps of Engineers, and the U.S. Coast Guard, although most statutes, particularly the Administrative Procedures Act, generally provide for a private cause of action to enforce the statute when an agency opts not to do so. Various states have additional environmental statutes, most of which integrate into the federal statutes but a few of which provide for local protections beyond the federal requirements.

Suggested Readings

Two works on U.S. environmental law are W. Rodgers, *Environmental Law* (2d ed. 1994), a one-volume treatise, and F. Grad, *Treatise on Environmental Law* (loose leaf), a multi-volume work. For international law, see P. Sands, *Principles of International Environmental Law* (2d ed. 2003). An excellent history is R. Lazarus, *The Making of Environmental Law* (2006). On the regulatory basis for environmental law, see R. Revesz & M. Livermore, *Retaking Rationality: How Cost Benefit Analysis Can Better Protect the Environment and Our Health* (2008).

Appendices

Reading Case Law and Statutes

The careful reading of a case and of a statute are essential skills for the lawyer, and American lawyers follow certain customary approaches to reading the text, parsing its meaning, and putting them both in the contexts of the prior and later law and legal policy. Law students are often taught to brief a case according to a standard outline, but whether this approach is taken or not, reading the case with an understanding of its facts, its issues, the law that is cited as the source of the decision, the decision made, and the outcomes that followed are essential. Likewise, reading a statute requires not only an understanding of its text but the relationship of the statute to other related laws and to the judicial experience of interpretation of similar statutes. The exercises below are useful introductions to these problems. For more detailed treatment, see the appendices of G. Fletcher & S. Sheppard, *American Law in a Global Context* (2005).

Case Law

In the following opinion, the Supreme Court of Oklahoma joins other jurisdictions in adopting the doctrine of "informed consent." This doctrine affects the liability in tort of a physician who has furnished medical treatment to a patient.

As the court points out, a physician who obtains a patient's consent to medical treatment is not liable in tort for a battery. Under the doctrine of informed consent, however, the physician, in obtaining the patient's consent, must inform the patient of the options as to treatment and of the risks involved in those options. If the physician fails to do this, the patient's consent is defective, and the physician is liable for any injury that results from the treatment even though there was no lack of care in the treatment itself.

Note that the court is strongly influenced by *Canterbury v. Spence*, a case decided in another jurisdiction but that the court declines to follow the "reasonable man" test of that case. Note also that the court limits its decision so as to be prospective only.

Scott v. Bradford

Supreme Court of Oklahoma, 1979.
606 P.2d 554.
DOOLIN, J:
This appeal is taken by plaintiffs in trial below, from a judgment in favor of defendant rendered on a jury verdict in a medical malpractice action.

Mrs. Scott's physician advised her she had several fibroid tumors on her uterus. He referred her to defendant surgeon. Defendant admitted her to the hospital where she signed a routine consent form prior to defendant's performing a hysterectomy. After surgery, Mrs. Scott experienced problems with incontinence. She visited another physician who discovered she had a vesico-vaginal fistula which permitted urine to leak from her bladder into the vagina. This physician referred her to an urologist who, after three surgeries, succeeded in correcting her problems.

Mrs. Scott, joined by her husband, filed the present action alleging medical malpractice, claiming defendant failed to advise her of the risks involved or of available alternatives to surgery. She further maintained had she been properly informed she would have refused the surgery.

The case was submitted to the jury with instructions to which plaintiffs objected. The jury found for defendant and plaintiffs appeal.

[The court quoted the instructions that the plaintiffs said the judge should have given.]

The issue involved is whether Oklahoma adheres to the doctrine of informed consent as the basis of an action for medical malpractice, and if so did the present instructions adequately advise the jury of defendant's duty.

Anglo-American law starts with the premise of thoroughgoing self-determination, each man considered to be his own master. This law does not permit a physician to substitute his judgment for that of the patient by any form of artifice.[1] The doctrine of informed consent arises out of this premise.

Consent to medical treatment, to be effective, should stem from an understanding decision based on adequate information about the treatment, the available alternatives, and the collateral risks. This requirement, labeled "informed consent," is, legally speaking, as essential as a physician's care and skill in the *performance* of the therapy. The doctrine imposes a duty on a physician or surgeon to inform a patient of his options and their attendant risks. If a physician breaches this duty, patient's consent is defective, and physician is responsible for the consequences.[2]

If treatment is completely unauthorized and performed without any consent at all, there has been a battery.[3] However, if the physician obtains a patient's consent but has breached his duty to inform, the patient has a cause of action sounding in negligence for failure to inform the patient of his options, regardless of the due care exercised at treatment, assuming there is injury.[4]

Until today, Oklahoma has not officially adopted this doctrine. In *Martin v. Stratton*, 515 P.2d 1366 (Okla. 1973), this Court discussed a physician's duty in this area but reversed the trial court on other grounds. It impliedly approved the doctrine and stated its basic principles but left its adoption until a later time.

---

[1] *See* Natanson v. Kline, 186 Kan. 393, 350 P.2d 1093, *reh'g denied*, 187 Kan. 186, 354 P.2d 670 (1960). *Also see* Rolaler v. Strain, 390 Okla. 572, 137 P. 96 (1913).

[2] Martin v. Stratton, 515 P.2d 1366 (Okla. 1973).

[3] *See* Rolater v. Strain, *supra*, n. 1; Wilkinson v. Vesey, 110 R.I. 606. 295 A.2d 676 (1972).

[4] Wilkinson v. Vesey, *supra*, n. 3.

The first buds of court decisions heralding this new medical duty are found in *Salgo v. Leland Stanford, Jr., University Board of Trustees*, 154 Cal. App. 2d 560, 317 P.2d 170 (1957). That court grounded the disclosure requirement in negligence law holding a physician violates a duty to his patient and subjects himself to liability if he withholds any facts which are necessary to form the basis of an intelligent consent by the patient to the proposed treatment. The court strongly suggested a physician is obligated not only to disclose *what* he intends to do, but to supply information which addresses the question of *whether* he should do it. This view was a marked divergence from the general rule of "professional standard of care" in determining what must be disclosed. Under that standard, earlier decisions seemed to perpetuate medical paternalism by giving the profession sweeping authority to decide unilaterally what is in the patient's best interest.[5] Under the "professional standard of care" a physician needed only to inform a patient in conformance with the prevailing medical practice in the community.[6]

More recently, in perhaps one of the most influential informed consent decisions, *Canterbury v. Spence*, 150 U.S. App. 263, 464 F.2d 772 (D.C. Cir. 1972), *cert. denied*, 409 U.S. 1064, 93 S. Ct. 560, 34 L.Ed.2d 518, the doctrine received perdurable impetus.[7] Judge Robinson observed that suits charging failure by a physician adequately to disclose risks and alternatives of proposed treatment were not innovative in American law. He emphasized the fundamental concept in American jurisprudence that every human being of adult years and sound mind has a right to determine what shall be done with his own body. True consent to what happens to one's self is the informed exercise of a choice. This entails an opportunity to evaluate knowledgeably the options available and the risks attendant upon each. It is the prerogative of every patient to chart his own course and determine which direction he will take.

The decision in *Canterbury* recognized the tendency of some jurisdictions to turn this duty on whether it is the custom of physicians

---

[5] *See* Katz, *Informed Consent—A Fairy Tale?* 39 U. Pitt. L. Rev. 137, 143 (1977).

[6] See list of jurisdictions still maintaining this standard of care as of 1976, found in an excellent discussion of the problem, Seidelson, *Medical Malpractice; Informed Consent Cases in "Full-Disclosure" Jurisdictions*, 14 Duq. L. Rev. 309 (1976).

[7] [In other words, became more long-lived and significant.]

practicing in the community to make the particular disclosure to the patient. That court rejected this standard and held the standard measuring performance of the duty of disclosure is conduct which is reasonable under the circumstances: "[We can not] ignore the fact that to bind disclosure obligations to medical usage is to arrogate the decision on revelation to the physician alone." We agree. A patient's right to make up his mind whether to undergo treatment should not be delegated to the local medical group. What is reasonable disclosure in one instance may not be reasonable in another.[8] We decline to adopt a standard based on the professional standard. We, therefore, hold the scope of a physician's communications must be measured by his patient's need to know enough to enable him to make an intelligent choice. In other words, full disclosure of all *Material risks* incident to treatment must be made. There is no bright line separating the material from the immaterial; it is a question of fact. A risk is material if it would be likely to affect patient's decision. When non-disclosure of a particular risk is open to debate, the issue is for the finder of facts.[9]

This duty to disclose is the first element of the cause of action in negligence based on lack of informed consent. However, there are exceptions creating a privilege of a physician not to disclose. There is no need to disclose risks that either ought to be known by everyone or are already known to the patient.[10] Further, the primary duty of a physician is to do what is best for his patient and where full disclosure would be detrimental to a patient's total care and best interests a physician may withhold such disclosure,[11] for example, where disclosure would alarm an emotionally upset or apprehensive patient. Certainly too, where there is an emergency and the patient is in no condition to determine for himself whether treatment should be administered, the privilege may be invoked.[12]

[8] Wilkinson v. Vesey, *supra*, n.3.

[9] Woods v. Brumlop, 71 N.M. 221. 377 P.2d 520 (1962); Canterbury v. Spence, 150 U.S. App. D.C. 263, 464 F.2d 772 (D.C. Cir. 1972); Natanson v. Kline, 187 Kan. 186, 354 P.2d 670 (1960).

[10] Yeates v. Harms, 193 Kan. 320, 393 P.2d 982 (1964).

[11] Nishi v. Hartwell, 52 Haw. 188, 473 P.2d 116 (1970).

[12] Woods v. Brumlop, *supra*, n.8.

The patient has the burden of going forward with evidence tending to establish prima facie the essential elements of the cause of action. The burden of proving an exception to his duty and thus a privilege not to disclose, rests upon the physician as an affirmative defense.

The cause of action, based on lack of informed consent, is divided into three elements: the duty to inform being the first, the second is causation, and the third is injury. The second element, that of causation, requires that plaintiff patient would have chosen no treatment or a different course of treatment had the alternatives and material risks of each been made known to him. If the patient would have elected to proceed with treatment had he been duly informed of its risks, then the element of causation is missing. In other words, a casual connection exists between physician's breach of the duty to disclose and patient's injury when and only when disclosure of material risks incidental to treatment would have resulted in a decision against it.[13] A patient obviously has no complaint if he would have submitted to the treatment if the physician had complied with his duty and informed him of the risks. This fact decision raises the difficult question of the correct standard on which to instruct the jury.

The court in *Canterbury v. Spence, supra*, although emphasizing principles of self-determination permits liability only if non-disclosure would have affected the decision of a fictitious "reasonable patient," even though actual patient testifies he would have elected to forego therapy had he been fully informed.

Decisions discussing informed consent have emphasized the disclosure element but paid scant attention to the consent element of the concept, although this is the root of causation. Language in some decisions suggest the standard to be applied is a subjective one, *i.e.*, whether that particular patient would still have consented to the treatment, reasonable choice or otherwise. See *Woods v. Brumlop, supra*, n. 8; *Wilkinson v. Vesey, supra*, n.3; *Gray v. Grunnogle*, 423 Pa. 144, 223 A.2d 663 (1966); *Poulin v. Zartman*, 542 P.2d 251 (Alaska 1975), *reh'g denied*, 548 P.2d 1299 (Alaska 1976).

---

[13]   Martin v. Stratton, *supra*, n.2; *see also* Holt v. Nelson, II, Wash. App. 230. 523 P.2d 211 (1974).

Although the *Canterbury* rule is probably that of the majority,[14] its "reasonable man" approach has been criticized by some commentators[15] as backtracking on its own theory of self-determination. The *Canterbury* view certainly severely limits the protection granted an injured patient. To the extent the plaintiff, given an adequate disclosure, would have declined the proposed treatment, and a reasonable person in similar circumstances would have consented, a patient's right of self-determination is *irrevocably lost*. This basic right to know and decide is the reason for the full-disclosure rule. Accordingly, we decline to jeopardize this right by the imposition of the "reasonable man" standard.

If a plaintiff testifies he would have continued with the proposed treatment had he been adequately informed, the trial is over under either the subjective or objective approach. If he testifies he would not, then the causation problem must be resolved by examining the credibility of plaintiff's testimony. The jury must be instructed that it must find plaintiff would have refused the treatment if he is to prevail.

Although it might be said this approach places a physician at the mercy of a patient's hindsight, a careful practitioner can always protect himself by insuring that he has adequately informed each patient he treats. If he does not breach this duty, a causation problem will not arise.

The final element of this case of action is that of injury. The risk must actually materialize and plaintiff must have been injured as a result of submitting to the treatment. Absent occurrence of the undisclosed risk, a physician's failure to reveal its possibility is not actionable.[16]

In summary, in a medical malpractice action, a patient suing under the theory of informed consent must allege and prove:

1. defendant physician failed to inform him adequately of a material risk before securing his consent to the proposed treatment;
2. if he had been informed of the risks, he would not have consented to the treatment;

---

[14] *See* Archer v. Galbraith. 18 Wash. App. 369, 567 P.2d 1155 (1977); Funke v. Fieldman, 212 Kan. 524, 512 P.2d 539 (1973); Cobbs v. Grant, 8 Cal.3d 229,104 Cal. Rptr. 505, 502 P.2d 1(1972).

[15] Seidekon, *Medical Malpractice: Informed Consent Cases in "Full-Disclosure" Jurisdictions*, 14 Duq. L. Rev. 309 (1976); Kara, *Informed Consent—A Fairy Tale?* 39 U. Pitt. L. Rev. 137 (1977).

[16] Downer v. Veilleux, 322 A.2d 82 (Me. 1974); Hales v. Pittman, 576 P.2d 493 (Ariz. 1978).

3. the adverse consequences that were not made known did in fact occur, and he was injured as a result of submitting to the treatment.

As a defense, a physician may plead and prove plaintiff knew of the risks, full disclosure would be detrimental to patient's best interests or that an emergency existed requiring prompt treatment, and patient was in no condition to decide for himself.[17]

Because we are imposing a new duty on physicians, we hereby make this opinion prospective only, affecting those causes of action arising after the date this opinion is promulgated.[18]

The trial court in the case at bar gave rather broad instructions upon the duty of a physician to disclose. The instructions objected to did instruct that defendant should have disclosed material risks of the hysterectomy and feasibility of alternatives. Instructions are sufficient when considered as a whole, they present the law applicable to the issues.[19] Jury found for defendant. We find no basis for reversal.

AFFIRMED.

LAVENDER, C.J. AND HODGES, HARGRAVE AND OPALA, JJ., CONCUR.

BARNES, JUSTICE, CONCURRING IN PART, DISSENTING IN PART:

I concur with the majority opinion in all respects except I would adopt the reasonable man test set out in *Canterbury v. Spence*, 150 U.S. App. D.C. 263, 464 F.2d772 (D.C. Cir. 1972), *cert. denied*, 409 U.S. 1064, 93 S. Ct. 560, 34 L.Ed.2d 508.

I am authorized to state that IRWIN, V.C.J., SIMMS, J., AND REYNOLDS, Special Justice, join in the views expressed in this opinion.

Statutes

The following opinion well illustrates a variety of techniques of statutory interpretation. It concerns the Safety Appliance Act of March 2, 1893, one of the early industrial safety acts that preceded workers' compensation legislation. The act, which as amended, is found today in sections 1–7 of

---

[17] We do not hold these to be the sole defenses, as others may be presented in the future.

[18] *See* First National Bank of Porter v. Howard, 550 P 2d 561 (Okla. 1976).

[19] Fields v. Volkswagen, 555 P.2d 48 (Okla. 1976).

Title 45 of the United States Code, suggests the detail common to much American legislation.

Workers seeking to recover from their employers under case law for injuries sustained during their employment had been met not only by the defense of contributory negligence but also by the defense of assumption of risk. This latter defense was developed by the courts on the premise that the employee, conscious of the hazards of the employment, had impliedly agreed to assume the risk of injury which resulted from them when entering on employment. In this case, the injured workman relied on the Safety Appliance Act in order to avoid the defense.

The statute in its entirety, as enacted in 1893, is set out below, followed by the opinion of the Court.

AN ACT to promote the safety of employees and travelers upon railroads by compelling common carriers engaged in interstate commerce to equip their cars with automatic couplers and continuous brakes and their locomotives with driving-wheel brakes and for other purposes.

Be it enacted by the Senate and House of Representatives of the United States of America in Congress assembled. That from and after the first day of January, eighteen hundred and ninety-eight, it shall be unlawful for any common carrier engaged in interstate commerce by railroad to use on its line any locomotive engine in moving interstate traffic not equipped with a power driving-wheel brake and appliances for operating the train-brake system, or to run any train in such traffic after said date that has not a sufficient number of cars in it so equipped with power or train brakes that the engineer on the locomotive drawing such train can control its speed without requiring brakemen to use the common hand brake for that purpose.

Sec. 2. That on and after the first day of January, eighteen hundred and ninety-eight, it shall be unlawful for any such common carrier to haul or permit to be hauled or used on its line any car used in moving interstate traffic not equipped with couplers coupling automatically by impact and which can be uncoupled without the necessity of men going between the ends of the cars.

Sec. 3. That when any person, firm, company, or corporation engaged in interstate commerce by railroad shall have equipped a sufficient number of its cars so as to comply with the provisions of section one of this act, it may lawfully refuse to receive from connecting lines of road or shippers any car not equipped sufficiently, in accordance with the first section of this act, with such power or train brakes as will work and readily interchange with the brakes in use on its own cars, as required by this act.

Sec. 4. That from and after the first day of July, eighteen hundred and ninety-five, until otherwise ordered by the Interstate Commerce Commission, it shall be unlawful for any railroad company to use any car in interstate commerce that is not provided with secure grab irons or handholds in the ends and sides of each car for greater security to men in coupling and uncoupling cars.

Sec. 5. That within ninety days from the passage of this act, the American Railway Association is authorized hereby to designated to the Interstate Commerce Commission the standard height of drawbars for freight cars, measured perpendicular from the level of the tops of the rails to the centers of the drawbars, for each of the several gauges of railroads in use in the United States, and shall fix a maximum variation from such standard height to be allowed between the drawbars of empty and loaded cars. Upon their determination being certified to the Interstate Commerce Commission, said Commission shall at once give notice of the standard fixed upon to all common carriers, owners, or leases engaged in interstate commerce in the United States by such means as the Commission may deem proper. But should said association fail to determine a standard as above provided, it shall be the duty of the Interstate Commerce Commission to do so, before July first, eighteen hundred and ninety-four, and immediately to give notice thereof as aforesaid. And after July first, eighteen hundred and ninety-five, no cars, either loaded or unloaded, shall be used in interstate traffic which do not comply with the standard above provided for.

Sec. 6. That any such common carrier using any locomotive engine, running any train, or hauling or permitting to be hauled or used on its line any car in violation of any of the provisions of this act, shall be liable to a penalty of one hundred dollars for each and every violation, to be recovered in a suit or suits to be brought by the United States district attorney in the district court of the United States having jurisdiction in the locality where such violation shall have been committed, and it shall be the duly of such district attorney to bring such suits upon duly verified information being lodged with him of such violation having occurred. And it shall also be the duty of the Interstate Commerce Commission to lodge with the proper district attorneys information of any such violations as may come to its knowledge: Provided, that nothing in this act contained shall apply to trains composed of four-wheel cars or to locomotives used in hauling such trains.

Sec. 7. That the Interstate Commerce Commission may from time to time upon full hearing and for good cause extend the period within which any common carrier shall comply with the provisions of this act.

Sec. 8. That any employee of any such common carrier who may be injured by any locomotive, car, or train in use contrary to the provision of this act shall not be deemed thereby to have assumed the risk thereby occasioned, although continuing in the employment of such carrier after the unlawful use of such locomotive car, or train had been brought to his knowledge.

Approved, March 2, 1893.

JOHNSON v. SOUTHERN PACIFIC CO.

Supreme Court of the United States, 1904.
196 U.S. 1, 25 S. Ct. 158, 49 L. Ed. 363.
Johnson brought this action in the District Court of the First Judicial District of Utah against the Southern Pacific Company to recover damages for injuries received while employed by that company as a brakeman. The case was removed to the Circuit Court of the United States for the District of Utah by defendant on the ground of diversity of citizenship.

The facts were briefly these: August 5, 1990, Johnson was acting as head brakeman on a freight train of the Southern Pacific Company, which was making its regular trip between San Francisco, California, and Ogden, Utah. On reaching the town of Promontory, Utah, Johnson was directed to uncouple the engine from the train and couple it to a dining car, belonging to the company, which was standing on a side track, for the purpose of turning the car around preparatory to its being picked up and put on the next westbound passenger train. The engine and the dining car were equipped respectively, with the Janney coupler and the Miller hook, so called, which would not couple together automatically by impact, and it was, therefore, necessary for Johnson, and he was ordered, to go between the engine and the dining car, to accomplish the coupling. In so doing Johnson's hand was caught between the engine bumper and the dining car bumper and crushed, which necessitated amputation of the hand above the wrist.

On the trial of the case, defendant, after plaintiff had rested, moved the court to instruct the jury to find in its favor, which motion was granted, and the jury found a verdict accordingly, on which judgment was entered. Plaintiff carried the case to the Circuit Court of Appeals for the Eighth Circuit and the judgment was affirmed. 117 Fed. Rep. 462.

Mr. Chief Justice Fuller, after making the foregoing statement, delivered the opinion of the court.

This case was brought here on certiorari, and also on writ of error, and will be determined on the merits, without discussing the question of jurisdiction as between the one writ and the other. *Pullman's Car Company v. Transportation Company*, 171 U.S. 138, 145.

The plaintiff claimed that he was relieved of assumption of risk under common law rules by the act of Congress of March 2, 1893, 27 Stat. 531, c. 196, entitled "An act to promote the safety of employees and travelers upon railroads by compelling common carriers engaged in interstate commerce to equip their cars with automatic couplers and continuous brakes and their locomotives with driving-wheel brakes, and for other purposes."

The issues involved questions deemed of such general importance that the Government was permitted to file brief and be heard at the bar.

The act of 1893 provided: [Here the Court quoted from sections 1, 2, 6, and 8 of the act.]

The Circuit Court of Appeals held, in substance, Sanborn J., delivering the opinion and Lochren, J., concurring, that the locomotive and car were both equipped as required by the act, as the one had a power driving-wheel brake and the other a coupler; that section 2 did not apply to locomotives; that at the time of the accident the dining car was not "used in moving interstate traffic" and, moreover, that the locomotive, as well as the dining car, was furnished with an automatic coupler so that each was equipped as the statute required if section 2 applied to both. Thayer, J., concurred in the judgment on the latter ground, but was of opinion that locomotives were included by the words "any car" in the second section, and that the dining car was being "used in moving interstate traffic."

We are unable to accept these conclusions, not withstanding the able opinion of the majority, as they appear to us to be inconsistent with the plain intention of Congress, to defeat the object of the legislation, and to be arrived at by an inadmissible narrowness of construction.

The intention of Congress, declared in the preamble and in sections one and two of the act, was "to promote the safety of employees and travelers upon railroads by compelling common carriers engaged in interstate commerce to equip their cars with automatic couplers and continuous brakes and their locomotives with driving-wheel brakes," those brakes to be accompanied with "appliances for operating the train-brake system;" and every car to be "equipped with couplers coupling automatically by impact, and which can be uncoupled without the necessity of men going between the ends of the cars," whereby the danger and risk consequent on the existing system was averted as far as possible.

The present case is that of an injured employee, and involves the application of the act in respect of automatic couplers, the preliminary question being whether locomotives are required to be equipped with such couplers. And it is not to be successfully denied that they are so required if the words "any car" of the second section were intended to embrace, and do embrace, locomotives. But it is said that this cannot be so because locomotives were elsewhere in terms required to be equipped with power driving-wheel brakes, and that the rule that the expression of one thing excludes another applies. That, however, is a question of intention, and as there was special reason for requiring locomotives to be equipped with power driving-wheel brakes, if it were also necessary that locomotives should be equipped with automatic couplers, and the word "car" would cover locomotives, then the intention to limit the equipment of locomotives to power driving-wheel brakes, because they were separately mentioned, could not be imputed. Now it was as necessary for the safety of employees in coupling and uncoupling, that locomotives should be equipped with automatic couplers, as it was that freight and passenger and dining cars should be, perhaps more so, as Judge Thayer suggests, "since engines have occasion to make couplings more frequently."

And manifestly the word "car" was used in its generic sense. There is nothing to indicate that any particular kind of car was meant. Tested by context, subject matter and object, "any car" meant all kinds of cars running on the rails, including locomotives. And this view is supported by the dictionary definitions and by many judicial decisions, some of them having been rendered in construction of this act. *Winkler v. Philadelphia & Reading Railway Company*, 53 Atl. Rep. 90; 4 Penn. (Del.) 387; *Fleming v. Southern Railway Company*, 131 N. Car. 476; *East St. Louis Connecting Railway Company v. O'Hara*, 150 Illinois, 580; *Kansas City &c. Railroad Company v. Crocker*, 95 Alabama, 412; *Thomas v. Georgia Railroad and Banking Company*, 38 Georgia, 222; *Mayor & c. v. Third Ave. R. R. Co.*, 117 N.Y. 404; *Benson v. Railway Company*, 75 Minnesota, 163.

The result is that if the locomotive in question was not equipped with automatic couplers, the company failed to comply with the provisions of the act. It appears, however, that this locomotive was in fact equipped with automatic couplers, as well as the dining car, but that the couplers on each, which were of different types, would not couple with each other automatically by impact so as to render it unnecessary for men to go between the cars to couple and uncouple.

Nevertheless, the Circuit Court of Appeals was of opinion that it would be an unwarrantable extension of the terms of the law to hold that where the couplers would couple automatically with couplers of their own kind, the couplers must so couple with couplers of different kinds. But we think that what the act plainly forbade was the use of cars which could not be coupled together automatically by impact, by means of the couplers actually used on the cars to be coupled. The object was to protect the lives and limbs of railroad employees by rendering it unnecessary for a man operating the couplers to go between the ends of the cars, and that object would be defeated, not necessarily by the use of automatic couplers of different kinds, but if those different kinds would not automatically couple with each other. The point was that the railroad companies should be compelled, respectively, to adopt devices, whatever they were, which would act so far uniformly as to eliminate the danger consequent on men going between the cars.

If the language used were open to construction, we are constrained to say that the construction put upon the act by the Circuit Court of Appeals was altogether too narrow.

This strictness was thought to be required because the commonlaw rule as to the assumption of risk was changed by the act, and because the act was penal.

The dogma as to the strict construction of statutes in derogation of the common law only amounts to the recognition of a presumption against an intention to change existing law, and as there is no doubt of that intention here, the extent of the application of the change demands at least no more rigorous construction than would be applied to penal laws. And, as Chief Justice Parker remarked, conceding that statutes in derogation of the common law are to be construed strictly, "they are also to be construed sensibly, and with a view to the object aimed at by the legislature." *Gibson v. Jenney*, 15 Massachusetts, 205.

The primary object of the act was to promote the public welfare by securing the safety of employees and travelers, and it was in that aspect remedial, while for violations a penalty of one hundred dollars, recoverable in a civil action, was provided for, and in that aspect it was penal. But the design to give relief was more dominant than to inflict punishment, and the act might well be held to fall within the rule applicable to statutes to prevent fraud upon the revenue, and for the collection of customs, that rule not requiring absolute strictness of construction. Taylor v. United States, 3 How. 197; United States v. Stowell, 133 U.S. 1, 12, and cases cited. And *see Farmers' and Merchants' National Bank v. Dearing*, 91 U.S. 29, 35; Gray v. Bennett, 3 Met. (Mass.) 522.

Moreover, it is settled that "though penal laws are to be construed strictly, yet the intention of the legislation must govern in the construction of penal as well as other statutes; and they are not to be construed so strictly as to defeat the obvious intention of the legislature." *United States v. Lacher*, 134 U.S. 624. In that case we cited and quoted from *United States v. Winn*, 3 Sumn. 209, in which Mr. Justice Story, referring to the rule that penal statutes are to be construed strictly, said:

> I agree to that rule in its true and sober sense; and that is, that penal statutes are not to be enlarged by implication, or extended to cases not obviously within their words and purport. But where the words are general, and include various classes of persons, I know of no authority, which would justify the court in restricting them to one class, or in giving them the narrowest interpretation, where the mischief to be redressed by the statute is equally applicable to all of them. And where a word is used in a statute, which has various known significations, I know of no rule, that requires the court to adopt one in preference to another, simply because it is more restrained, if the objects of the statute equally apply to the largest and broadest sense of

the word. In short, it appears to me, that the proper course in all these cases, is to search out and follow the true intent of the legislature, and to adopt that sense of the words which harmonizes best with the context, and promotes in the fullest manner, the apparent policy and objects of the legislature.

Tested by these principles, we think the view of the Circuit Court of Appeals, which limits the second section to merely providing automatic couplers, does not give due effect to the words "coupling automatically by impact, and which can be uncoupled without the necessity of men going between the cars," and cannot be sustained.

We dismiss as without merit the suggestion, which has been made, that the words "without the necessity of men going between the ends of the cars," which are the test of compliance with section two, apply only to the act of uncoupling. The phrase literally covers both coupling and uncoupling, and if read, as it should be, with a comma after the word "uncoupled," this becomes entirely clear. *Chicago, Milwaukee & St. Paul Railway Company v. Voelker*, 129 Fed. Rep. 522; *United States v. Lacher, supra*.

The risk in coupling and uncoupling was the evil sought to be remedied, and that risk was to be obviated by the use of couplers actually coupling automatically. True, no particular design was required, but whatever the devices used they were to be effectively interchangeable. Congress was not paltering in a double sense. And its intention is found "in the language actually used, interpreted according to its fair and obvious meaning." *United States v. Harris*, 177 U.S. 305, 309.

That this was the scope of the statute is confirmed by the circumstances surrounding its enactment, as exhibited in public documents to which we are at liberty to refer. *Binns v. United States*, 194 U.S. 486, 495; *Holy Trinity Church v. United States*, 143 U.S. 457, 463.

President Harrison, in his annual messages of 1889, 1890, 1891 and 1892, earnestly urged upon Congress the necessity of legislation to obviate and reduce the loss of life and the injuries due to the prevailing method of coupling and braking. In his first message he said: "It is competent, I think, for Congress to require uniformity in the construction of cars used in interstate commerce, and the use of improved safety appliances upon such trains. Time will be necessary to make the needed changes, but an earnest and intelligent beginning should be made at once.

It is a reproach to our civilization that any class of American workmen should, in the pursuit of a necessary and useful vocation, be subjected to a peril of life and limb as great as that of a soldier in time of war."

And he reiterated his recommendation in succeeding messages, saying in that for 1892: "Statistics furnished by the Interstate Commerce Commission show that during the year ending June 30, 1891, there were forty-seven different styles of car couplers reported to be in use, and that during the same period there were 2,660 employees killed and 26,140 injured. Nearly 16 percent of the deaths occurred in the coupling and uncoupling of cars, and over 36 per cent of the injuries had the same origin."

The Senate report of the first session of the Fifty-second Congress (No. 1049), and the House report of the same session (No. 1678), set out the numerous and increasing casualties due to coupling, the demand for protection, and the necessity of automatic couplers, coupling interchangeably. The difficulties in the case were fully expounded and the result reached to require an automatic coupling by impact so as to render it unnecessary for men to go between the cars, while no particular device or type was adopted, the railroad companies being left free to work out the details for themselves, ample time being given for that purpose. The law gave five years, and that was enlarged, by the Interstate Commerce Commission as authorized by law, two years, and subsequently seven months, making seven years and seven months in all.

The diligence of counsel has called our attention to changes made in the bill in the course of its passage and to the debates in the Senate on the report of its committee. 24 Cong. Rec., pt. 2, pp. 1246, 1273 et seq. These demonstrate that the difficulty as to interchangeability was fully in the mind of Congress and was assumed to be met by the language which was used. The essential degree of uniformity was secured by providing that the couplings must couple automatically by impact without the necessity of men going between the ends of the cars.

In the present case, the couplings would not work together. Johnson was obliged to go between the cars, and the law was not complied with.

March 2, 1903, 32 Stat. 943, c. 976, an act in amendment of the act of 1893 was approved, which provided, among other things, that the provisions and requirements of the former act "shall be held to apply to common carriers by railroads in the Territories and the District of Columbia and shall apply in all cases, whether or not the couplers brought together are of the same kind, make, or type;" and "shall be held to apply to all trains, locomotives, tenders, cars, and similar vehicles used on any railroad engaged in interstate commerce."

This act was to take effect September first, nineteen hundred and three, and nothing in it was to be held or construed to relieve any common carrier "from any of the provisions, powers, duties, liabilities, or requirements" of the act of 1893, all of which should apply except as specifically amended.

As we have no doubt of the meaning of the prior law, the subsequent legislation cannot be regarded as intended to operate to destroy it. Indeed, the latter act is affirmative, and declaratory, and, in effect, only construed and applied the former act. *Bailey v. Clark*, 21 Wall. 284; *United States v. Freeman*, 3 How. 556; *Cope v. Cope*, 137 U.S. 682; *Wetmore v. Markoe*, post, p. 68. This legislative recognition of the scope of the prior law fortifies and does not weaken the conclusion at which we have arrived.

Another ground on which the decision of the Circuit Court of Appeals was tested remains to be noticed. That court held by a majority that as the dining car was empty and had not actually entered upon its trip, it was not used in moving interstate traffic, and hence was not within the act. The dining car had been constantly used for several years to furnish meals to passengers between San Francisco and Ogden and for no other purpose. On the day of the accident, the eastbound train was so late that it was found that the car could not reach Ogden in time to return on the next westbound train according to intention, and it was therefore dropped off at Promontory to be picked up by that train as it came along that evening.

The presumption is that it was stocked for the return, and as it was not a new car, or a car just from the repair shop, on its way to its field of labor, it was not "an empty," as that term is sometimes used. Besides, whether cars are empty or loaded, the danger to employees is practically the same, and we agree with the observation of District Judge Shiras in *Voelker v. Railway Company*, 116 Fed. Rep. 867, that "it cannot be true that on the eastern trip the provisions of the act of Congress would be binding upon the company, because the cars were loaded, but would not be binding upon the return trip, because the cars are empty."

Counsel urges that the character of the dining car at the time and place of the injury was local only and could not be changed until the car was actually engaged in interstate movement or being put into a train for such use, and *Coe v. Errol*, 116 U.S. 517, is cited as supporting that contention. In *Coe v. Errol*, it was held that certain logs cut in New Hampshire, and hauled to a river in order that they might be transported to Maine were subject to taxation in the former State before transportation had begun.

The distinction between merchandise which may become an article of interstate commerce, or may not, and an instrument regularly used in moving interstate commerce, which has stopped temporarily in making its trip between two points in different states, renders this and like cases inapplicable.

Confessedly, this dining car was under the control of Congress while in the act of making its interstate journey, and in our judgment it was equally so when waiting for the train to be made up for the next trip. It was being regularly used in the movement of interstate traffic and so within the law.

Finally, it is argued that Johnson was guilty of such contributory negligence as to defeat recovery, and that, therefore, the judgment should be affirmed. But the Circuit Court of Appeals did not consider this question nor apparently did the Circuit Court, and we do not feel constrained to inquire whether it could have been open under Section 8, or if so, whether it should have been left to the jury under proper instructions.

The judgment of the Circuit Court of Appeals is reversed; the judgment of the Circuit Court is also reversed, and the cause remanded to that court with instructions to set aside the verdict and award a new trial.

Selected Readings by
E. Allan Farnsworth

Professor Farnsworth published over one hundred articles and book chapters. This sample is provided for the benefit of readers of this book interested in his fuller discussion of some of the topics raised and of his views on comparative and international law.

Books

Reporter for the American Law Institute, Restatement (Second) Contracts (1981) (3 vols.) (with J. Braucher).

Alleviating Mistakes: Reversal and Forgiveness for Flawed Perceptions (2004).

Farnsworth on Contracts (2d ed. 1998) (3 vols.).

Contracts (3d ed. 1998).

Selections for Contracts: Uniform Commercial Code, Restatement Second, UN Sales Convention, UNIDROIT Forms (1998).

Cases and Materials on Contracts (5th ed. 1995) (with W. Young).

Changing Your Mind: The Law of Regretted Decisions (1998).

Cases and Materials on Commercial Transactions (5th ed. 1993) (with J. Honnold, S. Harris, C. Mooney, Jr. & C. Reitz).

Cases and Materials on Commercial Paper (4th ed. 1993).

Contract Law in the USSR and the United States: History and General Concept
    (1987) (with V. Mozolini) (also Dogovornoe Pravo v SSShA i SSSR:
    Istoriia i Obschie Kontseptsii).

United States Contract Law (1992).

Chapters in Books, and Articles

"Comparative Contract Law," *in Oxford Handbook of Comparative Law* 899
    (with L. Garvin) (M. Reimann & R. Simmermann eds., 2007).

"Oops! The Waxing Of Alleviating Mistakes," 30 Ohio N.U. L. Rev. 167
    (2004).

"Parables about Promises: Religious Ethics and Contract Enforceability,"
    71 Fordham L. Rev. 695 (2002).

"Promises and Paternalism," 41 Wm. & Mary L. Rev. 385 (2000).

"The UNIDROIT Principles: A new lingua franca for the drafting of
    international commercial contracts?" *in The UNIDROIT Principles: A
    Common Law of Contracts for the Americas?* 193 (F. Mestre & P. de Seume
    eds., 1998).

"The American Provenance of the UNIDROIT Principles," 72 Tul. L. Rev.
    1985 (1998).

"Law Is A Sometime Autonomous Discipline," 21 Harv. J.L. & Pub. Pol'y
    95 (1997).

"An International Restatement: The UNIDROIT Principles of Interna-
    tional Commercial Contracts," 26 U. Balt. L. Rev. 1 (1997).

"Unification and Harmonization of Private Law," 27 Can. Bus. L.J. 48
    (1996).

"A Common Lawyer's View of His Civilian Colleagues," 57 La. L. Rev.
    227 (1996).

"Promises To Make Gifts," 43 Am. J. Comp. L. 359 (1995).

"Duties of Good Faith and Fair Dealing Under the UNIDROIT
    Principles, Relevant International Conventions, And National Laws," 3
    Tul. J. Int'l & Comp. L. 47 (1995).

"Freedom of Contract and Constitutional Law," *in Proceedings of the
    Colloquium of the International Association of Legal Science in Jerusalem,*
    September 1994 (A. Rabello & P. Sarcevic eds., 1998).

"Reasons for Regret," *in* 3 Scintillae juris. *Studi in Memoria di Gino Gorla* 1877 (1994).

"The Concept of Good Faith in American Law," Saggi, Conferenze e Seminari #10 (Centro di studie ricerche di diritto comparato e straniero in Rome 1993).

"Closing Remarks–Principles for International Commercial Contracts," 40 Am. J. Comp. L. 699 (1992).

"Contracts Is Not Dead," 77 Cornell L. Rev. 1034 (1992).

"Comments on Professor Waddams' "Precontractual Duties of Disclosure," 19 Can. Bus. L.J. 351 (1991).

"Developments in Contract Law During the 1980s: The Top Ten," 41 Case W. Res. L. Rev. 203 (1990).

"Casebooks and Scholarship: Confessions of an American Opinion Clipper," 42 Sw. L.J. 903 (1988).

"Review of Standard Forms or Terms Under the Vienna Convention," 21 Cornell Int'l L.J. 439 (1988).

"A Fable and a Quiz on Contracts," 37 J. Legal Ed. 206 (1987).

"Bečka Konvencija o Međunarodnoj Prodaji Robe (Americiko Stanoviste)," 37 Pravni _Ivot 1075 (1987).

"Precontractual Liability and Preliminary Agreements: Fair Dealing and Failed Negotiations," 87 Colum. L. Rev. 217 (1987).

"Your Loss or My Gain? The Dilemma of the Disgorgement Principle in Breach of Contract," 94 Yale L.J. 1339 (1985).

"Comment on Michael Bridge's Paper: Does Anglo-Canadian Contract Law Need a Doctrine of Good Faith?," 9 Can. Bus. L.J. 426 (1984).

"The Vienna Convention: History and Scope," 18 Int'l Lawyer 17 (1984).

"The Vienna Convention: An International Law for the Sale of Goods, Private Investors Abroad," 121 (1983).

"Ingredients in the Redaction of the Restatement (Second) of Contracts," 81 Colum. L. Rev. 1 (1981).

"The Convention on the International Sale of Goods from the Perspective of the Common Law Countries," in *La Vendita Internationale: La Convenzione di Vienna dell'll Aprile 1980*," 39 Quaderni di Giurisprudenza Commerciale 3 (1981).

"Contracts During the Half Century Between Restatements," 30 Cleveland St. L. Rev. 371 (1981).

"Damages and Specific Relief," 27 Am. J. Comp. L. 247 (1979).

"The Uniform Commercial Code and the Global Unification of International Trade Law," in *International Economic and Trade Law* 97 (C. M. Schmittoff & K. R. Simmonds eds., 1976).

"UNCITRAL and the Progressive Development of International Trade," in *Law and International Trade/Recht und Internationaler Handel* (Festschrift for Clive M. Schmitthoff) (F. Fabricius ed., 1973).

"UNCITRAL: Why? What? How? When?" 20 Am. J. Comp. L. 314 (1972).

"Legal Remedies for Breach of Contract," 70 Colum. L. Rev. 1145 (1970).

"The Development of the Civil Law of Obligations in New States: Senegal, Madagascar, and Ethiopia," in *Essays on the Civil Law of Obligations* (J. Dainow ed., 1969) (Bailey Lecture at Louisiana State University).

"The Past of Promise: An Historical Introduction to Contract," 69 Colum. L. Rev. 576 (1969).

"Formation of Contracts: A Study of the Common Core of Legal Systems," 69 Colum. L. Rev. 339 (1969).

"Disputes Over Omission in Contracts," 68 Colum. L. Rev. 860 (1968).

"Documentary Drafts Under the Uniform Commercial Code," 30 Rabels Zeitschrift 414 (1966), rev'd in 22 Bus. Law. 479 (1967) and in 84 Banking L.J. 189 (1967).

"'Meaning' in the Law of Contracts," 76 Yale L.J. 939 (1967).

"Le Nouveau Code des Obligations du Sénégal," 1963 Annales Africaines 73 [The New Code of Obligations of Senegal] rev'd & trans. as "Law Reform in a Developing Country: A New Code of Obligations for Senegal," 8 J. African L. 6 (1964).

"Good Faith Performance and Commercial Reasonableness under the Uniform Commercial Code," 30 U. Chi. L. Rev. 666 (1963).

"Formation of International Sales Contracts: Three Attempts at Unification," 110 U. Pa. L. Rev. 305 (1962).

"Review of A.N. Yiannopoulos, Negligence Clauses in Ocean Bills of Lading, Conflict of Laws, and the Brussels Convention: A Comparative Study (1962)," 55 L. Lib. J. 454 (1962).

"Le Droit Commercial aux États-Unis d'Amérique [Commercial Law in the United States of America]," [1962] Revue Internationale de Droit Comparé 309.

"Amerika Birleşik Devletlerinde Hukuk Meslekî [The American Legal Profession]," 35 Istanbul 52 (1961).

"John Hanna—An Appreciation," 60 Colum. L. Rev. 587 (1960).

"Implied Warranties of Quality in Non-Sales Cases," 57 Colum. L. Rev. 653 (1957).